CONTENTS

Contents continued

DISCRIMINATION

A GUIDE TO THE RELEVANT CASE LAW ON
SEX, RACE, DISABILITY AND SEXUAL ORIENTATION DISCRIMINATION,
AND EQUAL PAY

EIGHTEENTH EDITION

Michael Rubenstein

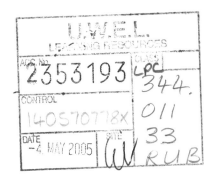

LexisNexis·
Butterworths

Members of the LexisNexis Group worldwide

United Kingdom	LexisNexis Butterworths, a Division of Reed Elsevier (UK) Ltd, Halsbury House, 35 Chancery Lane, LONDON, WC2A 1EL, and RSH, 1–3 Baxter's Place, Leith Walk EDINBURGH EH1 3AF
Argentina	LexisNexis Argentina, BUENOS AIRES
Australia	LexisNexis Butterworths, CHATSWOOD, New South Wales
Austria	LexisNexis Verlag ARD Orac GmbH & Co KG, VIENNA
Canada	LexisNexis Butterworths, MARKHAM, Ontario
Chile	LexisNexis Chile Ltda, SANTIAGO DE CHILE
Czech	Republic Nakladatelství Orac sro, PRAGUE
France	Editions du Juris-Classeur SA, PARIS
Germany	LexisNexis Deutschland GmbH, FRANKFURT and MUNSTER
Hong Kong	LexisNexis Butterworths, HONG KONG
Hungary	HVG-Orac, BUDAPEST
India	LexisNexis Butterworths, NEW DELHI
Italy	Giuffrè Editore, MILAN
Malaysia	Malayan Law Journal Sdn Bhd, KUALA LUMPUR
New Zealand	LexisNexis Butterworths, WELLINGTON
Poland	Wydawnictwo Prawnicze LexisNexis, WARSAW
Singapore	LexisNexis Butterworths, SINGAPORE
South Africa	LexisNexis Butterworths, Durban
Switzerland	Stämpfli Verlag AG, BERNE
USA	LexisNexis, DAYTON, Ohio

© Reed Elsevier (UK) Ltd 2005

Published by LexisNexis UK

A CIP Catalogue record for this book is available from the British Library.

ISBN 1-405-70778-X

9 781405 707787

Printed by Hobbs the Printers Ltd

Visit LexisNexis Butterworths at www.lexisnexis.co.uk

CASE INDEX

INTRODUCTION

The 18th edition of the *Discrimination Guide* takes into account the effect on the case law of 41 discrimination cases reported in *Industrial Relations Law Reports* (IRLR) during 2004.

Since the Equal Pay Act 1970, Sex Discrimination Act 1975, Race Relations Act 1976 and Disability Discrimination Act 1995 came into force, there have been some 800 significant decisions by the appellate courts reported in *Industrial Relations Law Reports* interpreting the statutory provisions. A major purpose of this Guide is to extract from these cases the main principles concerning employment discrimination that still can be regarded as binding authority. My hope is that this will assist those advising, acting or adjudicating in this jurisdiction on the current approach of the courts to the range of problems of interpretation posed by the statutes.

Discrimination cases have assumed increasing prominence in IRLR, and now represent the largest subject area covered by the reports, having eclipsed unfair dismissal several years ago. This has been due to the influence of EU law, the great increase in the number of cases and a corresponding increase in appeals, and the introduction of disability discrimination as a major new jurisdiction. Key points from cases reported in IRLR, and many other discrimination decisions of interest, can be found in *Equal Opportunities Review* (EOR) as they become available during the year.

The discrimination cases reported during 2004 were spread evenly over the main established jurisdictions: 15 cases raising issues of sex discrimination law, 11 equal pay cases, eight DDA cases, and eight race discrimination cases (some cases concerned more than one jurisdiction). We also reported the first case brought in connection with the sexual orientation Regulations, the judicial review application.

During 2004, we reported five decisions of the European Court of Justice on discrimination law, two decisions of the House of Lords, 13 discrimination law decisions of the English Court of Appeal, one decision each of the Court of Session in Scotland, the Court of Appeal in Northern Ireland, and the English High Court. The growth in the number of Court of Appeal decisions reported reflects a general trend which is continuing into 2005 of more cases in the discrimination field being appealed. There were 18 EAT decisions on aspects of discrimination law reported. These came from courts presided over by 10 different judges: four decisions each from Mrs Justice Cox and Judge McMullen QC, two decisions of Mr Justice Burton and Judge Peter Clark, and one decision each from Judge Ansell, Judge J Burke QC, Mr Justice Keith, Mr Justice Rimer, Judge Richardson, and Judge Wilkie QC.

2004 saw some major changes in statute law with the Disability Discrimination Act (Amendment) Regulations 2003 coming into force. The Employment Act 2002 (Dispute Resolution) Regulations 2004 and the Employment Tribunals (Constitution and Rules of Procedure) Regulations 2004 now apply to most discrimination claims, in the same way as they apply to other causes of action. In addition, there are special new provisions for dealing with equal pay claims to be found in the Equal Pay Act 1970 (Amendment) Regulations 2004 and the Employment Tribunals (Constitution and Rules of Procedure) (Amendment) Regulations 2004.

To take these changes and the decisions reported in IRLR in 2004 into account has meant deleting 28 entries which appeared in the 17th edition of the Guide, but which are no longer considered relevant, while adding 61 new principles in light of the new case law or new legislation. The Guide takes the law as it stood at the end of 2004.

Where essentially the same point has been enunciated in more than one reported case, the highest authority has been cited or, where that is not possible, the most recent or the most frequently quoted decision. For this and other purposes, therefore, the Guide distinguishes between the principle and the case. The principle, if still relevant, should be found in the Guide. A particular case may not be referred to either because it is no longer relevant or because the principle enunciated is better captured by another reference

Conflicting lines of authority inevitably present a difficult problem for an exercise such as this. Where the issue can be said to be open to serious doubt, I have included both conflicting sets of decisions. On the other hand, where a case has clearly been overruled implicitly, the principle has been removed even though the case has not been expressly disapproved.

Finally, since there has to be a cut-off point in preparing a publication such as this, I have only included cases reported in IRLR up to the end of 2004. Inevitably, however, because this area of the law is developing so rapidly, the Guide may include some principles which been have overruled by the courts by the time this edition reaches your hands. The Guide thus should be seen as an adjunct to *Industrial Relations Law Reports* and *Equal Opportunities Review*, rather than a replacement for regular perusal of these journals.

Michael Rubenstein
February 2005

1. SEX AND RACE DISCRIMINATION

EC SEX DISCRIMINATION LAW

Remedies under EC law

In order to carry out their task the Council and the Commission shall in accordance with the provisions of this Treaty, make regulations, issue directives, take decisions, make recommendations or deliver opinions.

A regulation shall have general application. It shall be binding in its entirety and directly applicable in all Member States.

A directive shall be binding, as to the result to be achieved, upon each Member State to which it is addressed, but shall leave to the national authorities the choice of form and methods.

A decision shall be binding in its entirety upon those to whom it is addressed.

Recommendations and opinions shall have no binding force.

EC TREATY – Article 189

Member States shall introduce into their national legal systems such measures as are necessary to enable all persons who consider themselves wronged by failure to apply to them the principle of equal treatment within the meaning of Articles 3, 4 and 5 to pursue their claims by judicial process after possible recourse to other competent authorities.

EQUAL TREATMENT DIRECTIVE – Article 6

Direct enforcement

Marshall v   **[1986] IRLR 140 ECJ**
Southampton and South-West
  Hampshire Area Health Authority
A Directive may not of itself impose obligations on an individual, as opposed to a State authority, and a provision of a Directive may not be relied upon as against an individual. According to Article 189 of the EC Treaty, the binding nature of a Directive, which constitutes the basis for the possibility of relying on the Directive before a national court, exists only in relation to "each Member State to which it is addressed". Whether a respondent must be regarded as having acted as an individual is for the national court to determine according to the circumstances of each case.

Marshall v   **[1986] IRLR 140 ECJ**
Southampton and South-West
  Hampshire Area Health Authority
Wherever the provisions of an EC Directive appear, as far as their subject-matter is concerned, to be unconditional and sufficiently precise, those provisions may be relied upon by an individual against the State where that State fails to implement the Directive in national law by the end of the period prescribed, or where it fails to implement the Directive correctly.

Verholen v   **[1992] IRLR 38 ECJ**
Sociale Verzekeringsbank Amsterdam
Community law does not preclude a national court from examining of its own motion whether national legal rules comply with the precise and unconditional provisions of a Directive, the period for whose implementation has elapsed.

Marshall v   **[1986] IRLR 140 ECJ**
Southampton and South-West
  Hampshire Area Health Authority
Where a person involved in legal proceedings is able to rely on a Directive as against the State, he may do so regardless of the capacity in which the latter is acting, whether employer or public authority.

Foster v   **[1990] IRLR 354 ECJ**
British Gas plc
Unconditional and sufficiently precise provisions of a Directive can be relied on against an organisation, whatever its legal form, which is subject to the authority or control of the State or which has been made responsible, pursuant to a measure adopted by the State, for providing a public service under the control of the State and has for that purpose special powers beyond those which result from the normal rules applicable in relations between individuals.

Foster v   **[1991] IRLR 268 HL**
British Gas plc
The sole questions under the test laid down by the European Court are whether the employer, pursuant to a measure adopted by the State, provides a public service under the control of the State and exercises special powers. That the employer engages in commercial activities, does not perform any of the traditional functions of the State and is not the agent of the State is not relevant to this test.

Foster v   **[1991] IRLR 268 HL**
British Gas plc
The principle laid down by the European Court of Justice was that the State must not be allowed to take advantage of its own failure to comply with Community law. There is no justification for a narrow or strained construction of the ruling of the European Court, which was couched in terms of broad principle and purposive language.

Foster v   **[1991] IRLR 268 HL**
British Gas plc
The British Gas Corporation, prior to its privatisation, was a body whose employees were entitled to rely directly upon the requirements of Article 5(1) of the EC Equal Treatment Directive.

Doughty v   **[1992] IRLR 126 CA**
Rolls-Royce plc
The three criteria formulated by the European Court in *Foster* for determining whether a particular entity is such that the provisions of a Directive are directly enforceable against it are

cumulative requirements rather than alternative. The power of control is only one of the cumulative criteria.

Doughty v [1992] IRLR 126 CA
Rolls-Royce plc

Rolls-Royce, prior to its privatisation, was not a body whose employees were entitled to rely directly upon the requirements of Article 5(1) of the EC Equal Treatment Directive, notwithstanding that the State was the sole shareholder in the company at the relevant time. It was a commercial undertaking which could not be said to have been "made responsible, pursuant to a measure adopted by the State for providing a public service". Nor was there any evidence that Rolls-Royce claimed to exercise any "special powers" of the type enjoyed by the British Gas Corporation.

Cotter v [1991] IRLR 380 ECJ
Minister for Social Welfare

In the absence of measures implementing a directly enforceable provision of an EC Directive, women are entitled to have the same rules applied to them as are applied to men who are in the same situation since, where the Directive has not been implemented, those rules remain the only valid point of reference. This principle applies even if it infringes a prohibition on unjust enrichment laid down by national law.

Jesuthasan v [1998] IRLR 372 CA
London Borough of Hammersmith & Fulham

Legislative measures which have been declared incompatible with EC law on account of their indirectly discriminatory effects must be disapplied in respect of all employees, regardless of sex. Therefore, even though the applicant is a man, he was entitled to rely on the decision of the House of Lords in *R v Secretary of State for Employment ex parte EOC* that the hours per week qualifying thresholds to claim unfair dismissal were incompatible with EC law because they indirectly discriminated against women.

Secretary of State for Scotland v [1991] IRLR 187 EAT
Wright

An employment tribunal has jurisdiction to hear a claim brought under directly applicable provisions of the Equal Treatment Directive in circumstances where the applicant has no remedy under domestic legislation. Accordingly, the tribunal had jurisdiction to hear the employees' complaint that their exclusion from the right to a contractual redundancy payment contravened Article 5(1) of the Equal Treatment Directive.

Blaik v [1994] IRLR 280 EAT
Post Office

If there is a sufficient remedy given by domestic law, it is unnecessary and impermissible to explore the same complaint under the equivalent provisions in a Directive. It is only if there is a disparity between the two that it becomes necessary to consider whether the provisions in EC law are directly enforceable by the complainant in his proceedings against the respondent.

Time limits

Emmott v [1991] IRLR 387 ECJ
Minister for Social Welfare

In the absence of Community rules on the subject, it is for the domestic legal system of each Member State to determine the procedural conditions governing actions at law intended to ensure the protection of rights which individuals derive from the direct effect of Community law, provided that such conditions are not less favourable than those relating to similar actions of a domestic nature, nor framed so as to render virtually impossible the exercise of rights conferred by Community law. The laying down of reasonable time limits, which if unobserved bar proceedings, in principle satisfies these two conditions.

Emmott v [1991] IRLR 387 ECJ
Minister for Social Welfare

Until such time as a Directive has been properly transposed into domestic law, a defaulting Member State may not rely on an individual's delay in initiating proceedings against it in order to protect rights conferred upon him by the provisions of the Directive, and a period laid down by national law within which proceedings must be initiated cannot begin to run before that time.

Steenhorst-Neerings v [1994] IRLR 244 ECJ
Bestuur van de Bedrijfsvereniging
voor Detailhandel, Ambachten en
Huisvrouwen

A national rule of law restricting the retroactive effect of claims is not precluded by EC law where an individual seeks to rely on rights conferred directly by an EC Directive and where on the date the claim for benefit was made the Member State concerned had not yet properly transposed that provision into national law. The principle set out by *Emmott*, that the time limits for proceedings brought by individuals seeking to avail themselves of their rights are applicable only when a Member State has properly transposed the Directive, did not apply in such a case. The right to claim benefits conferred upon women by the direct effect of a Directive must be exercised under the conditions determined by national law, provided those conditions are no less favourable than those relating to similar domestic actions and that they are not framed so as to render virtually impossible the exercise of rights conferred by Community law.

Johnson v [1995] IRLR 157 ECJ
Chief Adjudication Officer (No.2)

It is compatible with European Community law to apply a national rule, which limits the period in respect of which arrears of benefit are payable, to a claim based on the direct effect of an EC Directive, even where that Directive has not been properly transposed within the prescribed period in the Member State. The solution adopted in

Emmott was justified by the particular circumstances of that case, in which a time bar had the result of depriving the applicant of any opportunity whatever to rely on her right to equal treatment under the Directive. This was to be contrasted with application of a rule which merely limited the retroactive effect of claims for benefits to one year, and therefore did not make it virtually impossible to exercise rights based on the Directive.

Setiya v   **[1995] IRLR 348 EAT**
East Yorkshire Health Authority
The principle laid down in *Emmott* relates only to time limits for initiating proceedings, and has no application to national time limits for appealing against a decision.

Agreement precluding complaint

Livingstone v   **[1992] IRLR 63 EAT**
Hepworth Refractories plc
The procedural provisions of UK domestic law comply with the conditions indicated by the European Court in *Emmott*. Therefore, the proper approach is to apply the procedures of the Sex Discrimination Act, including that relating to time limits and the code intended to protect employees against bad bargains, to claims of sex discrimination brought directly under Community law.

Grounds of sex

(1) For the purposes of the following provisions, the principle of equal treatment shall mean that there shall be no discrimination whatsoever on grounds of sex either directly or indirectly by reference in particular to marital or family status.
EQUAL TREATMENT DIRECTIVE – Article 2

P v   **[1996] IRLR 347 ECJ**
S
The scope of the Equal Treatment Directive cannot be confined simply to discrimination based on the fact that a person is one or other sex. In view of its purpose and the fundamental nature of the rights which it seeks to safeguard, the scope of the Directive also applies to discrimination based essentially, if not exclusively, on the sex of the person concerned.

Pregnancy

Dekker v   **[1991] IRLR 27 ECJ**
VJV-Centrum
Whether a refusal to employ results in direct discrimination on grounds of sex depends on whether the most important reason is one which applies without distinction to employees of both sexes or whether it exclusively applies to one sex. As employment can only be refused because of pregnancy to women, such a refusal is direct discrimination on grounds of sex. Therefore, an employer is acting in direct contravention of the principle of equal treatment embodied in the EC Equal Treatment Directive if he refuses to enter into a contract of employment with a female applicant, found suitable by him for the post in question, because of the possible adverse consequences to him of employing a pregnant woman.

Handels- og Kontorfunktionærernes   **[1991] IRLR 31 ECJ**
  Forbund i Danmark
  (acting for Hertz) v
Dansk Arbejdsgiverforening
  (acting for Aldi Marked K/S)
The dismissal of a female worker because of her pregnancy constitutes direct discrimination on grounds of sex, in the same way as does the refusal to recruit a pregnant woman. Therefore, a woman is protected from dismissal because of her absence during the maternity leave from which she benefits under national law.

Webb v   **[1994] IRLR 482 ECJ**
EMO Air Cargo (UK) Ltd
Dismissal of a woman on grounds of pregnancy constitutes direct discrimination on grounds of sex. In determining whether there is discrimination on grounds of sex contrary to the Directive, the situation of a woman who finds herself incapable by reason of pregnancy of performing the task for which she was recruited cannot be compared with that of a man similarly incapable for medical or other reasons.

Sexual orientation

Grant v   **[1998] IRLR 206 ECJ**
South-West Trains Ltd
Discrimination based on sexual orientation does not constitute discrimination based on the sex of the worker within the meaning of Article 141. European Community law does not cover discrimination based on sexual orientation. Therefore, a refusal by an employer to allow travel concessions to a person of the same sex with whom a worker has a stable relationship is not contrary to EU law, even if such concessions are allowed to a person of the opposite sex with whom a worker has a stable relationship.

R v   **[1998] IRLR 508 HC**
Secretary of State for Defence
  ex parte Perkins (No.2)
Although the decision in *Grant* that Community law does not cover or render unlawful discrimination based on sexual orientation was a decision on the meaning of the word "sex" in the Equal Pay Directive, it must reasonably be inferred that the same word has the same meaning in the Equal Treatment Directive.

Transsexualism

P v   [1996] IRLR 347 ECJ
S
Where such discrimination arises from the gender reassignment of the person concerned, he or she is treated unfavourably by comparison with persons of the sex to which he or she was deemed to belong before undergoing gender reassignment.

Exclusions

Perceval-Price v   [2000] IRLR 380 NICA
Department of Economic Development
The term "worker" in the context of Community law must be interpreted broadly and in a purposive fashion so as to include within the definition all persons who are engaged in a relationship which is broadly that of employment rather than being self-employed or independent contractors.

Perceval-Price v   [2000] IRLR 380 NICA
Department of Economic Development
Tribunal chairmen are "workers" who are in "employment" within the meaning of European Community law, and are therefore entitled to bring equal pay and sex discrimination complaints, notwithstanding that they do not fall within the definition of "employment" under domestic equal pay and sex discrimination legislation because they are holders of statutory office.

Sex as determining factor

(2) This Directive shall be without prejudice to the right of Member States to exclude from its field of application those occupational activities and, where appropriate, the training leading thereto, for which, by reason of their nature or the context in which they are carried out, the sex of the worker constitutes a determining factor.

EQUAL TREATMENT DIRECTIVE – Article 2

Johnston v   [1986] IRLR 263 ECJ
The Chief Constable of the Royal
Ulster Constabulary
Article 2(2) of the Equal Treatment Directive, being a derogation from an individual right laid down in the Directive, must be interpreted strictly, and in determining the scope of any derogation, the principle of proportionality must be observed. That principle requires that derogations remain within the limits of what is appropriate and necessary for achieving the aim in view and requires the principle of equal treatment to be reconciled as far as possible with the requirement which constituted the decisive factor as regards the context of the activity in question. It is for the national court to ensure that the principle of proportionality is observed.

Sirdar v   [2000] IRLR 47 ECJ
The Army Board
There is no general exception in the EC Treaty covering all measures taken by Member States for reasons of public security. Therefore, application of the principle of equal treatment is not subject to any general reservation as regards measures for the organisation of the armed forces. However, the UK Government might be entitled under Article 2(2) of the Equal Treatment Directive to exclude women from service in special combat units such as the Royal Marines.

Commission of the European   [1984] IRLR 29 ECJ
  Communities v
United Kingdom of Great Britain
  and Northern Ireland
Reconciliation of the principle of equality of treatment with the principle of respect for private life is one of the factors which must be taken into consideration in determining the scope of the exception provided for in Article 2(2) of the Equal Treatment Directive.

Pregnancy

(3) This Directive shall be without prejudice to provisions concerning the protection of women, particularly as regards pregnancy and maternity.

EQUAL TREATMENT DIRECTIVE – Article 2

Johnston v   [1986] IRLR 263 ECJ
The Chief Constable of the Royal
  Ulster Constabulary
The differences in treatment between men and women that Article 2(3) of the Equal Treatment Directive allows out of a concern to protect women, do not include risks and dangers that do not specifically affect women as such. Article 2(3) must be interpreted strictly. It is clear from the express reference to pregnancy and maternity that the Directive is intended to protect a woman's biological condition and the special relationship which exists between a woman and her child. That provision of the Directive does not therefore allow women to be excluded from a certain type of employment on the ground that public opinion demands that women be given greater protection than men against risks which affect men and women in the same way and which are distinct from women's specific needs of protection, such as those expressly mentioned in Article 2(3).

Positive action

(4) With a view to ensuring full equality in practice between men and women in working life, the principle of equal treatment shall not prevent any Member State from maintaining or adopting measures providing for specific advantages in order to make it easier for the underrepresented sex to pursue a vocational activity or to prevent or compensate for disadvantages in professional careers.

EC TREATY – Article 141

4. This Directive shall be without prejudice to measures to promote equal opportunity for men and women, in particular by removing existing inequalities which affect women's opportunities in the areas referred to in Article 1(1).

EQUAL TREATMENT DIRECTIVE – Article 2

Kalanke v   [1995] IRLR 660 ECJ
Freie Hansestadt Bremen
National rules which guarantee women absolute and unconditional priority for appointment or promotion go beyond promoting equal opportunities and overstep the limits of the exception to the principle of equal treatment in Article 2(4) of the Equal Treatment Directive. As a derogation from an individual right laid down in the Directive, Article 2(4) must be interpreted strictly. It permits national measures relating to access to employment, including promotion, which give a specific advantage to women with a view to improving their ability to compete on the labour market and to pursue a career on an equal footing with men.

EFTA Surveillance Authority v   [2003] IRLR 318 EFTA Ct
Kingdom of Norway
The Equal Treatment Directive is based on the recognition of the right to equal treatment as a fundamental right of the individual. National rules and practices derogating from that right can only be permissible when they show sufficient flexibility to allow a balance between the need for the promotion of the under-represented gender and the opportunity for candidates of the opposite gender to have their situation objectively assessed. There must, as a matter of principle, be a possibility that the best-qualified candidate obtains the post. Therefore, national legislation which allows a number of academic posts to be reserved exclusively for women because they are under-represented in the particular post went beyond the scope of Article 2(4) of the Directive insofar as it gave absolute and unconditional priority to female candidates.

Marschall v   [1998] IRLR 39 ECJ
Land Nordrhein-Westfalen
It is not contrary to the Equal Treatment Directive for equally-qualified women to be given preference for promotion where there are fewer women than men in the relevant post, so long as male candidates are guaranteed that women are not to be given priority if reasons specific to an individual equally-qualified man tilt the balance in his favour.

Application by Badek   [2000] IRLR 432 ECJ
A measure which is intended to give priority in promotion to women in sectors of the public service where they are under-represented is compatible with Community law if it does not automatically and unconditionally give priority to women when women and men are equally qualified, and the candidatures are the subject of an objective assessment which takes account of the specific personal situations of all candidates.

Application by Badek   [2000] IRLR 432 ECJ
The Equal Treatment Directive does not preclude a rule for the public service which allocates at least half the training places to women in occupations in which women are under-represented and for which the State does not have a monopoly of training. Nor does it preclude a rule for the public service which guarantees, in sectors in which women are underrepresented, that where male and female candidates have equal qualifications, either all women who are qualified will be given an interview, or that no more male candidates than female candidates will be interviewed.

Abrahamsson v   [2000] IRLR 732 ECJ
Fogelqvist
The Equal Treatment Directive precludes national legislation which provides for positive discrimination in recruitment in favour of candidates of the under-represented sex by automatically granting preference to candidates belonging to the under-represented sex, so long as they are sufficiently qualified, subject only to the proviso that the difference between the merits of the candidates of each sex is not so great as to result in a breach of the requirement of objectivity in making appointments. Such legislation was ultimately based on the mere fact of belonging to the under-represented sex.

Abrahamsson v   [2000] IRLR 732 ECJ
Fogelqvist
Although Article 141(4) allows the Member States to maintain or adopt measures providing for special advantages intended to prevent or compensate for disadvantages in professional careers in order to ensure full equality between men and women in professional life, it cannot be inferred that it allows a selection method which is disproportionate to the aim pursued.

Abrahamsson v   [2000] IRLR 732 ECJ
Fogelqvist
The Equal Treatment Directive does not preclude a rule of national case law under which a candidate belonging to the underrepresented sex may be granted preference over a competitor of the opposite sex, provided that the candidates possess equivalent or substantially equivalent merits and the candidatures are subjected to an objective assessment which takes account of the specific personal situations of all the candidates.

Lommers v   [2002] IRLR 430 ECJ
Minister van Landbouw,
Natuurbeheer en Visserij
Provision of a limited number of subsidised nursery places to female staff only is permissible in principle under Article 2(4) of the Equal Treatment Directive, where the scheme has been set up by the employer to tackle extensive under-representation of women, in a context characterised by a proven insufficiency of proper, affordable child-care facilities, so long as male employees who take care of their children by themselves are allowed to have access to the scheme on the same conditions as female employees. The fact that the policy did not guarantee access to nursery

places to employees of both sexes on an equal footing was not contrary to the principle of proportionality.

Access to jobs

(1) Application of the principle of equal treatment means that there shall be no discrimination whatsoever on grounds of sex in the conditions, including selection criteria, for access to all jobs or posts, whatever the sector or branch of activity, and to all levels of the occupational hierarchy.

EQUAL TREATMENT DIRECTIVE – Article 3

Johnston v   **[1986] IRLR 263 ECJ**
The Chief Constable of the Royal
  Ulster Constabulary
The application of the principle of equal treatment to the conditions governing access to jobs, as set out in Article 3(1) of the Equal Treatment Directive, is unconditional and sufficiently precise so that it may be relied upon by individuals as against a Member State where that Member State fails to implement it correctly.

Gerster v   **[1997] IRLR 699 ECJ**
Freistaat Bayern
Legislation which treats part-time employees less favourably than full-time employees by providing for them to accrue length of service more slowly, and perforce gain promotion later, results in discrimination against women as compared with men and must in principle be regarded as contrary to the Equal Treatment Directive, unless the distinction is justified by objective reasons unrelated to any discrimination on grounds of sex. There would be no infringement of the Equal Treatment Directive if the national court found that part-time employees are generally slower than full-time employees in acquiring job-related abilities and skills, and that the competent authorities were in a position to establish that the measures chosen reflected a legitimate social policy aim, were an appropriate means of achieving that aim and were necessary in order to do so. However, a requirement that part-time employees must complete a longer period of service than a full-time employee in order to have approximately the same chance of promotion must be regarded as contrary to the Equal Treatment Directive if the national court concludes that there is no special link between length of service and acquisition of a certain level of knowledge or experience.

Kording v   **[1997] IRLR 710 ECJ**
Senator Für Finanzen
Legislation which treats a part-time employee less favourably than a full-time employee, by providing that the total length of professional experience required for exemption from a qualifying examination is to be extended on a pro-rata basis for part-time workers, gives rise to indirect discrimination against women if substan-

tially fewer men than women work part-time and must in principle be regarded as contrary to the Equal Treatment Directive. However, such inequality of treatment would be compatible with the Directive if it were justified by objective factors unrelated to any discrimination on grounds of sex.

Meyers v   **[1995] IRLR 498 ECJ**
Adjudication Officer
A benefit such as family credit in the UK falls within the scope of Article 3 of the Equal Treatment Directive, since its subject-matter is access to employment in that the benefit is intended to keep poorly-paid workers in employment. The fact that a scheme of benefits is part of a national social security system cannot exclude it from the scope of the Directive.

Pregnancy discrimination

Dekker v   **[1991] IRLR 27 ECJ**
VJV-Centrum
A refusal to employ because of the financial consequences of absence connected with pregnancy must be deemed to be based principally on the fact of the pregnancy. Such discrimination cannot be justified by the financial detriment that would be suffered by the employer during the woman's maternity leave.

Dekker v   **[1991] IRLR 27 ECJ**
VJV-Centrum
If the reason a woman is not selected is because she is pregnant, the decision is directly related to the applicant's sex and it is not important that there were no male applicants.

Mahlburg v   **[2000] IRLR 276 ECJ**
Land Mecklenburg-Vorpommern
It is contrary to Article 2(1) of the Equal Treatment Directive for an employer to refuse to appoint a pregnant woman to a post of an unlimited duration on the ground that a statutory prohibition on employment arising on account of her pregnancy would prevent her from being employed in that post from the outset and for the duration of the pregnancy.

Busch v   **[2003] IRLR 625 ECJ**
Klinikum Neustadt GmbH & Co Betriebs-KG
It is contrary to Article 2(1) of the Equal Treatment Directive to require an employee who wishes to return to work before the end of parental leave to inform her employer that she is pregnant, even though she will be unable to carry out all of her duties because of legislative provisions. Such discrimination cannot be justified by the fact that a woman is temporarily prevented from performing all of her duties by a legislative prohibition imposed because of pregnancy. That would be contrary to the objective of protection pursued by the Equal Treatment Directive and the Pregnant Workers Directive and would rob them of any practical effect.

Access to training

Application of the principle of equal treatment with regard to access to all types, and to all levels of vocational guidance, vocational training, advanced vocational training and retraining, means that Member States shall take all necessary measures to ensure that:

> *(a) any laws, regulations and administrative provisions contrary to the principle of equal treatment shall be abolished;*
>
> *(b) any provisions contrary to the principle of equal treatment which are included in collective agreements, individual contracts of employment, internal rules of undertakings or in rules governing the independent occupations and professions shall be, or may be declared, null and void or may be amended;*
>
> *(c) without prejudice to the freedom granted in certain Member States to certain private training establishments, vocational guidance, vocational training, advanced training and retraining shall be accessible on the basis of the same criteria and at the same levels without any discrimination on grounds of sex.*

EQUAL TREATMENT DIRECTIVE – Article 4(1)

Johnston v   **[1986] IRLR 263 ECJ**
The Chief Constable of the Royal
  Ulster Constabulary

The application of the principle of equal treatment to the conditions governing access to training, as set out in Article 4(1) of the Equal Treatment Directive, is unconditional and sufficiently precise so that it may be relied upon by individuals as against a Member State where that Member State fails to implement it correctly.

Working conditions and dismissal

(1) Application of the principle of equal treatment with regard to working conditions, including the conditions governing dismissal, means that men and women shall be guaranteed the same conditions without discrimination on grounds of sex.

EQUAL TREATMENT DIRECTIVE – Article 5

Marshall v   **[1986] IRLR 140 ECJ**
Southampton and South-West
  Hampshire Area Health Authority

Article 5(1) of the Equal Treatment Directive may be relied upon as against a State authority acting in its capacity as employer, in order to avoid the application of any national provision which does not conform to Article 5(1). Article 5(1) is sufficiently precise and unconditional to be relied on by individuals and to be applied by national courts. The provision, taken by itself, prohibits any discrimination on grounds of sex with regard to working conditions in a general manner and in unequivocal terms. It does not confer on Member States the right to limit the application of the principle of equality of treatment in its field of operation or to subject it to conditions.

Meyers v   **[1995] IRLR 498 ECJ**
Adjudication Officer

To confine the concept of a working condition within the meaning of Article 5 solely to those working conditions which are set out in the contract of employment or applied by the employer in respect of a worker's employment would remove situations directly covered by an employment relationship from the scope of the Directive. Therefore, a benefit such as family credit, which is necessarily linked to an employment relationship, constitutes a working condition within the meaning of Article 5 of the Directive.

Discriminatory retirement ages

Burton v   **[1982] IRLR 116 ECJ**
British Railways Board

"Dismissal" for the purposes of Article 5(1) of the Equal Treatment Directive must be widely construed.

Marshall v   **[1986] IRLR 140 ECJ**
Southampton and South-West
  Hampshire Area Health Authority

A general policy concerning dismissal involving the dismissal of a woman solely because she has attained the qualifying age for a State pension, which age is different under national legislation for men and women, constitutes discrimination on grounds of sex contrary to Article 5(1) of the Equal Treatment Directive. In accordance with the decision of the European Court in *Burton v British Railways Board*, the term "dismissal" in Article 5(1) must be given a wide meaning. An age limit for the compulsory dismissal of workers pursuant to an employer's general policy concerning retirement relates to the conditions governing dismissal, to be determined in accordance with the Equal Treatment Directive, even if the dismissal involved the grant of a retirement pension.

Pensions

(1) The purpose of this Directive is to put into effect in the Member States the principle of equal treatment for men and women as regards access to employment, including promotion, and to vocational training and as regards working conditions and, on the conditions referred to in paragraph 2, social security. This principle is hereinafter referred to as "the principle of equal treatment".

(2) With a view to ensuring the progressive implementation of the principle of equal treatment in matters of social security, the Council, acting on a proposal from the Commission, will adopt provisions defining its substance, its scope and the arrangements for its application.

EQUAL TREATMENT DIRECTIVE – Article 1

(1) This Directive shall be without prejudice to the right of Member States to exclude from its scope:

> *(a) the determination of pensionable age for the purposes of granting old-age and retirement pensions and the possible consequences thereof for other benefits;*

*(b) advantages in respect of old-age pension schemes grant-
ed to persons who have brought up children; the acquisition of benefit entitlements following periods of interrup-
tion of employment due to the bringing up of children;*

*(c) the granting of old-age or invalidity benefit entitle-
ments by virtue of the derived entitlements of a wife;*

*(d) the granting of increases of long-term invalidity, old-
age, accidents at work and occupational disease benefits for a dependent wife;*

*(e) the consequences of the exercise, before the adoption
of this Directive, of a right of option not to acquire
rights to incur obligations under a statutory scheme.*

SOCIAL SECURITY DIRECTIVE – Article 7

Marshall v   **[1986] IRLR 140 ECJ**
Southampton and South-West
Hampshire Area Health Authority
The exclusion of social security matters from the scope of the
Equal Treatment Directive must be interpreted strictly so that
the exception to the prohibition of discrimination on grounds of
sex provided for in Article 7(1) of the Social Security Directive
79/7 applies only to the determination of pensionable age for
the purposes of granting old-age and retirement pensions and
the possible consequences thereof for other benefits.

Burton v   **[1982] IRLR 116 ECJ**
British Railways Board
The conditions of access to a voluntary redundancy benefit
paid by an employer to a worker wishing to leave his
employment are covered by the principle of equal treatment
contained in Article 5(1).

Roberts v   **[1986] IRLR 150 ECJ**
Tate & Lyle Industries Ltd
A contractual provision which lays down a single age for the
dismissal of both men and women under a mass redundancy
involving the grant of an early retirement pension, in circumstances where the normal retirement age is different for men
and women, does not constitute discrimination on grounds of
sex contrary to Article 5(1) of the Equal Treatment Directive.
The fixing of the same age for both sexes for the grant of an
early pension does not amount to discrimination on grounds
of sex even though under the statutory social security scheme
the pensionable age for men and women is different.

R v   **[1992] IRLR 376 ECJ**
Secretary of State for Social Security
ex parte Equal Opportunities Commission
Article 7(1)(a) of EC Social Security Directive 79/7, which
allows Member States to exclude from the principle of equal
treatment "the determination of pensionable age for the purposes of granting old-age and retirement pensions and the
possible consequences thereof for other benefits", authorises
the maintenance of different contribution periods for male
and female workers under a State pension scheme such as in
the UK. The power of derogation conferred by Article
7(1)(a) does not merely allow men and women to be treated
unequally with respect to the moment at which they become

entitled to a pension. It also covers other forms of discrimination if they are found to be necessary in order to achieve
the objectives which the Directive is intended to pursue.

Pregnancy

Brown v   **[1998] IRLR 445 ECJ**
Rentokil Ltd
Dismissal of a woman at any time during her pregnancy for
absences due to incapacity for work caused by an illness
resulting from that pregnancy is direct discrimination on
grounds of sex contrary to the EC Equal Treatment Directive.

Webb v   **[1994] IRLR 482 ECJ**
EMO Air Cargo (UK) Ltd
It is contrary to the Equal Treatment Directive to dismiss
a woman employed for an unlimited term who, shortly
after her recruitment is found to be pregnant, even though
she was recruited initially to replace another employee
during the latter's maternity leave and notwithstanding
that the employer would have dismissed a male employee
engaged for this purpose who required leave of absence at
the relevant time for medical or other reasons.

Webb v   **[1994] IRLR 482 ECJ**
EMO Air Cargo (UK) Ltd
Dismissal of a pregnant woman recruited for an indefinite period cannot be justified on grounds relating to her inability to
fulfil a fundamental condition of her contract of employment.

Tele Danmark v   **[2001] IRLR 853 ECJ**
HK (acting on behalf of Brandt-Nielsen)
Article 5 of the Equal Treatment Directive and Article 10
of the Pregnant Workers Directive preclude a worker from
being dismissed on the ground of pregnancy, notwithstanding that she was recruited for a fixed period, failed to
inform the employer that she was pregnant even though she
was aware of this when the contract of employment was
concluded, and because of her pregnancy was unable to
work during a substantial part of the term of that contract.
Dismissal of a worker on account of pregnancy constitutes
direct discrimination on grounds of sex, whatever the
nature and extent of the economic loss incurred by the
employer as a result of her absence because of pregnancy.
Whether the contract was concluded for a fixed or an indefinite period has no bearing on the discriminatory character
of the dismissal. In either case the employee's inability to
perform her contract of employment is due to pregnancy.

Brown v   **[1998] IRLR 445 ECJ**
Rentokil Ltd
It is direct discrimination on grounds of sex to dismiss a
pregnant woman because of absences resulting from pregnancy in accordance with a contractual term providing that
an employer may dismiss workers of either sex after a stip-
ulated number of weeks of continuous absence.

Brown v   **[1998] IRLR 445 ECJ**
Rentokil Ltd

The Equal Treatment Directive affords a woman protection against dismissal on grounds of her absence throughout the period of pregnancy and during the maternity leave accorded to her under national law. Where a woman is absent owing to illness resulting from pregnancy or childbirth, and that illness arose during pregnancy and persisted during and after maternity leave, her absence not only during maternity leave but also during the period extending from the start of her pregnancy to the start of her maternity leave cannot be taken into account for computation of the period justifying her dismissal under national law. Absence after maternity leave may be taken into account under the same conditions as a man's absence through incapacity for work of the same duration.

Habermann-Beltermann v   **[1994] IRLR 364 ECJ**
Arbeiterwohlfahrt, Bezirksverband
  Ndb/Opf eV

Termination of a contract without a fixed term on account of a woman's pregnancy cannot be justified on the ground that a statutory prohibition, imposed because of pregnancy, temporarily prevents the employee from performing night work.

Jiménez Melgar v   **[2001] IRLR 848 ECJ**
Ayuntamiento de Los Barrios

Non-renewal of a fixed-term contract is a refusal of employment and, where non-renewal of a fixed-term contract is based on the worker's pregnancy, it constitutes direct discrimination on grounds of sex contrary to Articles 2(1) and 3(1) of the Equal Treatment Directive.

Handels- og Kontorfunktionærernes   **[1991] IRLR 31 ECJ**
  Forbund i Danmark
  (acting for Hertz) v
Dansk Arbejdsgiverforening
  (acting for Aldi Marked K/S)

The Equal Treatment Directive does not preclude dismissals resulting from absence due to an illness which originated in pregnancy or confinement and which appears after maternity leave.

CNAVTS v   **[1998] IRLR 399 ECJ**
Thibault

The principle of non-discrimination on grounds of sex in working conditions requires that a woman who continues to be bound to her employer by her contract of employment during maternity leave should not be deprived of the benefit of working conditions which apply to both men and women and are the result of that employment relationship. The exercise by women of pregnancy and maternity rights cannot be the subject of unfavourable treatment regarding their access to employment or their working conditions.

Gillespie v   **[1996] IRLR 214 ECJ**
Northern Health and Social
  Services Board

The Equal Treatment Directive does not apply to pay. Since the benefit paid during maternity leave constitutes pay and falls within the scope of Article 141 and the Equal Pay Directive, it cannot be covered by the Equal Treatment Directive as well.

CNAVTS v   **[1998] IRLR 399 ECJ**
Thibault

It is contrary to the Equal Treatment Directive for a woman to be accorded unfavourable treatment regarding her working conditions by being deprived of the right to an annual assessment of her performance and, therefore, of the opportunity of qualifying for promotion to a higher pay grade as a result of her absence on account of maternity leave.

Boyle v   **[1998] IRLR 717 ECJ**
Equal Opportunities Commission

A contractual term according to which a worker who does not return to work after childbirth is required to repay the difference between the pay received by her during her maternity leave and the Statutory Maternity Pay to which she was entitled does not constitute discrimination on grounds of sex contrary to EC law, notwithstanding that for other forms of paid leave, such as sick leave, workers are entitled to their salary without having to undertake to return to work at the end of their leave. The situation of a pregnant woman cannot be compared to that of a man or a woman on sick leave.

Boyle v   **[1998] IRLR 717 ECJ**
Equal Opportunities Commission

EC law does not preclude a clause in a contract of employment which requires a woman who is on sick leave with a pregnancy-related illness to take paid maternity leave if the period of sick leave occurs within six weeks of the expected date of childbirth, notwithstanding that any other worker who is sick is entitled to exercise their right to unconditional paid sick leave.

Boyle v   **[1998] IRLR 717 ECJ**
Equal Opportunities Commission

EC law does not preclude a clause in a contract of employment which limits the period during which annual holiday accrues to the statutory minimum 14 weeks' maternity leave period and which provides that annual holiday ceases to accrue during any period of supplementary maternity leave granted by the employer.

Transsexuals

P v   **[1996] IRLR 347 ECJ**
S

Dismissal of a transsexual for a reason related to a gender reassignment must be regarded as contrary to Article 5(1) of the Directive.

Indirect discrimination under EC law

R v   **[1999] IRLR 253 ECJ**
Secretary of State for Employment
    ex parte Seymour-Smith
In order to establish whether a measure adopted by a Member State has disparate effect as between men and women to such a degree as to amount to indirect discrimination for the purposes of Article 141, the national court must verify whether the statistics indicate that a considerably smaller percentage of women than men is able to satisfy the condition required. That would be evidence of apparent sex discrimination. That could also be the case if the statistical evidence revealed a lesser but persistent and relatively constant disparity over a long period between men and women who satisfy the requirement.

R v   **[2000] IRLR 363 HL**
Secretary of State for Employment
    ex parte Seymour-Smith (No.2)
The approach adopted by the European Court is similar to that provided in s.1(1)(b) of the Sex Discrimination Act. A considerable disparity can be more readily established if the statistical evidence covers a long period and the figures show a persistent and relatively constant disparity. In such a case, a lesser statistical disparity may suffice to show that the disparity is considerable than if the statistics cover only a short period or if they present an uneven picture.

R v   **[1999] IRLR 253 ECJ**
Secretary of State for Employment
    ex parte Seymour-Smith
The best approach for determining whether a rule has a more unfavourable impact on women than on men is to consider the respective proportions of men in the workforce able to satisfy the requirement and those unable to do so, and to compare those proportions as regards women in the workforce.

R v   **[2000] IRLR 363 HL**
Secretary of State for Employment
    ex parte Seymour-Smith (No.2)
The applicants had shown that at the time of their dismissal in 1991 the two-year qualifying period to bring an unfair dismissal complaint had a disparately adverse impact on women so as to amount to indirect discrimination contrary to Article 141 in circumstances in which, from 1985 up to and including 1991, the ratio of men and women who qualified was roughly 10:9. A persistent and constant disparity of that order in respect of the entire male and female labour forces was adequate to demonstrate that the extension of the qualifying period from one to two years had a considerably greater adverse impact on women than men.

Jørgensen v   **[2000] IRLR 726 ECJ**
Foreningen af Speciallæger
In order to determine whether a collective agreement indi-

rectly discriminates on grounds of sex, the Equal Treatment Directive requires a separate assessment to be made of each of the key conditions laid down in the contested provisions, in so far as those key elements constitute in themselves specific measures based on their own criteria of application and affecting a significant number of persons belonging to a determined category. An overall assessment of all the elements which might be involved in a scheme or a set of provisions would not allow effective review of the application of the principle of equal treatment and might not comply with the rules governing the burden of proof in matters relating to indirect discrimination on grounds of sex.

R v   **[1999] IRLR 253 ECJ**
Secretary of State for Employment
    ex parte Seymour-Smith
If a considerably smaller percentage of women than men is capable of fulfilling a statutory requirement, such as the service qualification for unfair dismissal, it is for the Member State, as the author of the allegedly discriminatory rule, to show that the said rule reflects a legitimate aim of its social policy, that that aim is unrelated to any discrimination based on sex, and that it could reasonably consider that the means chosen were suitable for attaining that aim.

Nolte v   **[1996] IRLR 225 ECJ**
Landesversicherungsanstalt
    Hannover
A legislative measure is based on objective factors unrelated to discrimination on grounds of sex where the measure chosen reflects a legitimate social policy of the Member State, is appropriate to achieve that aim and necessary in order to do so. However, social policy is a matter for the Member States. Consequently, the Member States have a broad margin of discretion in exercising their competence to choose the measures capable of achieving the aim of their social and employment policy.

Kruger v   **[1999] IRLR 808 ECJ**
Kreiskrankenhaus Ebersberg
The exclusion of persons in "minor" employment from the scope of a collective agreement providing for the grant of a special annual bonus was indirect discrimination within the meaning of Article 141 where it affected a considerably higher percentage of women than men. The exclusion was not justified since an exclusion from the benefit of a collective agreement is a different situation from that in *Nolte* and *Megner*, in which the Court held that the exclusion of persons in minor employment from social insurance fell within the broad margin of discretion of Member States to choose the measures for achieving the aims of their social and employment policy.

R v   **[1999] IRLR 253 ECJ**
Secretary of State for Employment
    ex parte Seymour-Smith
In order to show that a measure is justified by objective factors unrelated to any discrimination based on sex, it is not

sufficient for a Member State to show that it was reasonably entitled to consider that the measure would advance a social policy aim. Although, in the *Nolte* case, the Court observed that, in choosing the measures capable of achieving the aims of their social and employment policy, the Member States have a broad margin of discretion, that cannot have the effect of frustrating the implementation of a fundamental principle of Community law such as that of equal pay for men and women. Mere generalisations concerning the capacity of a specific measure to encourage recruitment are not enough to show that the aim of the disputed rule is unrelated to any discrimination based on sex nor to provide evidence on the basis of which it could reasonably be considered that the means chosen were suitable for achieving that aim.

Jørgensen v   **[2000] IRLR 726 ECJ**
Foreningen af Speciallæger
Budgetary considerations cannot in themselves justify discrimination on grounds of sex. Although budgetary considerations may underlie a Member State's choice of social policy and influence the nature or scope of the social protection measures which it wishes to adopt, they do not in themselves constitute an aim pursued by that policy and cannot therefore justify discrimination against one of the sexes.

Kutz-Bauer v   **[2003] IRLR 368 ECJ**
Freie und Hansestadt Hamburg
An employer cannot justify discrimination solely because avoidance of such discrimination would involve increased costs.

Kachelmann v   **[2001] IRLR 49 ECJ**
Bankhaus Hermann Lampe KG
The Equal Treatment Directive does not preclude a selection process for dismissal when a part-time job is abolished on economic grounds that does not compare full-time workers with part-time workers, even though this may create an indirect disadvantage for part-time workers. If comparability between full-time and part-time workers were to be introduced in the selection process, that would have the effect of placing part-time workers at an advantage, while putting full-time workers at a disadvantage since, in the event of their jobs being abolished, part-time workers would have to be offered a full-time job, even if their employment contract did not entitle them to one.

R v   **[2000] IRLR 363 HL**
Secretary of State for Employment
   ex parte Seymour-Smith (No.2)
The onus is on the Member State to show (1) that the allegedly discriminatory rule reflects a legitimate aim of its social policy, (2) that this aim is unrelated to any discrimination based on sex, and (3) that the Member State could reasonably consider that the means chosen were suitable for attaining that aim. Governments must be able to govern and are to be afforded a broad measure of discretion. Generalised assumptions, lacking any factual foundation, are not

good enough, but national courts, acting with hindsight, are not to impose an impracticable burden on governments which are proceeding in good faith.

R v   **[2000] IRLR 363 HL**
Secretary of State for Employment
   ex parte Seymour-Smith (No.2)
If the Government introduces a measure which proves to have a disparately adverse impact, it is under a duty to take reasonable steps to monitor the working of the measure and review the position periodically. The requirements of Community law must be complied with at all relevant times. The retention of a measure having a disparately adverse impact may no longer be objectively justifiable.

R v   **[2000] IRLR 363 HL**
Secretary of State for Employment
   ex parte Seymour-Smith (No.2)
The Secretary of State had discharged the burden of showing that he was reasonably entitled in 1985 to consider that the extension of the unfair dismissal qualifying period from one to two years was justified by objective factors unrelated to sex, and that the 1985 Order was still objectively justified in 1991.

R v   **[1987] IRLR 53 HC**
Secretary of State for Education
   ex parte Schaffter
Statutory eligibility requirements for education grants which distinguished between single and married lone parents and had a disproportionate impact upon women had not been shown to be objectively justified for the purposes of the Equal Treatment Directive where the argument relied upon by the Secretary of State did not give reasons for the distinction drawn but merely stated that the purpose of the Regulations was to benefit married lone parents. That did not amount to a justification. Therefore, the requirements infringed the principle of equal treatment for men and women as regards access to vocational training embodied in the Equal Treatment Directive.

Qualifying thresholds

R v   **[1994] IRLR 176 HL**
Secretary of State for Employment
   ex parte Equal Opportunities Commission
The provisions of the Employment Protection (Consolidation) Act whereby employees who work for fewer than 16 hours per week were subject to different conditions in respect to qualification for redundancy pay from those which apply to employees who work for 16 hours per week or more are incompatible with Article 141 of the EC Treaty and EC Equal Pay Directive 75/11.

R v   **[1994] IRLR 176 HL**
Secretary of State for Employment
   ex parte Equal Opportunities Commission
The provisions of the Employment Protection (Consoli-

dation) Act whereby employees who work for fewer than 16 hours per week were subject to different conditions in respect of the right to compensation for unfair dismissal are incompatible with EC Equal Treatment Directive 76/207.

R v   **[1994] IRLR 176 HL**
Secretary of State for Employment
   ex parte Equal Opportunities Commission
No objective justification for the hours per week qualifying thresholds in the Employment Protection (Consolidation) Act had been established by the Secretary of State where, on the evidence, the threshold provisions had not been proved actually to result in greater availability of part-time work than would be the case without them.

R v   **[1996] IRLR 464 CA**
Secretary of State for Trade & Industry
   ex parte Unison
It was lawful under EC law for the 1995 Regulations to exempt employees with less than two years' continuous service from the protection against dismissal by reason of a transfer guaranteed by Article 4 of Directive 77/187, since the two-year qualifying period could not be regarded as having a disparate adverse impact on women. Evidence that the disparity between the percentage of female employees who could comply with a two-year service qualification with their employer compared with the percentage of male employees who could comply was only four percentage points suggested that this fell within the de minimis exception and was not a considerable difference. Thus if the Secretary of State had considered, or if he were to consider, this question, it would be open to him to conclude that the disparity was less than considerable and there would be no obligation upon him to consider objective justification.

Sanctions

Member States shall introduce into their national legal systems such measures as are necessary to enable all persons who consider themselves wronged by failure to apply to them the principle of equal treatment within the meaning of Articles 3, 4 and 5 to pursue their claims by judicial process after possible recourse to other competent authorities.

                              EQUAL TREATMENT DIRECTIVE – Article 6

Coote v   **[1998] IRLR 656 ECJ**
Granada Hospitality Ltd
By virtue of Article 6, all persons have the right to obtain an effective remedy in a competent court against measures which they consider interfere with the equal treatment for men and women laid down in the Directive. It is for the Member States to ensure effective judicial control of compliance with the applicable provisions of Community law and of national legislation intended to give effect to the rights for which the Directive provides.

Marshall v   **[1993] IRLR 445 ECJ**
Southampton and South-West Hampshire
   Area Health Authority (No.2)
Article 6 of EC Equal Treatment Directive 76/207 must be interpreted as meaning that compensation for the loss and damage sustained by a victim of discrimination may not be limited by national law to an upper limit fixed a priori or by excluding an award of interest to compensate for the loss sustained by the recipient as a result of the effluxion of time until the capital sum awarded is actually paid. Financial compensation must be adequate, in that it must enable the loss and damage actually sustained as a result of discrimination to be made good in full in accordance with the applicable national rules.

Marshall v   **[1993] IRLR 445 ECJ**
Southampton and South-West Hampshire
   Area Health Authority (No.2)
Article 6 of the Equal Treatment Directive may be relied upon by individuals before the national courts as against an authority of the State acting in its capacity as an employer in order to set aside a national provision which imposes limits on the amount of compensation recoverable by way of reparation.

Dekker v   **[1991] IRLR 27 ECJ**
VJV-Centrum
The Equal Treatment Directive does not make the liability of the discriminator in any way dependent upon evidence of fault on the part of the employer, nor require that it be established that there are no grounds for justification which he can take advantage of. Accordingly, where a Member State chooses a civil law sanction, any breach of the prohibition of discrimination must in itself be sufficient to impose full liability on the discriminator and no account can be taken of grounds for justification provided for under national law.

Drӕhmpӕhl v   **[1997] IRLR 538 ECJ**
Urania Immobilenservice ohG
The Equal Treatment Directive precludes provisions of domestic law which, unlike other provisions of domestic civil and labour law, place an upper limit of three months' salary for the job in question as the amount of compensation which may be claimed by an applicant discriminated against on grounds of sex in the making of an appointment, where that applicant would have obtained the vacant position if the selection process had been carried out without discrimination. A Member State must ensure that infringements of Community law are penalised under procedural and substantive conditions which are analogous to those applicable to infringements of domestic law of a similar nature and importance.

EC law and UK law

General principles

Webb v   **[1993] IRLR 27 HL**
EMO Air Cargo (UK) Ltd

Although an EC Directive does not have direct effect upon the relationship between a worker and an employer who is not an emanation of the State, it is for a United Kingdom court to construe domestic legislation in any field covered by a Community Directive so as to accord with the interpretation of the Directive as laid down by the European Court, if that can be done without distorting the meaning of the domestic legislation. That is so whether the domestic legislation came after or preceded the Directive. However, as the European Court said in the *Marleasing* case, a national court must construe a domestic law to accord with the terms of a Directive in the same field only if it is possible to do so. That means that the domestic law must be open to an interpretation consistent with the Directive.

Porter v   **[1993] IRLR 329 NICA**
Cannon Hygiene Ltd

If in a given situation there are two possible interpretations of a provision in national law and one of them accords with the wording and purpose of a relevant EC Directive while the other does not do so, the national court's duty under the EC Treaty is to prefer the interpretation which accords with the Directive. However, there is no "usual method of interpretation" which enables or permits a court simply to disregard a statutory provision or interpret it in a sense directly opposite to that which the House of Lords has said is the correct interpretation.

Specific examples

Duke v   **[1988] IRLR 118 HL**
GEC Reliance

As s.6(4) of the Sex Discrimination Act 1975 was intended to preserve discriminatory retirement ages, it was not possible to construe it in a manner which gave effect to EC Equal Treatment Directive 76/207 as interpreted by the European Court of Justice in the first *Marshall* decision.

Finnegan v   **[1990] IRLR 299 HL**
Clowney Youth Training Programme Ltd

The exclusion of complaints relating to retirement in Article 8(4) of the Sex Discrimination (Northern Ireland) Order 1976 was indistinguishable from the exclusion in s.6(4) of the Sex Discrimination Act 1975 which the House of Lords, in *Duke v GEC Reliance,* held was not to be construed so as to conform to the EC Equal Treatment Directive 76/207.

EXCLUSIONS AND EXCEPTIONS

Meaning of "employment"

(1) In this Act, unless the context otherwise requires –
"employment" means employment under a contract of service or of apprenticeship or a contract personally to execute any work or labour, and related expressions shall be construed accordingly;
SEX DISCRIMINATION ACT – s.82
RACE RELATIONS ACT – s.78

Mirror Group Newspapers Ltd v   **[1986] IRLR 27 CA**
Gunning

The words "a contract personally to execute any work or labour" in the extended definition of "employment" in s.82(1) of the Sex Discrimination Act contemplates a contract whose dominant purpose is that the party contracting to provide services under it performs personally the work or labour which forms the subject-matter of the contract. What falls to be determined, therefore, looking at the contract as a whole, is firstly whether there is some obligation by one contracting party personally to execute any work or labour and, secondly, whether that is the dominant purpose of the contract. The word "any" in the phrase "a contract personally to execute any work or labour" refers to the kind of work or labour to be performed rather than the amount or quantity. Therefore, it could not be accepted that any obligation personally to execute any work or labour, however limited in amount the work or labour might be, is sufficient to bring the contract containing that obligation within the statutory definition.

Mingeley v   **[2004] IRLR 373 CA**
Pennock and Ivory

On the plain words of the statute and the authorities, an applicant has to establish that his contract placed him under an obligation "personally to execute any work or labour".

Quinnen v   **[1984] IRLR 227 EAT**
Hovells

The inclusion in the definition of "employment" in s.82(1) of the Sex Discrimination Act of a third limb covering employment under "a contract personally to execute any work or labour" is a wide and flexible concept and was intended to enlarge upon the ordinary connotation of "employment" so as to include persons outside the master-servant relationship.

BP Chemicals Ltd v   **[1995] IRLR 128 EAT**
Gillick

The extended definition of "employment" in s.82, referring to employment under a contract personally to execute work, must be taken to refer to a contract between the party doing the work and the party for whom the work is done. A contract worker does not enter into an "employment" relationship with the principal.

Hall v
Woolston Hall Leisure Ltd
[2000] IRLR 578 CA

Where the performance by the employer of a contract of employment involves illegality of which the employee is aware, public policy does not bar the employee, when discriminated against on grounds of sex by dismissal, from recovering compensation under the Sex Discrimination Act. A complaint of sex discrimination by dismissal is not based on the contract of employment. Although the employee must establish that she was employed and was dismissed from that employment, it is the sex discrimination which is the core of the complaint. The correct approach is for the tribunal to consider whether the applicant's claim arises out of or is so inextricably bound up with her illegal conduct that the court could not permit the applicant to recover compensation without appearing to condone that conduct.

Claim in time

An employment tribunal shall not consider a complaint under [s.63 – SDA; s.54 – RRA] unless it is presented to the tribunal before the end of the period of three months beginning when the act complained of was done . . .

A court or tribunal may nevertheless consider any such complaint, claim or application which is out of time if, in all the circumstances of the case, it considers that it is just and equitable to do so.

For the purposes of this section –

(a) When the inclusion of any term in a contract renders the making of the contract an unlawful act, that act shall be treated as extending throughout the duration of the contract; and

(b) any act extending over a period shall be treated as done at the end of that period; and

(c) a deliberate omission shall be treated as done when the person in question decided upon it;

and in the absence of evidence establishing the contrary a person shall be taken for the purposes of this section to decide upon an omission when he does an act inconsistent with doing the omitted act or, if he has done no such inconsistent act, when the period expires within which he might reasonably have been expected to do the omitted act if it was to be done.

SEX DISCRIMINATION ACT – s.76(1), (5), (6)
RACE RELATIONS ACT – s.68(1), (6), (7)

Dodd v
British Telecom plc
[1988] IRLR 16 EAT

An originating application is "presented" when the application arrives at the Office of Employment Tribunals. In order to commence proceedings, it is not necessary for the application to be registered by the Office of Employment Tribunals.

Dodd v
British Telecom plc
[1988] IRLR 16 EAT

In order to be a valid complaint sufficient to stop time running, the written application must contain sufficient to identify who is making it and against whom it is made, and must contain sufficient to show what sort of complaint it is. An application whose contents did not comply with those broad minimum requirements would not be capable of being described as an originating application at all. However, the requirements of rule 1(a), (b) and (c) of the Employment Tribunals Rules of Procedure, which specify that an originating application shall set out the name and address of the applicant and of the person against whom relief is sought and the grounds, with particulars thereof, on which relief is sought, are not mandatory but are directory only. Therefore, where an application indicates that the claimant is making a complaint of discrimination in relation to her rejection for a particular post, a failure to specify whether the complaint is of sex discrimination or race discrimination or both is not fatal to the efficacy of the originating application.

Quarcoopome v
Sock Shop Holdings Ltd
[1995] IRLR 353 EAT

An originating application that makes a claim for race discrimination incorporates any claim for race discrimination, whether it be under s.1(1)(a), or s.1(1)(b) or s.2 (discrimination by way of victimisation), or any other claim that may be made under the Act. Therefore, it was an error to treat the reference to race discrimination in the appellant's originating application as not covering his later attempt to add a claim of indirect discrimination to his complaint.

Clarke v
Hampshire Electro-plating Co Ltd
[1991] IRLR 490 EAT

In determining when "the act complained of was done", the question is whether the cause of action had crystallised on the relevant date, not whether the complainant felt that he had suffered discrimination on that date. The phrase "the act complained of was done" indicates that there was at that time an act of discrimination and that the cause of action could properly be said to be complete at that time, because otherwise there would be no point in bringing proceedings. Every case must depend upon its own facts as to the clarity of the crystallisation of any cause of action.

Cast v
Croydon College
[1998] IRLR 318 CA

A decision by an employer may be a separate act of discrimination for time limit purposes, whether or not it is made on the same facts as before, providing it results from a further consideration of the matter and is not merely a reference back to an earlier decision. If the matter is reconsidered in response to a further request, time begins to run again. Therefore, the appellant's complaint that the respondents had discriminated against her on grounds of sex by refusing to permit her to work part-time after she returned from maternity leave was not out of time, even though her request to work part-time was first refused prior to her maternity leave, and her originating application was not submitted until after she returned from maternity leave when her further requests to work part-time were again refused. Each decision amounted to a fresh refusal of a fresh request to work part time.

Swithland Motors plc v   **[1994] IRLR 276 EAT**
Clarke

An unlawful act of discrimination by omitting to offer employment cannot be committed until the alleged discriminator is in a position to offer such employment. Accordingly, the only sensible construction of s.76(6)(c) of the Sex Discrimination Act, which provides that "a deliberate omission shall be treated as done when the person in question decided upon it", is that "decides" means "decides at a time and in circumstances when he is in a position to implement that decision" and not "decides on the hypothetical basis that he will implement the decision when and if circumstances arise in which he is able to do so".

Aniagwu v   **[1999] IRLR 303 EAT**
London Borough of Hackney

An applicant must be able to identify the detriment to which he has been subjected before he can present a complaint. Therefore, the time limit for bringing a complaint of discrimination in respect of an employer's refusal to accept a grievance began to run from the date the decision of a grievance panel was communicated to the employee rather than the date on which that decision was taken.

Adekeye v   **[1993] IRLR 324 EAT**
Post Office

If a dismissed black employee complains that he or she did not succeed upon an internal appeal in circumstances where a white comparator would have succeeded such that there is an allegation of unlawful discrimination on racial grounds in the result of the appeal, that is an "act complained of".

Extension

Robertson v   **[2003] IRLR 434 CA**
Bexley Community Centre

An employment tribunal has a very wide discretion in determining whether or not it is just and equitable to extend time. It is entitled to consider anything that it considers relevant. However, time limits are exercised strictly in employment cases. When tribunals consider their discretion to consider a claim out of time on just and equitable grounds, there is no presumption that they should do so unless they can justify failure to exercise the discretion. On the contrary, a tribunal cannot hear a complaint unless the applicant convinces it that it is just and equitable to extend time. The exercise of discretion is thus the exception rather than the rule.

Hutchison v   **[1977] IRLR 69 EAT**
Westward Television Ltd

The formula provided by s.76(5) of the Sex Discrimination Act allowing an employment tribunal to consider a complaint which is out of time "if, in all the circumstances of the case, it considers that it is just and equitable to do so", entitles the tribunal to take into account anything which it judges to be relevant. The employment tribunal is to do what it thinks is fair in the circumstances.

Mills v   **[1998] IRLR 494 EAT**
Marshall

The words "just and equitable" in the discrimination legislation giving power to extend time could not be wider or more general. The discretion to extend time is unfettered and may include a consideration of the date from which the complainant could reasonably have become aware of her right to present a worthwhile complaint.

London Borough of Southwark v   **[2003] IRLR 220 CA**
Afolabi

In considering whether it is just and equitable to extend time, a tribunal is not required to go through the matters listed in s.33(3) of the Limitation Act 1980, provided that no significant factor has been left out of account by the tribunal in exercising its discretion.

Mills v   **[1998] IRLR 494 EAT**
Marshall

Where a person was reasonably unaware of the fact that they had the right to being proceedings until shortly before the complaint was filed, whether it is just and equitable to extend time is for the employment tribunal to determine, balancing all the relevant factors, including whether it is possible to have a fair trial of the issues raised by the complaint. Unawareness of the right to sue might stem from a failure by the lawyers to appreciate that a claim lay, or because the law "changed" or was differently perceived after a decision of another court.

Chohan v   **[2004] IRLR 685 EAT**
Derby Law Centre

Delay in bringing a claim in time due to incorrect legal advice ought not defeat an applicant's contention that the claim ought to be heard. The failure by a legal adviser to enter proceedings in time should not be visited upon the claimant for otherwise the defendant would be in receipt of a windfall.

British Coal Corporation v   **[1997] IRLR 336 EAT**
Keeble

It was "just and equitable" to allow the applicants to bring their complaints under Sex Discrimination Act concerning a discriminatory voluntary redundancy payment scheme outside the requisite three-month time limit, notwithstanding that the reason for the delay was the applicants' mistake of law as to their position. If the only reason for a long delay is a wholly understandable misapprehension of the law, that must have been a matter which Parliament intended the tribunal to take into account when considering "all the circumstances of the case". The statement in *Biggs v Somerset County Council* that "it would be contrary to the principle of legal certainty to allow past transactions to be reopened and limitation periods to be circumvented because the existing law at the relevant time had not been explained or had not been fully understood" was intended to apply only in the context of the time limit provisions relating to unfair dismissal and the consideration of whether it was "reasonably practicable" for the applicant to present her complaint in time. The discretion conferred by s.76(5) of the Sex Discrimination Act is very much wider than relating to unfair dismissal.

Apelogun-Gabriels v   **[2002] IRLR 116 CA**
London Borough of Lambeth
The correct law for whether it is just and equitable to extend the time limit for presenting a discrimination complaint which is out of time because the applicant was pursuing internal proceedings was laid down by *Robinson v Post Office* rather than by *Aniagwu v London Borough of Hackney*. The fact, if it be so, that the employee had deferred proceedings in the tribunal while awaiting the outcome of domestic proceedings is only one factor to be taken into account. To the extent that *Aniagwu* lays down some general principle that one should always await the outcome of internal grievance procedures before embarking on litigation, it was plainly wrong.

Robinson v   **[2000] IRLR 904 EAT**
Post Office
When delay on account of an incomplete internal appeal is relied upon as a reason for failing to lodge a tribunal application in time, it will ordinarily suffice for the employment tribunal to put this into the balance when the justice and equity of the matter is being considered.

Hutchison v   **[1977] IRLR 69 EAT**
Westward Television Ltd
The words "in all the circumstances of the case" in s.76(5) refer to the actual facts of the matter in so far as they are relevant to the matter under consideration in s.76(5). The employment tribunal is not required to hear the entire case before making its decision as to whether time should be extended, although it may want to form some fairly rough idea as to whether it is a strong complaint or a weak complaint.

Dimtsu v   **[1991] IRLR 450 EAT**
Westminster City Council
An employment tribunal is not obliged to raise the question of whether a complainant wishes to apply under s.68(6) of the Race Relations Act for an extension of the time limit, so as to enable events which took place more than three months before the originating application was presented to form part of the substantive complaint, in circumstances in which the complainant's representative had not requested an extension of the time limit.

Continuing discrimination

Barclays Bank plc v   **[1991] IRLR 136 HL**
Kapur
To maintain a continuing regime which adversely affects an employee is an act which continues so long as it is maintained.

Hendricks v   **[2003] IRLR 96 CA**
Commissioner of Police for the Metropolis
In determining whether there was "an act extending over a period", as distinct from a succession of unconnected or isolated specific acts, for which time would begin to run from the date when each specific act was committed, the focus should be on the substance of the complaints that the employer was responsible for an ongoing situation or a continuing state of affairs. The concepts of policy, rule, practice, scheme or regime in the authorities were given as examples of when an act extends over a period. They should not be treated as a complete and constricting statement of the indicia of "an act extending over a period".

Robertson v   **[2003] IRLR 434 CA**
Bexley Community Centre
To establish a continuing act it must be shown that the employer had a practice, policy, rule or regime governing the act said to constitute it.

Cast v   **[1998] IRLR 318 CA**
Croydon College
Application of a discriminatory policy or regime pursuant to which decisions may be taken from time to time is an act extending over a period. There can be a policy even though it is not of a formal nature or expressed in writing, and even though it is confined to a particular post or role.

Cast v   **[1997] IRLR 14 EAT**
Croydon College
The mere repetition of a request cannot convert a single managerial decision into a policy, practice or rule.

Hendricks v   **[2003] IRLR 96 CA**
Commissioner of Police for the Metropolis
The burden is on the applicant to prove, either by direct evidence or by inference from primary facts, that alleged incidents of discrimination were linked to one another and were evidence of a continuing discriminatory state of affairs covered by the concept of "an act extending over a period."

Tyagi v   **[2001] IRLR 465 CA**
BBC World Service
A job applicant cannot complain of a policy of "continuing discrimination" extending over a period. The statutory language relating to selection arrangements, which refers to discrimination in the arrangements which the employer makes "for the purpose of determining who should be offered that employment", makes it clear that what is being complained about is not employment generally but the particular employment that is being offered.

Examples

Barclays Bank plc v   **[1991] IRLR 136 HL**
Kapur
An employer's refusal to allow an employee's previous service to count towards a pension is an "act extending

over a period" within the meaning of s.68(7)(b) of the Race Relations Act rather than a "deliberate omission" within the meaning of s.68(7)(c). A man works not only for his current wage but also for his pension and to require him to work on less favourable terms as to pension is as much a continuing act as to require him to work for lower wages.

Sougrin v   **[1992] IRLR 416 CA**
Haringey Health Authority
In *Kapur*, in stating that there would be a continuing act lasting throughout the period of employment if an employer continued to pay lower wages to coloured employees, Lord Griffiths was clearly referring to the case of an employer who has a policy of paying coloured employees less than their white counterparts.

Sougrin v   **[1992] IRLR 416 CA**
Haringey Health Authority
A grading decision is a one-off act with continuing consequences rather than a continuing act of discrimination.

Rovenska v   **[1997] IRLR 367 CA**
General Medical Council
If the General Medical Council's regime for exemption from a test set for registration as a medical practitioner was indirectly discriminatory, then it would be committing an act of unlawful discrimination on every occasion that it refused to allow the applicant limited registration without first taking the test.

Owusu v   **[1995] IRLR 574 EAT**
London Fire & Civil Defence Authority
In alleging a failure by the employers over a number of years to re-grade him and a failure to give him an opportunity to act-up when such opportunities arose, the complainant was alleging a continuing act in the form of maintaining a practice which resulted in consistent discriminatory decisions.

Calder v   **[1989] IRLR 55 EAT**
James Finlay Corporation Ltd
By constituting a mortgage subsidy scheme under the rules of which a woman could not obtain benefit, the employers were discriminating against the appellant woman in the way they afforded her "access" to the benefit. It followed that so long as she remained in the employers' employ, there was a continuing discrimination against her. Alternatively, it could be said that so long as her employment continued, the employers were subjecting her to "any other detriment". As the rule of the scheme constituted a discriminatory act extending over the period of the appellant's employment, it was therefore to be treated as having been done at the end of her employment rather than on the last occasion on which she was deliberately refused access to the scheme. Consequently, as her complaint had been presented within three months of

leaving her employment, the employment tribunal had jurisdiction to entertain it.

Littlewoods Organisation plc v   **[1993] IRLR 154 EAT**
Traynor
A complaint of racial discrimination in respect of alleged racial abuse was not out of time, notwithstanding that the last incident took place more than three months before the complaint was filed, in circumstances in which remedial measures promised by the employers had not been fully implemented when the respondent resigned and made his complaint to the tribunal. So long as the remedial measures which had been agreed on were not actually taken, a situation capable of involving racial discrimination continued and allowing that situation to continue amounted to a continuing act.

Barclays Bank plc v   **[1991] IRLR 136 HL**
Kapur
A "deliberate omission" in s.68(7)(c) of the Race Relations Act was included by the draftsman as a sweeping-up provision intended for the protection of employees and addressed to activities peripheral to the employment rather than to the terms of the employment itself. It was intended to cover a one-off, rather than a continuing situation.

Agreement precluding complaint

(3) A term in a contract which purports to exclude or limit any provision of this Act [or the Equal Pay Act 1970 – SDA] is unenforceable by any person in whose favour the term would operate apart from this subsection.

(4) Subsection (3) does not apply –
    (a) to a contract settling a complaint to which [s.63(1) of this Act or s.2 of the Equal Pay Act – SDA; s.54(1) – RRA] applies where the contract is made with the assistance of a conciliation officer;
    (b) to a contract settling a claim which [s.66 – SDA; s.57 – RRA] applies.

SEX DISCRIMINATION ACT – s.77
RACE RELATIONS ACT – s.72

Lunt v   **[1999] IRLR 458 EAT**
Merseyside TEC Ltd
The requirement in s.77(4A)(b) of the Sex Discrimination Act that a compromise agreement "must relate to the particular complaint" is not limited to complaints that have been presented to an employment tribunal. However, a "blanket" agreement compromising claims which had never been indicated in the past is not permitted.

Lunt v   **[1999] IRLR 458 EAT**
Merseyside TEC Ltd
A single compromise agreement can cover claims under more than one statute.

Work ordinarily outside Great Britain

(1) For the purposes of this Part [and s.1 of the Equal Pay Act 1970 – SDA] ("the relevant purposes"), employment is to be regarded as being at an establishment in Great Britain unless the employee does his work wholly outside Great Britain.

(2) The reference to "employment" in subsection (1) includes –
 (a) employment on board a ship registered at a port of registry in Great Britain, and
 (b) employment on an aircraft or hovercraft registered in the United Kingdom and operated by a person who has his principal place of business, or is ordinarily resident, in Great Britain.
 SEX DISCRIMINATION ACT – s.10

(1) For the purposes of this Part, employment is to be regarded as being at an establishment in Great Britain if the employee –
 (a) does his work wholly or partly in Great Britain; or
 (b) does his work wholly outside Great Britain and subsection (1A) applies".
(1A) This subsection applies if, in a case involving discrimination on grounds of race or ethnic or national origins, or harassment –
 (a) the employer has a place of business at an establishment in Great Britain;
 (b) the work is for the purposes of the business carried on at that establishment; and
 (c) the employee is ordinarily resident in Great Britain –
 (i) at the time when he applies for or is offered the employment, or
 (ii) at any time during the course of the employment.
 RACE RELATIONS ACT 1976 (as amended) – s.8

(3) In the case of employment on board a ship registered at a port of registry in Great Britain (except where the employee does his work wholly outside Great Britain [and outside any area added under subsection (5) – SDA]), the ship shall for the relevant purposes be deemed to be the establishment.

(4) Where work is not done at an establishment it shall be treated for the relevant purposes as done at the establishment from which it is done or (where it is not done from any establishment) at the establishment with which it has the closest connection.
 SEX DISCRIMINATION ACT – s.10
 RACE RELATIONS ACT – s.8

Deria v [1986] IRLR 108 CA
General Council of British Shipping
Whether there has been a refusal to offer employment "at an establishment in Great Britain" so as to confer jurisdiction under the Race Relations Act is to be determined by what was contemplated by the parties at the date of the act complained of. Therefore, s.8(1) and (2) of the Act can be construed as meaning that "employment is to be regarded as being at an establishment in Great Britain unless the employee does *or is to do* his work wholly outside Great Britain".

Bossa v [1998] IRLR 284 EAT
Nordstress Ltd
Article 48 of the EC Treaty, which provides that freedom of movement of workers entails "the abolition of any discrimination based on nationality between workers of the Member States" as regards employment, has direct effect. The provisions of the Race Relations Act excluding a complaint relating to employment outside Great Britain must be disapplied where there is a conflict with the right to freedom of movement established by Article 48. Therefore, a tribunal had jurisdiction to hear the appellant's complaint that he had been discriminated against on grounds of nationality contrary to the Race Relations Act when he was not interviewed by an employer in Great Britain for a post based in Italy because he held Italian nationality.

Death of applicant

Harris v [2000] IRLR 320 CA
Lewisham & Guys
 Mental Health NHS Trust
A complaint brought under the discrimination statutes survives the death of the complainant.

Bankruptcy of applicant

Khan v [2004] IRLR 961 CA
Trident Safeguards Ltd
A claim for race discrimination is a "hybrid" claim, since it includes both a claim for pecuniary loss, which is property that is part of the bankrupt's estate, and a claim for injury to feelings, which is "personal" and does not form part of the bankrupt's estate, and therefore the whole of the hybrid claim vests in the trustee in bankruptcy in accordance with the decision in *Ord v Upton*. However, there is a public interest in claims of race discrimination being fully examined. Therefore, a bankrupt should be permitted to limit their claim for relief to a declaration and compensation for injury to feelings only. If that is done, the claim ceases to be a hybrid one.

Acts done under statutory authority

(1) Nothing in the following provisions, namely –
 (a) Part II,
 (b) Part III so far as it applies to vocational training, or
 (c) Part IV so far as it has effect in relation to the provisions mentioned in paragraphs (a) and (b),
shall render unlawful any act done by a person in relation to a woman if –

(i) it was necessary for that person to do it in order to comply with a requirement of an existing statutory provision concerning the protection of women, or

(ii) it was necessary for that person to do it in order to comply with a requirement of a relevant statutory provision (within the meaning of Part I of the Health and Safety at Work etc Act 1974) and it was done by that person for the purpose of the protection of the woman in question (or of any class of women that included that woman).

(2) In subsection (1) –

(a) the reference in paragraph (i) of that subsection to an existing statutory provision concerning the protection of women is a reference to any such provision having effect for the purpose of protecting women as regards –

(i) pregnancy or maternity, or

(ii) other circumstances giving rise to risks specifically affecting women,

whether the provision relates only to such protection or to the protection of any other class of persons as well; and

(b) the reference in paragraph (ii) of that subsection to the protection of a particular woman or class of women is a reference to the protection of that woman or those women as regards any circumstances falling within paragraph (a)(i) or (ii) above.

(3) In this section "existing statutory provision" means (subject to subsection (4)) any provision of –

(a) an Act passed before this Act, or

(b) an instrument approved or made by or under such an Act (including one approved or made after the passing of this Act).

(4) Where an Act passed after this Act re-enacts (with or without modification) a provision of an Act passed before this Act, that provision as re-enacted shall be treated for the purpose of subsection (3) as if it continued to be contained in an Act passed before this Act.

A(1) Nothing in –

(a) the relevant provisions of Part III, or

(b) Part IV so far as it has effect in relation to those provisions,

shall render unlawful any act done by a person if it was necessary for that person to do it in order to comply with a requirement of an existing statutory provision within the meaning of s.51.

(2) In subsection (1) "the relevant provisions of Part III" means the provisions of that Part except so far as they apply to vocational training.

SEX DISCRIMINATION ACT – s.51

(1) Nothing in Parts II to IV shall render unlawful any act of discrimination done –

(a) in pursuance of any enactment or Order in Council; or

(b) in pursuance of any instrument made under any enactment by a Minister of the Crown; or

(c) in order to comply with any condition or requirement imposed by a Minister of the Crown (whether before or after the passing of this Act) by virtue of any enactment.

References in this section to an enactment, Order in Council or instrument include an enactment, Order in Council or instrument passed or made after the passing of this Act.

(1A) Subsection (1) does not apply to an act which is unlawful, on grounds of race or ethnic or national origins, by virtue of a provision referred to in section 1(1B)

(2) Nothing in Parts II to IV shall render unlawful any act whereby a person discriminates against another on the basis of that other's nationality or place of ordinary residence or the length of time for which he has been present or resident in or outside the United Kingdom or an area within the United Kingdom, if that act is done –

(a) in pursuance of any enactment or Order in Council; or

(b) in pursuance of any instrument made under any enactment by a Minister of the Crown; or

(c) in order to comply with any requirement imposed by a Minister of the Crown (whether before or after the passing of this Act) by virtue of any enactment; or

(d) in pursuance of any arrangements made (whether before or after the passing of this Act) by or with the approval of, or for the time being approved by, a Minister of the Crown; or

(e) in order to comply with any condition imposed (whether before or after the passing of this Act) by a Minister of the Crown.

RACE RELATIONS ACT 1976 (as amended) – s.41

Hampson v   **[1990] IRLR 302 HL**
Department of Education and Science
The words "in pursuance of any instrument" are confined to acts done in necessary performance of an express obligation contained in the instrument and do not also include acts done in exercise of a power or discretion conferred by the instrument. An act is done "in pursuance of" an enactment, order or instrument so as to be protected by s.41 only if it is specified in the enactment, order or instrument.

General Medical Council v   **[1988] IRLR 425 EAT**
Goba
Section 41(1) does not provide a blanket defence whatever the act complained of and however heinous it may be in terms of discrimination. The correct construction of the phrase "in pursuance of" is that the act complained of, in its doing and in the way it was carried out, must have been one which was reasonably necessary in order to comply with any condition or requirement of the statute or order. This includes carrying out the duties or other necessary functions. Hampson v Department of Education was distinguishable on its facts because in Hampson the Minister was bound to take the decision in question.

Page v   **[1981] IRLR 13 EAT**
Freighthire (Tank Haulage) Ltd
The interests of safety are not a justification for discrimination on grounds of sex unless the act was done to comply with a pre-existing statutory requirement within the meaning of s.51 of the Sex Discrimination Act.

Page v   **[1981] IRLR 13 EAT**
Freighthire (Tank Haulage) Ltd
In order to satisfy the test of s.51, an employer does not have to show that debarring a woman from taking up a job was

inexorably the only method available to him of satisfying the requirements of the Health and Safety at Work Act to ensure, so far as is reasonably practicable, the health, safety and welfare at work of his employees. It is important to consider all the circumstances of the case, the risk involved and the measures which it can be said are reasonably necessary to eliminate the risk. There may be cases where one course which is suggested as being sufficient may leave open some doubt as to whether it is going to achieve the desired level of protection. In such a case, it may be that an employer is complying with the requirements of the legislation if, in all the circumstances, he thinks it right not to allow an employee, for his (or her) own protection or safety, to do the particular job.

Race discrimination

Genuine occupational requirements

(1) In relation to discrimination on grounds of race or ethnic or national origins –

> *(a) section 4(1)(a) or (c) does not apply to any employment; and*
>
> *(b) section 4(2)(b) does not apply to promotion or transfer to, or training for, any employment; and*
>
> *(c) section 4(2)(c) does not apply to dismissal from any employment;*

where subsection (2) applies.

(2) This subsection applies where, having regard to the nature of the employment or the context in which it is carried out –

> *(a) being of a particular race or of particular ethnic or national origins is a genuine and determining occupational requirement;*
>
> *(b) it is proportionate to apply that requirement in the particular case; and*
>
> *(c) either –*
>
>> *(i) the person to whom that requirement is applied does not meet it, or*
>>
>> *(ii) the employer is not satisfied, and in all the circumstances it is reasonable for him not to be satisfied, that that person meets it.".*

RACE RELATIONS ACT 1976 (as amended) – s.4A

(1) In relation to racial discrimination in cases where s.4A does not apply –

> *(a) s.4(1)(a) or (c) does not apply to any employment where being of a particular racial group is a genuine occupational qualification for the job; and*
>
> *(b) s.4(2)(b) does not apply to opportunities for promotion or transfer to, or training for, such employment.*

(2) Being of a particular racial group is a genuine occupational qualification for a job only where –

> *(a) the job involves participation in a dramatic performance or other entertainment in a capacity for which a person of that racial group is required for reasons of authenticity; or*
>
> *(b) the job involves participation as an artist's or photographic model in the production of a work of art, visual image or sequence of visual images for which a person of that racial group is required for reasons of authenticity; or*
>
> *(c) the job involves working in a place where food or drink is (for payment or not) provided to and consumed by members of the public or a section of the public in a particular setting for which, in that job, a person of that racial group is required for reasons of authenticity; or*
>
> *(d) the holder of the job provides persons of that racial group with personal services promoting their welfare, and those services can most effectively be provided by a person of that racial group.*

(3) Subsection (2) applies where some only of the duties of the job fall within paragraph (a), (b), (c) or (d) as well as where all of them do.

(4) Paragraph (a), (b), (c) or (d) of subsection (2) does not apply in relation to the filling of a vacancy at a time when the employer already has employees of the racial group in question –

> *(a) who are capable of carrying out the duties falling within that paragraph; and*
>
> *(b) whom it would be reasonable to employ on those duties; and*
>
> *(c) whose numbers are sufficient to meet the employer's likely requirements in respect of these duties without undue inconvenience.*

RACE RELATIONS ACT – s.5

London Borough of Lambeth v CRE [1989] IRLR 379 EAT

Section 5 provides an exception to s.4, and as a matter of principle should be narrowly or strictly construed. Section 5(2), in setting out the genuine occupational qualification exceptions, uses the word "only".

Tottenham Green Under-Fives' Centre v Marshall [1989] IRLR 147 EAT

In construing s.5 an employment tribunal needs to carry out a delicate balancing exercise, bearing in mind the need to guard against discrimination and the desirability of promoting racial integration. It is important not to give s.5 too wide a construction, which would enable it to provide an excuse or cloak for undesirable discrimination. On the other hand, where genuine attempts are being made to integrate ethnic groups into society, too narrow a construction might stifle such initiatives.

London Borough of Lambeth v CRE [1989] IRLR 379 EAT

In exercising their jurisdiction in s.5 cases, tribunals should take a broad commonsense approach on matters which are largely issues of fact. It should not be too difficult to identify genuine defences, and to distinguish specious defences which cloak undesirable discrimination.

Tottenham Green Under-Fives'   **[1991] IRLR 162 EAT**
Centre v
Marshall (No.2)

It is not open to an employment tribunal to disregard a duty in determining whether a genuine occupational qualification exception applies, unless the matter is de minimis or is a sham duty invented for the purpose of qualifying for the exception. Provided the employment tribunal is satisfied that the relevant duty is not so trivial that it can properly be disregarded altogether, it is not for the tribunal to make an evaluation of the importance of the duty. Section 5(3) indicates clearly that one of the duties of the job, if it falls within any of the relevant paragraphs, will operate to make the exception available.

London Borough of Lambeth v   **[1990] IRLR 230 CA**
CRE

The use of the word "personal" in s.5(2)(d), where the holder of the job provides "personal services", indicates that the identity of the giver and the recipient of the services is important and appears to contemplate direct contact between the giver and the recipient – mainly face to face or where there could be susceptibility in personal, physical contact.

London Borough of Lambeth v   **[1990] IRLR 230 CA**
CRE

If a person is providing persons of a racial group defined by colour (eg black people) with personal services promoting their welfare, it is open to an employment tribunal on the particular facts of the case to find that those services can be most effectively provided by a person of that colour, from whatever ethnic group he comes, and even though some of his clients may belong to other ethnic groups.

Tottenham Green Under-Fives'   **[1989] IRLR 147 EAT**
Centre v
Marshall

Where a defence is raised under s.5(2)(d), the holder of the post must be directly involved in the provision of the services, although this need not necessarily be on a one-to-one basis. If the post-holder provides several personal services to the recipient, the defence is established provided one of those genuinely falls within s.5(2)(d).

Tottenham Green Under-Fives'   **[1989] IRLR 147 EAT**
Centre v
Marshall

The phrase "promoting their welfare" in s.5(2)(d) is a very wide expression and it would be undesirable to seek to narrow the width of those words.

Tottenham Green Under-Fives'   **[1989] IRLR 147 EAT**
Centre v
Marshall

The phrase "those services can most effectively be provided by a person of that racial group" in s.5(2)(d) assumes that the personal services could be provided by others. The

words are not "must be provided" nor "can only be provided". Whether the services can be "most effectively provided" by a person of that racial group and whether they would be less effective if provided by others is a matter of fact for the tribunal. However, if a tribunal accepts that the conscious decision of a responsible employer to commit an act of discrimination and to rely upon s.5(2) is founded upon a genuinely held and reasonably based opinion that a genuine occupational requirement will best promote the welfare of the recipient, considerable weight should be given to that decision when reaching a conclusion whether or not the defence succeeds.

Sex discrimination

Genuine occupational qualifications

(1) In relation to sex discrimination –
> *(a) s.6(1)(a) or (c) does not apply to any employment where being a man is a genuine occupational qualification for the job; and*
> *(b) s.6(2)(a) does not apply to opportunities for promotion or transfer to, or training for, such employment.*

(2) Being a man is a genuine occupational qualification for a job only where –
> *(a) the essential nature of the job calls for a man for reasons of physiology (excluding physical strength or stamina) or, in dramatic performances or other entertainment, for reasons of authenticity, so that the essential nature of the job would be materially different if carried out by a woman; or*
> *(b) the job needs to be held by a man to preserve decency or privacy because –*
>> *(i) it is likely to involve physical contact with men in circumstances where they might reasonably object to its being carried out by a woman, or*
>> *(ii) the holder of the job is likely to do his work in circumstances where men might reasonably object to the presence of a woman because they are in a state of undress or are using sanitary facilities; or*
> *[(ba) the job is likely to involve the holder of the job doing his work, or living in a private home and needs to be held by a man because objection might reasonably be taken to allowing a woman –*
>> *(i) the degree of physical or social contact with a person living in the home, or*
>> *(ii) the knowledge of intimate details of such a person's life,*
>> *which is likely, because of the nature or circumstances of the job or of the home, to be allowed to, or available to, the holder of the job; or]*
> *(c) the nature or location of the establishment makes it impracticable for the holder of the job to live elsewhere than in premises provided by the employer, and –*
>> *(i) the only such premises which are available for persons holding that kind of job are lived in, or*

normally lived in, by men and are not equipped with separate sleeping accommodation for women and sanitary facilities which could be used by women in privacy from men, and

   (ii) it is not reasonable to expect the employer either to equip those premises with such accommodation and facilities or to provide other premises for women; or

(d) the nature of the establishment, or of the part of it within which the work is done, requires the job to be held by a man because –

   (i) it is, or is part of, a hospital, prison or other establishment for persons requiring special care, supervision or attention, and

   (ii) those persons are all men (disregarding any women whose presence is exceptional), and

   (iii) it is reasonable, having regard to the essential character of the establishment or that part, that the job should not be held by a woman; or

(e) the holder of the job provides individuals with personal services promoting their welfare or education, or similar personal services, and those services can most effectively be provided by a man; or

(f) . . . [repealed].

(g) the job needs to be held by a man because it is likely to involve the performance of duties outside the United Kingdom in a country whose laws or customs are such that the duties could not, or could not effectively, be performed by a woman; or

(h) the job is one of two to be held by a married couple.

(3) Subsection (2) applies where some only of the duties of the job fall within paragraphs (a) to (g) as well as where all of them do.

(4) Paragraph (a), (b), (c), (d), (e), (f) or (g) of subsection (2) does not apply in relation to the filling of a vacancy at a time when the employer already has male employees –

(a) who are capable of carrying out the duties falling within that paragraph; and

(b) whom it would be reasonable to employ on those duties; and

(c) whose numbers are sufficient to meet the employer's likely requirements in respect of those duties without undue inconvenience.

SEX DISCRIMINATION ACT – s.7

Timex Corporation v   **[1981] IRLR 530 EAT**
Hodgson
Where a man is selected for redundancy on grounds of his sex in circumstances in which a woman has been retained because her job has been given additional duties of a kind where being a woman may be a genuine occupational qualification, the discrimination by the employers is in selecting the woman to do the revised job, not in dismissing the man who is not selected. Therefore, although the defence under s.7 of the Sex Discrimination Act that there was a genuine occupational qualification does not extend to conduct falling within s.6(2)(b), in such a case the discrimination lies either in failing to "transfer" the man to the revised job within s.6(2)(a) or in "deliberately omitting to offer" the man employment in the revised job within s.6(1)(c), so that the exceptions in s.7(2) can apply.

Sisley v   **[1983] IRLR 404 EAT**
Britannia Security Systems Ltd
Section 7(2)(b)(ii) of the Sex Discrimination Act is not confined to cases where the job itself requires the holder to be in a state of undress. The reference in the subsection to "sanitary facilities" shows that the subsection is not confined to job duties. It deals with the situation where the holder of a particular job is likely to do his work, and all matters reasonably incidental to it, in circumstances where the holder might reasonably object to the presence of a member of the opposite sex because the holder is in a state of undress or is using sanitary facilities.

Sisley v   **[1983] IRLR 404 EAT**
Britannia Security Systems Ltd
Section 7(2)(b)(ii) does not extend to circumstances where someone other than the holder of the job might object to the presence of a member of the opposite sex, so that it does not cover cases where the holder of the job (for example, a man employed in a dress shop) is working in circumstances where women customers might object to a man doing that job because the women are in a state of undress.

Sisley v   **[1983] IRLR 404 EAT**
Britannia Security Systems Ltd
The words "to live in" in s.7(2)(c) of the Sex Discrimination Act involve the concept of residence either permanent or temporary and do not cover cases where an employee is obliged to remain on the premises for a limited period of time, eating and taking a period of rest. Whether there is the necessary feature of residence is a question of fact and degree in every case.

Timex Corporation v   **[1981] IRLR 530 EAT**
Hodgson
Once an employment tribunal is satisfied that additional duties have been genuinely added to a job, its function is to look at the duties involved in the job and, under s.7(3), to see whether some of those duties fall within s.7(2). The employment tribunal cannot tell the employers how to manage their business and that they need not have included the additional duties in the revised job.

Etam plc v   **[1989] IRLR 150 EAT**
Rowan
Being a woman was not a genuine occupational qualification for a sales assistant's job in a women's clothing shop so as to entitle the appellants to refuse to consider a man for the post, notwithstanding that it would have been impossible for a man to carry out the functions of a sales assistant within the shop's fitting room, where the case fell within the circumstances envisaged by s.7(4) in that a man would have been able to adequately carry out the bulk of the job of sales assistant, and such parts as he could not carry out could easily have been done by one of

the female sales assistants without causing any inconvenience or difficulty for the appellants.

Lasertop Ltd v   **[1997] IRLR 498 EAT**
Webster
The relevant time under s.7(4), which refers to the filling of a vacancy "at a time when the employer already has [female] employees", is when the prima facie discrimination takes place. The employer must already have sufficient female employees at that time who are capable of carrying out the prohibited duties and whom it would be reasonable to employ on those duties without undue inconvenience.

Lasertop Ltd v   **[1997] IRLR 498 EAT**
Webster
The provisions of s.7(4), which provide that s.7(2) does not apply when the employer already has sufficient male employees who could reasonably carry out the relevant duties, focuses solely on the contractual duties falling within s.7(2). The remaining contractual duties are irrelevant. In this case, the job in question required a salesperson to take prospective members on a tour of a women-only health club and that part of the post-holder's selling duties which took him into the changing room, sauna area, sunbed room and toilet could not be allocated to female members of staff without undue inconvenience.

Retirement or death provisions

(4) Subsections (1)(b) and (2) do not apply to provisions in relation to death or retirement [except in so far as, in their application to provision in relation to retirement, they render it unlawful for a person to discriminate against a woman –
> *(a) in such of the terms on which he offers her employment as make provision in relation to the way in which he will afford her access to opportunities for promotion, transfer or training or as provide for her dismissal or demotion; or*
> *(b) in the way he affords her access to opportunities for promotion, transfer or training or by refusing or deliberately omitting to afford her access to any such opportunities; or*
> *(c) by dismissing her or subjecting her to any detriment which results in her dismissal or consists in or involves her demotion.]*

SEX DISCRIMINATION ACT – s.6

Duke v   **[1988] IRLR 118 HL**
GEC Reliance
Section 6(4), prior to its amendment by the Sex Discrimination Act 1986, made discriminatory retirement ages between men and women lawful. It did not only apply to discriminatory benefits provided after retirement.

DIRECT DISCRIMINATION

(1) A person discriminates against another in any circumstances relevant for the purpose of any provision of this Act if –
> *(a) on racial grounds he treats that other less favourably than he treats or would treat other persons . . .*

RACE RELATIONS ACT – s.1

(1) A person discriminates against a woman in any circumstances relevant for the purposes of any provision of this Act if –
> *(a) on the ground of her sex he treats her less favourably than he treats or would treat a man . . .*

SEX DISCRIMINATION ACT – s.1

(1) This section applies where a complaint is presented under section 54 and the complaint is that the respondent –
> *(a) has committed an act of discrimination, on grounds of race or ethnic or national origins, which is unlawful by virtue of any provision referred to in section 1(1B)(a), (e) or (f), or Part IV in its application to those provisions, or*
> *(b) has committed an act of harassment.*

(2) Where, on the hearing of the complaint, the complainant proves facts from which the tribunal could, apart from this section, conclude in the absence of an adequate explanation that the respondent –
> *(a) has committed such an act of discrimination or harassment against the complainant, or*
> *(b) is by virtue of section 32 or 33 to be treated as having committed such an act of discrimination or harassment against the complainant,*

the tribunal shall uphold the complaint unless the respondent proves that he did not commit or, as the case may be, is not to be treated as having committed, that act.

RACE RELATIONS ACT 1976 (as amended) – s.54A

(1) This section applies to any complaint presented under section 63 to an employment tribunal.

(2) Where, on the hearing of the complaint, the complainant proves facts from which the tribunal could, apart from this section, conclude in the absence of an adequate explanation that the respondent –
> *(a) has committed an act of discrimination against the complainant which is unlawful by virtue of Part 2, or*
> *(b) is by virtue of section 41 or 42 to be treated as having committed such an act of discrimination against the complainant,*

the tribunal shall uphold the complaint unless the respondent proves that he did not commit, or, as the case may be, is not to be treated as having committed, that act.

SEX DISCRIMINATION ACT (as amended) – s.63A

Burden of proof

Barton v   **[2003] IRLR 332 EAT**
Investec Henderson Crosthwaite Securities Ltd
Observed: The correct approach to the burden of proof in sex discrimination cases, in light of the introduction of s.63A of the Sex Discrimination Act implementing the EC Burden of Proof Directive, is as follows:

(1) Pursuant to section 63A, it is for the applicant to prove on the balance of probabilities facts from which the tribunal could conclude, in the absence of an adequate explanation, that the respondents have committed an act of discrimination which is unlawful by virtue of Part II or which by virtue of section 41 or 42 is to be treated as having been committed against the applicant. These are referred to below as "such facts"

(2) If the applicant does not prove such facts he or she will fail.

(3) It is important to bear in mind in deciding whether the applicant has proved such facts that it is unusual to find direct evidence of sex discrimination. Few employers would be prepared to admit such discrimination, even to themselves. In some cases the discrimination will not be an intention but merely based on the assumption that "he or she would not have fitted in".

(4) In deciding whether the applicant has proved such facts, it is important to remember that the outcome at this stage of the analysis by the tribunal will therefore usually depend on what inferences it is proper to draw from the primary facts found by the tribunal.

(5) It is important to note the word is "could". At this stage the tribunal does not have to reach a definitive determination that such facts would lead it to the conclusion that there was an act of unlawful discrimination. At this stage a tribunal is looking at the primary facts proved by the applicant to see what inferences of secondary fact could be drawn from them.

(6) These inferences can include, in appropriate cases, any inferences that it is just and equitable to draw in accordance with s.74(2)(b) of the Sex Discrimination Act from an evasive or equivocal reply to a questionnaire or any other questions that fall within s.74(2).

(7) Likewise, the tribunal must decide whether any provision of any relevant code of practice is relevant and if so, take it into account in determining such facts pursuant to section 56A(10). This means that inferences may also be drawn from any failure to comply with any relevant code of practice.

(8) Where the applicant has proved facts from which inferences could be drawn that the respondents have treated the applicant less favourably on the grounds of sex, then the burden of proof moves to the respondent.

(9) It is then for the respondent to prove that he did not commit, or as the case may be, is not to be treated as having committed that act.

(10) To discharge that burden it is necessary for the respondent to prove, on the balance of probabilities, that the treatment was in no sense whatsoever on the grounds of sex, since "no discrimination whatsoever" is compatible with the Burden of Proof Directive.

(11) That requires a tribunal to assess not merely whether the respondent has proved an explanation for the facts from which such inferences can be drawn, but further that it is adequate to discharge the burden of proof on the balance of probabilities that sex was not any part of the reasons for the treatment in question.

(12) Since the facts necessary to prove an explanation would normally be in the possession of the respondent, a tribunal would normally expect cogent evidence to discharge that burden of proof. In particular the tribunal will need to examine carefully explanations for failure to deal with the questionnaire procedure and/or code of practice.

University of Huddersfield v Wolff   [2004] IRLR 534 EAT

The burden of proof moves where the applicant has proved facts from which inferences could be drawn that the respondents have treated the applicant less favourably on the grounds of sex. The tribunal must therefore arrive at a conclusion that there is a prima facie case that the respondent has treated the applicant less favourably on the grounds of sex. It is only if there are appropriate findings on the basis of which the prima facie case of less favourable treatment on the grounds of sex is made that the employer knows what it has to justify. Once the tribunal concludes that there is a prima facie case, it then considers the respondent's explanations. It must, if it has not already done so, make findings of fact, or draw inferences from findings of fact, for the purposes of concluding whether any of the explanations put forward by the respondent satisfy them, the burden being on the respondent to show that the less favourable treatment was not on the grounds of sex.

Chamberlin Solicitors v Emokpae   [2004] IRLR 592 EAT

Guideline 10 in *Barton* should be adjusted to read as follows: "To discharge that burden it is necessary for the respondent to prove, on the balance of probabilities, that the treatment was not significantly influenced, as defined in *Nagarajan v London Regional Transport* [1999] IRLR 572, by grounds of sex."

Sinclair Roche & Temperley v Heard   [2004] IRLR 763 EAT

In order to find discrimination, an employment tribunal must set out the relevant facts, draw its inferences if appropriate and then conclude that there is a prima facie case of unfavourable treatment by reference to those facts, and then look to the respondent for an explanation to rebut the prima facie case. If the tribunal satisfies itself that there has been on the face of it unfavourable treatment, it has effectively only reached halfway. It must set out clearly its conclusions as to the nature and extent of such unfavourable treatment, so that the respondent can understand what it is that it has to explain. It must then fully and carefully consider what the explanations of the employer were, and why, if such be the case, such explanations provide no answer. It may be that there is no explanation, or there may be an explanation which only confirms the existence of discrimination, or there may be a non-discriminatory explanation which redounds to its discredit such as it always behaves badly to everyone, or there may be a non-discriminatory explanation which is wholly admirable.

Meaning of "less favourable"

R v   [1989] IRLR 173 HL
Birmingham City Council ex parte
  Equal Opportunities Commission
In order to establish that there was less favourable treatment of members of one sex by reason of their having been
denied the same opportunities as the other sex, it is enough
that they are deprived of a choice which was valued by
them and which (even though others may take a different
view) is a choice obviously valued, on reasonable grounds,
by many others. It is not necessary to prove that that which
was lost was "better".

Simon v   [1987] IRLR 307 CA
Brimham Associates
Words or acts of discouragement can amount to treatment
of the person discouraged which is less favourable than that
given to other persons.

Burrett v   [1994] IRLR 7 EAT
West Birmingham Health
  Authority
The fact that a complainant honestly considers that she is
being less favourably treated does not of itself establish that
there is "less favourable treatment" within s.1(1)(a). Whether
there is less favourable treatment is for the employment tribunal to decide.

Stewart v   [1994] IRLR 440 EAT
Cleveland Guest (Engineering) Ltd
There is room for disagreement as to what is or is not less
favourable treatment and the employment tribunal, as industrial jury, is best placed to make a decision on the facts of a
particular case. If the error of law relied upon is the argument that the employment tribunal reached a decision which
no reasonable tribunal, on a proper appreciation of the facts
and law, would have reached, an overwhelming case to that
effect must be made out.

Discriminatory treatment

James v   [1990] IRLR 288 HL
Eastleigh Borough Council
The question to be considered under s.1(1)(a) is: "would
the complainant have received the same treatment from the
defendant but for his or her sex?" This test embraces both
the case where the treatment derives from the application of
a gender-based criterion and the case where it derives from
the selection of the complainant because of his or her sex.

Nagarajan v   [1999] IRLR 572 HL
London Regional Transport
The crucial question in a case of direct discrimination is why

the complainant received less favourable treatment. Was it on
grounds of race? Or was it for some other reason? If racial
grounds were the reason for the less favourable treatment,
direct discrimination under s.1(1)(a) is established. The reason
why the discriminator acted on racial grounds is irrelevant
when deciding whether an act of racial discrimination occurred.

Shamoon v   [2003] IRLR 285 HL
Chief Constable of the Royal Ulster Constabulary
Per Lord Nicholls: Employment tribunals may sometimes
be able to avoid arid and confusing disputes about the
identification of the appropriate comparator by concen-
trating primarily on why the claimant was treated as she
was, and postponing the less favourable treatment issue
until after they have decided why the treatment was
afforded. Was it on the proscribed ground or was it for
some other reason? If the former, there will usually be no
difficulty in deciding whether the treatment afforded to
the claimant on the proscribed ground was less favourable
than was or would have been afforded to others.

James v   [1990] IRLR 288 HL
Eastleigh Borough Council
Since the statutory pensionable age is itself a criterion which
directly discriminates between men and women in that it
treats women more favourably than men "on the ground of
their sex", any other differential treatment of men and
women which adopts the same gender-based criterion must
equally involve discrimination "on the ground of sex".

Sidhu v   [2000] IRLR 602 CA
Aerospace Composite Technology Ltd
In order to find direct discrimination under s.1(1)(a), the
complainant must show that he has been treated less
favourably by the discriminator than the discriminator treats
or would treat other persons in the same circumstances.
However, in certain cases the comparison need not be
demonstrated by evidence as to how a comparator was or
would be treated, because the very action complained of is in
itself less favourable treatment on sexual or racial grounds. If
a person is harassed or abused because of his race, that conduct is race-specific and it is not necessary to show that a
person of another race would be treated more favourably.

Sidhu v   [2000] IRLR 602 CA
Aerospace Composite Technology Ltd
A policy in relation to incidents of violence by one employee
against another which only looked at the fact of violence or
abusive language and disregarded provocation and other
mitigating factors, such as that the accused employee had
been provoked by a racial assault, was not a race-specific policy merely because it ignored the racial element in the attack.

Commissioners of   [2002] IRLR 776 EAT
  Inland Revenue v
Morgan
There is no statutory or other offence consisting of a body

being institutionally racist. While it would be possible to imagine a body whose habitual rules or practices were such that one could fairly say of the body that as an institution it was racist, the charge would be relevant only as a step in the reasoning toward a conclusion that the body was or was not guilty of some unlawful discrimination that fell within the Act.

Smith v   **[1996] IRLR 456 CA**
Safeway plc
There is an important distinction between discrimination between the sexes and discrimination against one or other of the sexes. Discrimination is not failing to treat men and women the same. If discrimination is to be established, it is necessary to show, not merely that the sexes are treated differently, but that the treatment accorded to one is less favourable than the treatment accorded to the other.

Jaffrey v   **[2002] IRLR 688 EAT**
Department of Environment, Transport and Regions
The facts of a case might give rise to claims both in respect of direct and indirect discrimination if different facts demonstrate the different types of discrimination, and the factual circumstances overlap but not precisely coincide.

Motive

R v   **[1989] IRLR 173 HL**
Birmingham City Council ex parte
  Equal Opportunities Commission
The intention or motive of the defendant to discriminate is not a necessary condition to liability. There is discrimination within the meaning of s.1(1)(a) of the Sex Discrimination Act if there is less favourable treatment on the ground of sex, in other words if the relevant woman or women would have received the same treatment as the men but for their sex. Were that not the case, it would be a good defence for an employer to show that he discriminated against a woman not because he intended to but (for example) because of customer preference, or to save money, or even to avoid controversy.

James v   **[1990] IRLR 288 HL**
Eastleigh Borough Council
The correct test under s.1(1)(a) is objective, not subjective. Whether or not the treatment is less favourable on the ground of sex is not saved from constituting unlawful discrimination by the fact that the defendant acted from a benign motive.

James v   **[1990] IRLR 288 HL**
Eastleigh Borough Council
Per Lord Goff: If it were necessary for the purpose of s.1(1)(a) to identify the requisite intention of the defendant, that intention is simply an intention to perform the relevant act of less favourable treatment. However, in the majority of cases, it is doubtful if it is necessary to focus upon the

intention or motive of the defendant in this way and the simple "but for" test avoids, in most cases at least, complicated questions relating to concepts such as intention, motive, reason or purpose, and the danger of confusion arising from the misuse of those elusive terms.

James v   **[1989] IRLR 318 CA**
Eastleigh Borough Council
There is direct discrimination if the overt basis for affording less favourable treatment was sex or, if the overt reason does not in terms relate to sex, it is shown that the overt reason was not the true reason and the true reason is the desire to treat women less favourably than men.

R v   **[1984] IRLR 230 HC**
Commission for Racial Equality
  ex parte Westminster City Council
An employer who treats a black employee less favourably on racial grounds for worthy motives is guilty of unlawful discrimination. Therefore an employer will be guilty of unlawful discrimination if he decides to change an employee's employment, not because he is prejudiced against that employee but because that employee is being discriminated against by his fellow employees contrary to the employer's wishes.

Din v   **[1982] IRLR 281 EAT**
Carrington Viyella Ltd
If an act of racial discrimination gives rise to actual or potential industrial unrest, an employer will or may be liable for unlawful discrimination if he simply seeks to remove that unrest by getting rid of the person against whom racial discrimination has been shown.

Stereotypical assumptions

Horsey v   **[1982] IRLR 395 EAT**
Dyfed County Council
The words "on the ground of" sex, marital status or race in the statutory definitions of discrimination cover cases where the reason for the discrimination was a generalised assumption that people of a particular sex, marital status or race possess or lack certain characteristics. They do not only cover cases where the sole factor influencing the decision of the alleged discriminator is the sex, marital status or race of the complainant. Most discrimination flows from generalised assumptions and not from a single prejudice dependent solely upon the sex or colour of the complainant. Therefore, a decision to treat a complainant in a particular way for reasons which, as an essential ingredient, contain a generalised assumption about a woman's behaviour is a decision made "on the ground of" her sex.

Coleman v   **[1981] IRLR 398 CA**
Skyrail Oceanic Ltd
An assumption that men are more likely than women to be the primary supporters of their spouses and children is an

assumption based on sex. Therefore, the dismissal of a woman based upon an assumption that husbands are bread-winners, and wives are not, can amount to discrimination under the Sex Discrimination Act.

Bradford Hospitals NHS Trust v   [2003] IRLR 4 EAT
Al-Shahib
Whilst it may sometimes be legitimate for a tribunal to take into account differences in behaviour which reflect racial and cultural differences, it is wrong for a tribunal to make findings based on the existence of such differences unless there is some evidential basis for them, such as expert evidence. For a tribunal simply to assume that a particular ethnic group has a specific characteristic is fundamentally wrong, even if the assumption is made for benign purposes.

Causation

Owen & Briggs v   [1982] IRLR 502 CA
James
That a racial consideration was an important factor in an employer's decision is sufficient to found a case of discrimination. It is not necessary that the racial factor be the sole reason for the employer's decision.

Nagarajan v   [1994] IRLR 61 EAT
Agnew
Where there are mixed motives for the doing of an act, not all of which constitute unlawful discrimination, there will be unlawful discrimination if the unlawful motive was of sufficient weight in the decision-making process to be treated as a cause of the act thus motivated. An important factor in the decision is well within that principle.

Lewis Woolf Griptight Ltd v   [1997] IRLR 432 EAT
Corfield
There is sex discrimination where the principal reason for dismissal is gender-neutral, but the means by which the employer sought to effect the termination of employment are gender-specific, such as reliance upon the statutory maternity leave provisions, and could not be relied upon in the case of a man. Therefore, the applicant was discriminated against when the employers used the expiry of the four-week period after maternity leave as an excuse for terminating the employment.

Seide v   [1980] IRLR 427 EAT
Gillette Industries Ltd
In determining whether there has been unlawful discrimination, the question is whether the activating cause of what happened is that the employer has treated a person less favourably than others on racial grounds. Where there is more than one ground for an employer's action, it might be enough if a substantial and effective cause for the action is a breach of the statute. However, it is not sufficient merely to consider whether the fact that the person is of a particular racial group is any part of the background or is a *causa sine qua non* of what happened. Therefore, an employee who was transferred in order to preserve good working relationships had not been discriminated against on racial grounds, notwithstanding that he might not have been transferred had he not been Jewish, since his being Jewish was not the activating cause of his transfer.

Statutory comparison

(3) A comparison of the cases of persons of different sex or marital status under s.1(1) or 3(1) must be such that the relevant circumstances in the one case are the same, or not materially different, in the other.

SEX DISCRIMINATION ACT – s.5

(4) A comparison of the case of a person of a particular racial group with that of a person not of that group under s.1(1) must be such that the relevant circumstances in the one case are the same, or not materially different, in the other.

RACE RELATIONS ACT – s.3

Macdonald v   [2003] IRLR 512 HL
Advocate General for Scotland
Pearce v
Governing Body of Mayfield Secondary School
The "relevant circumstances" for the purpose of the statutory comparison are those which the alleged discriminator takes into account when deciding to treat the woman or the man as he does. If the relevant circumstances are to be "the same or not materially different", within the meaning of s.5(3), all the characteristics of the complainant which are relevant to the way his case was dealt with must be found also in the comparator. They do not have to be precisely the same, but they must not be materially different. That is the basic rule, if one is to compare like with like. Characteristics that have no bearing on the way the woman was treated can be ignored, but those that do have a bearing on the way she was treated must be the same if one is to determine whether, but for her sex, she would have been treated differently.

Balamoody v   [2002] IRLR 288 CA
United Kingdom Central Council
for Nursing, Midwifery and Health
The task set by s.3(4) of the Race Relations Act is broadly to compare like with like. If the applicant can point to an actual person whose circumstances are the same or not materially different from their own, then so much the better. However, where there is no actual comparator who has been treated more favourably than the applicant, it is necessary to construct a hypothetical comparator to show how a person of the other racial group would have been treated. This is a matter of law because it goes to the manner in which the tribunal is to approach a case. If a hypothetical comparator is required and the tribunal does not direct itself to the need for that

control group against which to test the alleged discriminatory treatment, then the tribunal would err in principle.

Chief Constable of West Yorkshire Police v
Vento
[2001] IRLR 124 EAT

Where there is no evidence as to the treatment of an actual male comparator whose position is wholly akin to the applicant's, a tribunal has to construct a picture of how a hypothetical male comparator would have been treated in comparable surrounding circumstances. Inferences will frequently need to be drawn. One permissible way of judging a question such as that is to see how unidentical but not wholly dissimilar cases were treated in relation to other individual cases. It is not required that a minutely exact actual comparator has to be found. If that were the case then isolated cases of discrimination would almost invariably go uncompensated.

Marks & Spencer plc v
Martins
[1998] IRLR 326 CA

In order to determine whether there has been less favourable treatment of an unsuccessful job applicant, it is compulsory to make a comparison between the treatment of the complainant and the treatment of an applicant for the same job of the same age from a different racial group with similar experience and qualifications.

Bullock v
Alice Ottley School
[1992] IRLR 564 CA

The "relevant circumstances" are the circumstances which are relevant to the comparison. "Relevant" has to be judged by an objective standard.

Showboat Entertainment Centre Ltd v
Owens
[1984] IRLR 7 EAT

In judging whether there has been discrimination, although like has to be compared with like, the comparison is between the treatment actually meted out and the treatment which would have been afforded to a man having all the same characteristics as the complainant except his race or his attitude to race. Only by excluding matters of race can it be discovered whether the differential treatment was on racial grounds. Therefore, in a case where an employee was dismissed for refusing to carry out an unlawful discriminatory instruction, the correct comparison was between the employee dismissed and another employee who did not refuse to obey the unlawful discriminatory instruction rather than between the employee and how the employers would have treated another employee who refused to obey the instruction.

Re EOC for Northern Ireland's Application
[1989] IRLR 64 NIHC

To be relied upon, a material difference must be one which itself has not been created by discrimination on the ground of sex.

James v
Eastleigh Borough Council
[1990] IRLR 288 HL

Because pensionable age is itself discriminatory, it cannot be treated as a relevant circumstance in making the comparison.

Grieg v
Community Industry
[1979] IRLR 158 EAT

The relevant employment for the purposes of comparison under s.5(3) of the Sex Discrimination Act is the employment for which the applicant applied, not some hypothetical employment with totally different personnel concerned. Therefore, where a woman complains that she has been discriminated against in not getting a job where the other workers are men, the correct approach is to ask whether a man would have got the job, not what would have happened had all the other workers been women and a man had applied.

Dhatt v
McDonalds Hamburgers Ltd
[1991] IRLR 130 CA

The nationality of someone seeking work is a relevant circumstance within the meaning of s.3(4) because Parliament itself recognises and seeks to enforce by reference to nationality a general division between those who by reason of their nationality are free to work and those who require permission. Although nationality is itself discriminatory in racial terms, it is discrimination which has been sanctioned by statute.

Evidence

Standard of proof

King v
The Great Britain-China Centre
[1991] IRLR 513 CA

The following principles and guidance can be extracted from the authorities:

(1) It is for the applicant who complains of racial discrimination to make out his or her case. Thus if the applicant does not prove the case on the balance of probabilities he or she will fail.

(2) It is important to bear in mind that it is unusual to find direct evidence of racial discrimination. Few employers will be prepared to admit such discrimination even to themselves. In some cases the discrimination will not be ill-intentioned but merely based on an assumption "he or she would not have fitted in".

(3) The outcome of the case will therefore usually depend on what inferences it is proper to draw from the primary facts found by the tribunal. These inferences can include, in appropriate cases, any inferences that it is just and equitable to draw in accordance with s.65(2)(b) of the 1976 Act from an evasive or equivocal reply to a questionnaire.

(4) Though there will be some cases where, for example, the non-selection of the applicant for a post or for promotion is clearly not on racial grounds, a finding of discrimination and a

finding of a difference in race will often point to the possibility of racial discrimination. In such circumstances the tribunal will look to the employer for an explanation. If no explanation is then put forward, or if the tribunal considers the explanation to be inadequate or unsatisfactory, it will be legitimate for the tribunal to infer that the discrimination was on racial grounds.

Zafar v [1998] IRLR 36 HL
Glasgow City Council
The conduct of a hypothetical reasonable employer is irrelevant to deciding whether a discrimination claimant has been treated by the alleged discriminator "less favourably" than that person treats or would have treated another. It cannot be inferred only from the fact that an employer has acted unreasonably towards one employee that he would have acted reasonably if he had been dealing with another in the same circumstances

Anya v [2001] IRLR 377 CA
University of Oxford
Very little direct discrimination today is overt or even deliberate. The guidance from the case law tells tribunals to look for indicators from a time before or after the particular decision which may demonstrate that an ostensibly fair-minded decision was, or equally was not, affected by racial bias.

Rihal v [2004] IRLR 642 CA
London Borough of Ealing
In determining whether there were racial grounds for less favourable treatment, a tribunal is obliged to look at all the material put before it which is relevant to determination of that issue, which may include evidence about the conduct of the alleged discriminator before or after the act about which complaint is made. The total picture has to be looked at. In constructing a picture of how a hypothetical comparator would have been treated in comparable circumstances, the tribunal may have to look beyond the immediate circumstances of the incident about which complaint is made. Moreover, where there are allegations of discrimination by an employer over a substantial period of time, it would be wrong for a tribunal to treat the individual incidents complained of in isolation from one another. That would be a fragmented approach and would overlook the relevance which the wider profile may have to the decisions to be reached on those individual complaints.

Qureshi v [1991] IRLR 264 CA
London Borough of Newham
Incompetence does not, without more, become discrimination merely because the person affected by it is from an ethnic minority.

Anya v [2001] IRLR 377 CA
University of Oxford
Unreasonable behaviour by an employer towards a black employee may justify an inference of racial bias if there is nothing else to explain it. Whether the explanation is that

the employer behaves equally badly to employees of all races depends not on a theoretical possibility, but on evidence that he does.

Bahl v [2004] IRLR 799 CA
Law Society
Unreasonable treatment of a complainant alleging discrimination, if there is nothing else to explain it, cannot in itself lead to an inference of discrimination even in the absence of evidence from the employer that equally unreasonable treatment would have been meted out to the comparator. Racial or sex discrimination may be inferred if there is no explanation for unreasonable treatment. However, this is not an inference from unreasonable treatment itself but from the absence of any explanation for it. Proof of equally unreasonable treatment of all is merely one way of avoiding an inference of unlawful discrimination. It is not the only way.

Bahl v [2004] IRLR 799 CA
Law Society
In order to find discrimination on the ground of race or sex, the tribunal must find that subjectively racial or sexual considerations were in the mind of the discriminator.

West Midlands Passenger Transport [1988] IRLR 186 CA
Executive v
Singh
Statistical evidence may establish a discernible pattern in the treatment of a particular group: if that pattern demonstrates a regular failure of members of the group to obtain particular jobs and of underrepresentation in such jobs, it may give rise to an inference of discrimination against the group. Statistics obtained through monitoring of the workforce and of applications for recruitment and promotion are not conclusive in themselves, but if they show imbalances or disparities, they may indicate areas of discrimination.

West Midlands Passenger Transport [1988] IRLR 186 CA
Executive v
Singh
If a practice is being operated against a racial group then, in the absence of a satisfactory explanation in a particular case, it is reasonable to infer that the complainant, as a member of the group, has himself been treated less favourably on grounds of race. Evidence of discriminatory treatment against the group may be more persuasive of discrimination in a particular case than previous treatment of the complainant by the employer, which may be indicative of personal factors peculiar to the complainant and not necessarily racially motivated.

Rihal v [2004] IRLR 642 CA
London Borough of Ealing
If an employer institutes an arrangement which is discriminatory, that arrangement does not cease to be so merely because the manager in charge changes. It is the employers against whom the complaint is made, not the individual manager.

Robson v   **[1998] IRLR 186 EAT**
Commissioners of Inland Revenue
Whether someone is related by marriage to someone from an ethnic minority is not probative of whether they discriminated against someone from a different racial group.

Oxford v   **[1977] IRLR 225 EAT**
Department of Health and
    Social Security
Although the formal burden of proof lies upon the applicant, it would only be in exceptional or frivolous cases that it would be right for an employment tribunal to find at the end of the applicant's case that there was no case to answer and that it was not necessary to hear what the respondents had to say about it.

Scope of evidence

West Midlands Passenger Transport   **[1988] IRLR 186 CA**
    Executive v
Singh
As evidence from employers that both white and non-white persons hold responsible positions has been accepted as demonstrating that the employers have a policy of non-discrimination and as providing probative evidence from which an employment tribunal can decide that a particular applicant had not been discriminated against, so evidence of a discriminatory attitude on the employers' part may also have probative effect.

Din v   **[1982] IRLR 281 EAT**
Carrington Viyella Ltd
Section 68(1) of the Race Relations Act prevents an act which occurred more than three months before the start of proceedings being treated as the cause of action giving rise to a remedy under the Act. Section 68(1) does not say that no regard shall be had to any discriminatory acts done outside the period of three months. Though no damages or other relief can be obtained relying simply on acts done outside the period of three months, it does not follow that acts done within the three months' period which are related to acts done outside the three months' period are incapable of giving rise to a cause of action.

Chattopadhyay v   **[1981] IRLR 487 EAT**
The Headmaster of Holloway School
Evidence of events subsequent to an alleged act of discrimination is admissible where it is logically probative of a relevant fact.

Chattopadhyay v   **[1981] IRLR 487 EAT**
The Headmaster of Holloway School
If a person involved in an alleged act of discrimination had, before the act complained of, treated the complainant with hostility, that evidence of hostility would be admissible as showing circumstances consistent with a racialist attitude of that person, even though there might be another, innocent explanation for such hostility. There is no relevant distinction between hostility before the event and hostility after the event. Evidence of such hostility is admitted with a view to showing that the person involved was treating the complainant differently from other people, whether he was animated by racial considerations or not. In either case, it calls for an answer.

Chapman v   **[1994] IRLR 124 CA**
Simon
The jurisdiction of the employment tribunal is limited to complaints which have been made to it. If the act of which complaint is made is found to be not proven, it is not for the tribunal to find another act of discrimination of which complaint has not been made to give a remedy in respect of that other act.

Dimtsu v   **[1991] IRLR 450 EAT**
Westminster City Council
In determining a discrimination complaint, an employment tribunal does not have an inquisitorial role to investigate generally and see that the requirements of the Act have in all respects been observed. An employment tribunal's duty is to adjudicate upon the issues before it. A tribunal is not under a duty to investigate other possible complaints, even though they arise out of the same incident, unless it is asked to do so.

Zurich Insurance Co v   **[1998] IRLR 118 EAT**
Gulson
An employment tribunal was entitled to exercise its discretion not to allow the employers to cross-examine the applicant about her family outgoings, with a view to showing that she and her husband could stretch their income to pay for a full-time nanny so that she comply with a requirement to work on a rota basis.

Discovery and particulars
GENERAL PRINCIPLES

Nasse v   **[1979] IRLR 465 HL**
Science Research Council
Vyas v
Leyland Cars
In cases under the Sex Discrimination Act and the Race Relations Act, the necessary information and material to support or refute a claim will rarely be in the possession of the employee, but, on the contrary, is likely to be in the possession of the employer. Discrimination often involves an allegation that, although the unselected complainant is as well qualified as the person selected, or indeed better qualified, he was not chosen, an allegation which almost necessarily involves a careful comparison of qualifications and an inquiry into the selection process. The employer is likely to have information on these matters. There is a clear public interest, accepted and emphasised by Parliament in the Sex Discrimination and Race Relations Acts, that the fullest information should be before the tribunals.

West Midlands Passenger Transport   [1988] IRLR 186 CA
Executive v
Singh

Statistics of the number of white and non-white persons who applied for similar posts with the employers over a period, categorised as to whether or not they had been appointed, are discoverable by an unsuccessful applicant for promotion since they are logically probative of whether the employers discriminated against him on racial grounds when they denied him promotion. The statistical material was relevant in that it might assist the complainant in establishing a positive case that the treatment of non-white employees was on racial grounds, which was an effective cause for their, and his, failure to obtain promotion and it might assist the complainant to rebut the employers' contention that they operated an equal opportunities policy and applied it in his case.

Perera v   [1980] IRLR 233 EAT
Civil Service Commission

Since it is rare for there to be direct evidence or a direct admission of racial discrimination, tribunals will have to probe the facts which are put forward initially by the person against whom the proceedings are brought to consider whether there has been discrimination. Therefore, an applicant is entitled to have the opportunity of looking, in such form as is convenient and fair, at such material which is in the possession of the employer and which is necessary for the tribunal to consider the matter.

Rasul v   [1978] IRLR 203 EAT
Commission for Racial Equality

A complainant is entitled to discovery of documents from the respondents, which will enable him to make a comparative analysis between his own qualifications and history and that of his competitors for a job for which he applied unsuccessfully, in order that an employment tribunal can legitimately draw the inference that the reason for his non-success was that the respondents had discriminated against him on grounds of his race. It is not easy for a complainant in a discrimination case to give direct evidence to establish whether somebody has practised discrimination, since it is what happens in the decision-making process of the prospective employer that is, or is not, discrimination.

Commissioner of Police of   [1993] IRLR 319 EAT
the Metropolis v
Locker

Discovery of statements made in the course of the grievance procedure dealing with the employee's allegations of discrimination in respect of her non-selection for a post was necessary for fairly disposing of her employment tribunal complaints, notwithstanding that the statements sought to be inspected were about events which may have preceded the discriminatory conduct complained of, since the allegations went significantly wider than the conduct of the interview when she was not selected. She relied upon a background of discriminatory treatment which would, if proved, clearly be admissible material from which inferences could be drawn of discrimination on racial grounds, and the grievance procedure may well have produced statements that would tend to prove such background facts.

West Midlands Passenger Transport   [1988] IRLR 186 CA
Executive v
Singh

A tribunal may decide that a request for discovery is oppressive and not order discovery even where it is relevant if it is of the opinion that it is not necessary for disposing fairly of the proceedings or for saving costs. Discovery may be oppressive if it requires the provision of material not readily to hand, which can only be made available with difficulty and at great expense, or if it requires the party ordered to make discovery to embark on a course which will add unreasonably to the length and cost of the hearing.

Carrington v   [1990] IRLR 6 EAT
Helix Lighting Ltd

There are no powers under the Employment Tribunals Rules of Procedure to require an employer to prepare a schedule of evidence disclosing details of the ethnic composition of its workforce where this information is not available and can only be produced by carrying out a survey of the workforce. "Discovery" is limited to the production of documents in being.

CONFIDENTIAL DOCUMENTS

Nasse v   [1979] IRLR 465 HL
Science Research Council
Vyas v
Leyland Cars

There is no principle of law by which documents are protected from discovery by confidentiality in and of itself. If an employment tribunal is satisfied that discovery of a document is necessary in order to dispose fairly of proceedings or for saving costs, it must order the document to be disclosed, notwithstanding that the document is confidential.

Nasse v   [1979] IRLR 465 HL
Science Research Council
Vyas v
Leyland Cars

Where there is an objection by an employer to the disclosure of documents on the grounds of confidentiality, the employment tribunal should inspect the documents to decide whether disclosure is necessary for the fair disposal of the case or for saving costs. An employment tribunal should not order discovery without first inspecting the documents concerned. In exercising its discretion as to whether to order disclosure, the tribunal should have regard to the fact that documents are confidential and should consider whether the necessary information can be obtained by other means, not involving a breach of confidence. It should consider whether justice can be done by special measures such as "covering up" or substituting anonymous references for specific names.

British Railways Board v   **[1979] IRLR 45 EAT**
Natarajan

Before deciding whether an examination of confidential documents is necessary, an employment tribunal chairman should decide whether there is any prima facie prospect of the confidential material being relevant to an issue which arises in the litigation. If there is not, the examination of the documents should not take place. If it is reasonable to expect that there is a real likelihood of relevance emerging from the examination, it is a matter of convenience in each case as to whether the examination should take place at the interlocutory stage of discovery or immediately the matter arises at the trial.

The British Library v   **[1984] IRLR 306 EAT**
Palyza

In considering whether discovery sought is necessary for disposing fairly of the proceedings, a tribunal should confine its attention to matters which are, or might be, of assistance to the applicant. The tribunal is not required to order the disclosure against the employer's wishes of material which would or could help the employer's case. The "fair disposal of the proceedings" means a disposal which is fair to the applicant. The justification for ordering the disclosure of information which would otherwise remain confidential is that Parliament has seen fit to place upon the complainant of racial or sexual discrimination the burden of proving his or her case, notwithstanding that the bulk of the relevant evidence is likely to be in the possession of the respondent to the complaint. The procedure of discovery is designed to offset the probative disadvantages which the complainant would otherwise suffer. It is designed to do justice to the complainant, and there is no reason why it should seek to go further than that. The governing concept is fairness, not absolute justice, and it would be strange if one of the adversaries was compelled to adduce favourable evidence which he would rather withhold.

The British Library v   **[1984] IRLR 306 EAT**
Palyza

The decision of an employment tribunal as to whether or not it is necessary for fairly disposing of the proceedings that confidential reports should be disclosed in cases of alleged discrimination is one which the EAT is free to review and to substitute its own view. The decision whether discovery should be ordered is of such importance as to make it highly desirable that its review by the appellate court should be unfettered.

Commissioner of Police of   **[1993] IRLR 319 EAT**
   the Metropolis v
Locker

Whether public interest immunity exists depends upon whether the court is satisfied that the nature and status of the procedure in which the class of documents was generated is of a type to which public interest immunity should apply. On that basis, public interest immunity does not attach to statements made during the course of a police grievance procedure.

PARTICULARS

Carrington v   **[1990] IRLR 6 EAT**
Helix Lighting Ltd

An employment tribunal does not have power in a case of alleged discrimination to require a schedule of evidence to be produced by an employer where there is no documentation upon which the schedule is to be based and where the production of the schedule is in the nature of creating evidence. Such information cannot be regarded as "particulars" as particulars are the basis whereby a party may ascertain the way the other side is putting their case so that they can prepare accordingly. Particulars are not evidence.

FORMS FOR QUESTIONING

(1) With a view to helping a person ("the person aggrieved") who considers he may have been discriminated against in contravention of this Act to decide whether to institute proceedings and, if he does so, to formulate and present his case in the most effective manner, the Secretary of State shall by order prescribe –

    (a) forms by which the person aggrieved may question the respondent on his reasons for doing any relevant act, or on any other matter which is or may be relevant;

    (b) forms by which the respondent may if he so wishes reply to any questions.

(2) Where the person aggrieved questions the respondent (whether in accordance with an order under subsection (1) or not) –

    (a) the question, and any reply by the respondent (whether in accordance with such an order or not) shall, subject to the following provisions of this section, be admissible as evidence in the proceedings;

    (b) if it appears to the court or tribunal that the respondent deliberately, and without reasonable excuse omitted to reply within a reasonable period or that his reply is evasive or equivocal, the court or tribunal may draw any inference from that fact that it considers it just and equitable to draw, including an inference that he committed an unlawful act.

                     SEX DISCRIMINATION ACT – s.74
                      RACE RELATIONS ACT – s.65

Carrington v   **[1990] IRLR 6 EAT**
Helix Lighting Ltd

The statutory procedure by way of questionnaire is the way in which the legislature has made provision for an applicant to advance his or her case of discrimination. Tribunals are encouraged by the statutes to take a serious view of any unsatisfactory answering of questionnaires and have ample power to draw adverse inferences.

Carrington v   **[1990] IRLR 6 EAT**
Helix Lighting Ltd

It is a sensible and necessary part of the procedure that after any initial questionnaire, an applicant should be able to seek leave, on notice, to administer a further questionnaire.

Oxford v   **[1977] IRLR 225 EAT**
Department of Health and
  Social Security

There is no obligation on an employer, in answer to a form for questioning under s.74 of the Sex Discrimination Act, to provide a complainant with the names and addresses of successful applicants for the position for which the complainant applied. Information as to the qualifications of successful applicants and other relevant information should generally be disclosed, with the identity of the individuals being concealed and their address withheld.

Sex discrimination

Pregnancy discrimination

(1) Section 1, and the provisions of Parts II and III relating to sex discrimination against women, are to be read as applying equally to the treatment of men, and for that purpose shall have effect with such modifications as are requisite.

(2) In the application of subsection (1) no account shall be taken of special treatment afforded to women in connection with pregnancy or childbirth.

SEX DISCRIMINATION ACT – s.2

Webb v   **[1993] IRLR 27 HL**
EMO Air Cargo (UK) Ltd

To dismiss a woman because she is pregnant or to refuse to employ a woman of child-bearing age because she may become pregnant is unlawful direct discrimination since child-bearing and the capacity for child-bearing are characteristics of the female sex. To apply these characteristics as the criterion for dismissal or refusal to employ is to apply a gender-based criterion.

Webb v   **[1995] IRLR 645 HL**
EMO Air Cargo (UK) Ltd (No.2)

To dismiss a woman because she was found to be pregnant, in circumstances in which she had been recruited for an unlimited term with a view, initially, to replacing another employee during the latter's maternity leave and would not be available for work at the time when the task for which she was recruited fell to be performed, is unlawful discrimination contrary to the Sex Discrimination Act.

O'Neill v   **[1996] IRLR 372 EAT**
Governors of St Thomas More
  RCVA Upper School

The distinction between pregnancy per se and pregnancy in the circumstances of the case as motives is legally erroneous. The critical question is whether, on an objective consideration of all the surrounding circumstances, the dismissal or other treatment complained of is on the ground of pregnancy, or on some other ground. This must be determined by an objective

test of causal connection. The event or factor alleged to be causative of the matter complained of need not be the only or even the main cause of the result complained of. It is enough if it is an effective cause. The concept of pregnancy per se is misleading, because it suggests pregnancy as the sole ground for dismissal. Pregnancy always has surrounding circumstances. The Sex Discrimination Act requires the tribunal to decide a case by having regard to whether the treatment complained of was on the ground of sex, not by having regard to the subjective motives of the alleged discriminator.

O'Neill v   **[1996] IRLR 372 EAT**
Governors of St Thomas More
  RCVA Upper School

A religious education teacher who was dismissed after it became known that she had become pregnant by a Roman Catholic priest was dismissed on grounds of pregnancy and, therefore, discriminated against on grounds of sex. The factors surrounding the pregnancy – the paternity of the child, the publicity of that fact and the consequent untenability of the appellant's position as a religious education teacher – were all causally related to the fact that she was pregnant. Her pregnancy precipitated and permeated the decision to dismiss her. Therefore, it was not possible to say that the ground for dismissal was anything other than pregnancy.

Abbey National plc v   **[1999] IRLR 222 EAT**
Formoso

Where a woman is prevented from defending herself at a disciplinary hearing due to her absence for a pregnancy-related reason, that is direct sex discrimination.

Caledonia Bureau Investment   **[1998] IRLR 110 EAT**
  & Property v
Caffrey

Where a woman is dismissed by reason of an illness which is related to being pregnant, or having given birth, which illness arises or emerges during the course of the maternity leave period, the dismissal is still discriminatory even though it takes place after the expiry of that period, on the basis that at the time of dismissal the woman suffered from an illness from which a man could not suffer and thus was treated differently from her male counterparts.

Iske v   **[1997] IRLR 401 EAT**
P & O European Ferries (Dover) Ltd

The employers' failure to offer a pregnant seafarer a transfer to available and suitable shore work when she was no longer able to work at sea due to pregnancy, because alternative work was not given to women after the 28th week of pregnancy, was less favourable treatment on the grounds of her sex where such work would have been offered to a woman who was less than 28 weeks' pregnant or a man who was unfit for seagoing work.

Hardman v   **[2002] IRLR 516 EAT**
Mallon

A failure to carry out a risk assessment in respect of a pregnant woman, as required by the Management of Health and Safety Regulations, is sex discrimination, even where the employer has not carried out risk assessments in respect of any of its employees regardless of their sex. It is not necessary for the treatment of a pregnant woman to be compared with the employer's treatment of a comparable male employee, or a non-pregnant female employee.

Day v [1999] IRLR 217 EAT
T Pickles Farms Ltd
Failure to carry out a risk assessment in accordance with regs. 3(1) and 13A(1) of the Management of Health and Safety at Work Regulations 1992 that takes into account the risk to the health and safety of a new or expectant mother, or to that of her baby, can be a detriment contrary to the Sex Discrimination Act. The obligation to carry out a risk assessment is triggered by employing a woman of child-bearing age. It does not only apply when an employer has a pregnant employee.

GUS Home Shopping Ltd v [2001] IRLR 75 EAT
Green
An employer unlawfully discriminated against the applicants on grounds of sex when it treated them as disqualified from receiving payment under a loyalty bonus scheme because they were absent from work during the relevant period because of pregnancy-related illness or maternity leave.

British Telecommunications plc v [1996] IRLR 601 EAT
Roberts
A request to jobshare after maternity leave is not covered by the special protection against discrimination accorded to women during pregnancy and maternity leave. The period protected by statute is the period of the maternity leave. Once a woman returns to work after her leave, the statutory protection finishes, and her work thereafter is to be considered in the same circumstances as if she were a man. She is not permanently entitled to rely on having had babies as a protecting feature. Therefore, the employers' failure to give reasonable consideration to the applicants' requests to job share on returning from maternity leave could not be regarded as automatically direct discrimination on grounds of sex in accordance with the principles laid down by the European Court in the *Webb* decision.

Discrimination against transsexuals

(1) A person ("A") discriminates against another person ("B") in any circumstances relevant for the purposes of –
>   *(a) any provision of Part II,*
>   *(b) s.35A or 35B, or*
>   *(c) any other provision of Part III, so far as it applies to vocational training,*
> *if he treats B less favourably than he treats or would treat other persons, and does so on the ground that B intends to undergo, is undergoing or has undergone gender reassignment.*
(2) Subsection (3) applies to arrangements made by any person in
relation to another's absence from work or from vocational training.
(3) For the purposes of subsection (1), B is treated less favourably than others under such arrangements if, in the application of the arrangements to any absence due to B undergoing gender reassignment –
>   *(a) he is treated less favourably than he would be if the absence was due to sickness or injury, or*
>   *(b) he is treated less favourably than he would be if the absence was due to some other cause and, having regard to the circumstances of the case, it is reasonable for him to be treated no less favourably.*
(4) In subsections (2) and (3) "arrangements" includes terms, conditions or arrangements on which employment, a pupillage or tenancy or vocational training is offered.
(5) For the purposes of subsection (1), a provision mentioned in that subsection framed with reference to discrimination against women shall be treated as applying equally to the treatment of men with such modifications as are requisite.
SEX DISCRIMINATION ACT 1975 – s.2A

"Gender reassignment" means a process which is undertaken under medical supervision for the purpose of reassigning a person's sex by changing physiological or other characteristics of sex, and includes any part of such a process.
SEX DISCRIMINATION ACT 1975 – s.82

A v [2004] IRLR 573 HL
Chief Constable of West Yorkshire Police
EU law requires that a trans person must be recognised in her reassigned gender for the purposes of sex discrimination law. In sex discrimination cases, it is necessary to compare the applicant's treatment with that afforded to a member of the opposite sex. In gender reassignment cases, it is necessary to compare the applicant's treatment with that afforded to a member of the sex to which he or she used to belong. Thus, for the purposes of discrimination between men and women in the fields covered by the Equal Treatment Directive, a trans person is to be regarded as having the sexual identity of the gender to which he or she has been reassigned.

Chessington World of [1997] IRLR 556 EAT
Adventures Ltd v
Reed
The Sex Discrimination Act applies in a case where the complainant has been less favourably treated following notice of intention to undergo a gender reassignment. Discrimination arising from a declared intention to undergo gender reassignment is based on the person's sex. Where the reason for unfavourable treatment is sex-based, there is no requirement for a male/female comparison to be made. Therefore, the Sex Discrimination Act can be interpreted consistently with the purpose of the Directive as interpreted in *P v S*.

Croft v [2003] IRLR 592 CA
Royal Mail Group plc
By virtue of the definition in s.82 of the Sex Discrimination Act as amended, the category of persons who are not to be discriminated against on grounds of gender reassignment

includes persons at all stages of gender reassignment under medical supervision. However, acquiring the status of transsexual does not carry with it the right to choose which toilet to use. Conversely, it does not follow that, until the final stage is reached, an employee can necessarily be required, in relation to lavatories, to behave as if they were not undergoing gender reassignment. A judgment has to be made as to when a male to female transsexual employee becomes a woman and is entitled to the same facilities as other women. The moment at which a person at the "real life test" stage is entitled to use female toilets depends on all the circumstances. The employer must take into account the stage reached in treatment, including the employee's own assessment and presentation, although the employer is not bound by the employee's self-definition when making a judgment as to when the changes occurred. The employer is also entitled to take into account, though not to be governed by, the susceptibilities of other members of the workforce. Regard should also be had to the particular difficulties which arise with respect to toilet facilities, and the need for separate facilities for men and women. It is inherent in a situation in which two sets of facilities, male and female, are required and in which a category of persons changing from one sex to another is recognised, that there must be a period during which the employer is entitled to make separate arrangements for those undergoing the change.

Sexual orientation discrimination

Macdonald v   [2003] IRLR 512 HL
Advocate General for Scotland
Pearce v
Governing Body of Mayfield Secondary School
In the context of s.1 of the Sex Discrimination Act, "sex" means "gender" and does not include sexual orientation.

Discrimination against married persons

3. (1) In any circumstances relevant for the purposes of any provision of Part 2, a person discriminates against a married person of either sex if –
   (a) on the ground of his or her marital status he treats that person less favourably than he treats or would treat an unmarried person of the same sex, or
   (b) he applies to that person a provision, criterion or practice which he applies or would apply equally to an unmarried person, but –
      (i) which is such that it would be to the detriment of a considerably larger proportion of married persons than of unmarried persons of the same sex, and
      (ii) which he cannot show to be justifiable irrespective of the marital status of the person to whom it is applied, and
      (iii) which is to that person's detriment.

(2) For the purposes of subsection (1), a provision of Part 2 framed with reference to discrimination against women shall be treated as applying equally to the treatment of men, and for that purpose shall have effect with such modifications as are requisite."
                    SEX DISCRIMINATION ACT as amended – s.3

Chief Constable of the Bedfordshire   [2002] IRLR 239 EAT
   Constabulary v
Graham
A police force's policy which restricted officers married to each other or who are in relationships with each other from working together would be more likely to affect women than men, since a higher proportion of female officers were in relationships with male officers than male officers with female officers.

Hurley v   [1981] IRLR 208 EAT
Mustoe
In general, a condition excluding all members of a class from employment cannot be justified on the ground that some members of that class are undesirable employees. Parliament has legislated that women with children are not to be treated as a class but as individuals. No employer is bound to employ unreliable employees, whether men or women. But he must investigate each case and not simply apply a rule of convenience, or a prejudice, to exclude a whole class of women or married persons because some members of that class are not suitable employees. Therefore, a policy of not employing persons, of either sex, who had small children was indirectly discriminatory against married persons contrary to s.3(1)(b)(i) of the Sex Discrimination Act and could not be regarded as justifiable for the purposes of s.3(1)(b)(ii).

Race discrimination

Racial grounds

(1) In this Act, unless the context otherwise requires –
   "racial grounds" means any of the following grounds, namely colour, race, nationality or ethnic or national origins;
   "racial group" means a group of persons defined by reference to colour, race, nationality or ethnic or national origins, and references to a person's racial group refer to any racial group into which he falls.
(2) The fact that a racial group comprises two or more distinct racial groups does not prevent it from constituting a particular racial group for the purposes of this Act.

(3) In this Act –
   (a) references to discrimination refer to any discrimination falling within s.1 or 2; and
   (b) references to racial discrimination refer to any discrimination falling within s.1;
and related expressions shall be construed accordingly.
                    RACE RELATIONS ACT – s.3

Mandla v Lee   **[1983] IRLR 209 HL**

A group can be defined by reference to its "ethnic origins" within the meaning of s.3(1) if it constitutes a separate and distinct community by virtue of characteristics which are commonly associated with common racial origin. "Ethnic" is used in the Race Relations Act in a sense appreciably wider than strictly racial or biological.

Per Lord Fraser of Tullybelton: For a group to constitute an ethnic group for the purposes of the Race Relations Act, it must regard itself, and be regarded by others, as a distinct community by virtue of certain characteristics. It is essential that there is (1) a long shared history, of which the group is conscious as distinguishing it from other groups, and the memory of which keeps it alive; (2) a cultural tradition of its own, including family and social customs and manners, often but not necessarily associated with religious observance. In addition, there are other relevant characteristics, one or more of which will commonly be found and will help to distinguish the group from the secondary community; (3) either a common geographical origin, or descent from a small number of common ancestors; (4) a common language, not necessarily peculiar to the group; (5) a common literature peculiar to the group; (6) a common religion different from that of the neighbouring groups or from the general community surrounding it; (7) a sense of being a minority or being an oppressed or a dominant group within a larger community.

CRE v Dutton   **[1989] IRLR 8 CA**

Whether there is an identifiable group of persons who are defined by reference to ethnic origins is essentially a question of fact, to be determined on the evidence, applying the approach set out by Lord Fraser in *Mandla v Lee*.

CRE v Dutton   **[1989] IRLR 8 CA**

If there remains a discernible minority of a religious, racial or ethnic group which adheres to the group it may still be a "racial group" within Lord Fraser's criteria, even though a substantial proportion of the group have become assimilated in the general public.

London Borough of Lambeth v CRE   **[1990] IRLR 230 CA**

Section 3(1) provides that "racial group" can be defined by "colour" so that a racial group may be of more than one ethnic origin.

Mandla v Lee   **[1983] IRLR 209 HL**

Sikhs are a group defined by "ethnic origins" for the purposes of s.3(1) of the Race Relations Act.

CRE v Dutton   **[1989] IRLR 8 CA**

Gipsies, using the narrower meaning of the word "gipsies" as "a wandering race (by themselves called 'Romany'), of

Hindu origin" rather than the larger, amorphous group of "travellers" or "nomads", are an identifiable group defined by reference to "ethnic origins" within the meaning of the definition of "racial group".

CRE v Dutton   **[1989] IRLR 8 CA**

"Travellers" are not synonymous with "gipsies". Therefore, a notice in a pub stating "no travellers" did not indicate an intention by the licensee to discriminate on racial grounds, since the prohibited class included all those of a nomadic way of life and all nomads were treated equally whatever their race.

Dawkins v Department of the Environment   **[1993] IRLR 284 CA**

Rastafarians are not a separate "racial group" within the meaning of s.3(1). Although they are a separate group with identifiable characteristics, they have not established some separate identity by reference to their ethnic origins. "Ethnic" has a racial flavour. Comparing Rastafarians with the rest of the Jamaican community in England or with the rest of the Afro-Caribbean community, there was nothing to set them aside as a separate ethnic group.

BBC Scotland v Souster   **[2001] IRLR 150 CS**

Neither the English nor the Scots are an "ethnic group" within the meaning of the Race Relations Act because the distinctive racial element required for recognition as an ethnic group is lacking.

Seide v Gillette Industries Ltd   **[1980] IRLR 427 EAT**

Although discrimination on the ground of religion is outside the provisions of the Race Relations Act, being "Jewish" can mean a member of a race or a particular ethnic origin as well as being a member of a particular religious faith, and can therefore fall within the scope of the Act.

BBC Scotland v Souster   **[2001] IRLR 150 CS**

The phrase "national origins" in s.3(1) is not limited to "nationality" in the legal sense and thus to citizenship which an individual acquires at birth. An individual can become a member of a racial group defined by reference to "origins" through adherence, as for instance by marriage.

BBC Scotland v Souster   **[2001] IRLR 150 CS**

There can be direct or indirect racial discrimination within Great Britain arising from the fact that a person is of Scots or English national origins.

Tejani v The Superintendent Registrar for the District of Peterborough   **[1986] IRLR 502 CA**

"National origins" for the purpose of the Race Relations

Act refers only to a particular place or country of origin in accordance with the decision of the House of Lords in *Ealing London Borough Council v Race Relations Board* that "national origins" means "national" in the sense of "race" and not "citizenship". Therefore, there was no discrimination on grounds of "national origins" where the complainant was treated less favourably on grounds that he had been born abroad, without any particular reference to any particular place or country of origin, notwithstanding that a person born in the UK would not have been treated in the same way.

BBC Scotland v   **[2001] IRLR 150 CS**
Souster
"Nationality" is not defined exclusively by reference to citizenship. Nationality can encompass a change in nationality, and can be referable to present nationality.

BBC Scotland v   **[2001] IRLR 150 CS**
Souster
An applicant can be discriminated against on grounds of his English nationality where that nationality has been acquired by adherence or adoption since his birth or because he has been perceived to have become a member of the racial group, the English. It will be for the applicant to prove that he is English, whether that be because his national origins are English or because he has acquired English nationality or that he is perceived to be English.

Dhatt v   **[1991] IRLR 130 CA**
McDonalds Hamburgers Ltd
An application form which distinguished between British citizens and EC nationals on the one hand and applicants who were not British citizens or EC nationals on the other hand did not discriminate on grounds of nationality.

Simon v   **[1987] IRLR 307 CA**
Brimham Associates
In determining whether an act was done on "racial grounds", which means by reason of the racial group to which the complainant belongs, although it cannot be conclusive that the alleged discriminator did not know of the racial origin of the complainant, the knowledge or lack of knowledge of the alleged discriminator must be material.

Vicarious discrimination

Zarczynska v   **[1978] IRLR 532 EAT**
Levy
Discrimination on racial grounds can cover the case of a person who is discriminated against because of another person's race, such as where the complainant has been dismissed for refusing to comply with an instruction to discriminate, whereas another employee who complied with the instruction was not dismissed.

Weathersfield Ltd v   **[1999] IRLR 94 CA**
Sargent
An employee is unfavourably treated on racial grounds if they are required to carry out a racially discriminatory trading policy, even though the instruction concerns others of a different racial group to the complainant. That involved giving a broad meaning to the expression "racial grounds", but it was one which was justified and appropriate. The reasoning of the EAT in *Showboat Entertainment Centre Ltd v Owens*, that the words "on racial grounds" are capable of covering any reason or action based on race and that Parliament could not have intended that a person dismissed for refusing to obey an unlawful discriminatory instruction should be without a remedy, would be agreed with.

Showboat Entertainment Centre Ltd v   **[1984] IRLR 7 EAT**
Owens
Section 1(1)(a) of the Race Relations Act covers all cases of discrimination "on racial grounds" whether the racial characteristics in question are those of the person treated less favourably or of some other person. Therefore, dismissal of an employee because he refused to carry out a racially discriminatory instruction to exclude blacks was "on racial grounds" within the meaning of s.1(1)(a), notwithstanding that the employee was white.

Segregation

(2) It is hereby declared that, for the purposes of this Act, segregating a person from other persons on racial grounds is treating him less favourably than they are treated.

RACE RELATIONS ACT – s.1

PEL Ltd v   **[1980] IRLR 142 EAT**
Modgill
Segregation for the purposes of s.1(2) of the Race Relations Act means the employer keeping apart one person from others on grounds of his race. "Congregating" does not amount to "segregating". Where the fact that all the workers are of a particular racial group arises by the acts of those working in the particular shop themselves, the failure by the employer to intervene and to insist on workers of other racial groups going into the shop, to introduce their friends, contrary to the wishes of the employees in the shop, does not constitute the act of segregating persons on racial grounds.

Sex and race discrimination by employers

(1) It is unlawful for a person, in relation to employment by him at an establishment in Great Britain, to discriminate against a woman –
    (a) in the arrangements he makes for the purpose of determining who should be offered that employment; or
    (b) in the terms on which he offers her that employment; or
    (c) by refusing or deliberately omitting to offer her that employment.

(2) It is unlawful for a person, in the case of a woman employed by him at an establishment in Great Britain, to discriminate against her –

> *(a) in the way he affords her access to opportunities for promotion, transfer or training, or any other benefits, facilities or services, or by refusing or deliberately omitting to afford her access to them; or*
>
> *(b) by dismissing her, or subjecting her to any other detriment.*

SEX DISCRIMINATION ACT – s.6

(1) It is unlawful for a person, in relation to employment by him at an establishment in Great Britain, to discriminate against another –

> *(a) in the arrangements he makes for the purpose of determining who should be offered that employment; or*
>
> *(b) in the terms on which he offers him that employment; or*
>
> *(c) by refusing or deliberately omitting to offer him that employment.*

(2) It is unlawful for a person, in the case of a person employed by him at an establishment in Great Britain, to discriminate against that employee –

> *(a) in the terms of employment which he affords him; or*
>
> *(b) in the way he affords him access to opportunities for promotion, transfer or training, or to any other benefits, facilities or services, or by refusing or deliberately omitting to afford him access to them; or*
>
> *(c) by dismissing him, or subjecting him to any other detriment.*

RACE RELATIONS ACT – s.4

(4A) In subsection (2)(c) reference to the dismissal of a person from employment includes, where the discrimination is on grounds of race or ethnic or national origins, reference –

> *(a) to the termination of that person's employment by the expiration of any period (including a period expiring by reference to an event or circumstance), not being a termination immediately after which the employment is renewed on the same terms; and*
>
> *(b) to the termination of that person's employment by any act of his (including the giving of notice) in circumstances such that he is entitled to terminate it without notice by reason of the conduct of the employer.*

RACE RELATIONS ACT 1976 (as amended) – s.4

Selection arrangements

Nagarajan v   **[1999] IRLR 572 HL**
London Regional Transport
The reference to a "person" in s.4 of the Race Relations Act, which makes it unlawful for "a person, in relation to employment by him" to discriminate, is focused exclusively on the employer. On a complaint against an employer under s.4(1)(a), it does not matter that different employees were involved at different stages. The acts of both employees are treated as done by the respondent employer.

Nagarajan v   **[1999] IRLR 572 HL**
London Regional Transport
Interviewing and assessing candidates for a post can

amount to making arrangements for the purpose of determining who should be offered that employment. *Brennan v J H Dewhurst Ltd* correctly held that the arrangements an employer makes encompasses more than setting up the arrangements for interviewing applicants, and also includes the manner in which the arrangements are operated.

Brennan v   **[1983] IRLR 357 EAT**
J H Dewhurst Ltd
Arrangements made for the purpose of determining who should be offered employment are unlawful within the meaning of s.6(1)(a) of the Sex Discrimination Act if they operate so as to discriminate against a woman, even though they were not made with the purpose of so discriminating.

Cardiff Women's Aid v   **[1994] IRLR 390 EAT**
Hartup
Placing a discriminatory advertisement is not an act of discrimination by an employer within the meaning of Part II in respect of which an individual can make a complaint. Only the statutory enforcement agencies can bring proceedings in respect of causing an advertisement to be published which indicates "an intention" by a person to do an act of discrimination.

Saunders v   **[1977] IRLR 362 EAT**
Richmond upon Thames
  Borough Council
The Sex Discrimination Act does not make it automatically unlawful to ask a woman a question at an interview which would not be asked of a man. Whether such questions do constitute discrimination in the "arrangements" made by an employer for filling a position within the meaning of s.6(1)(a) depends upon whether, by asking the question, the woman was treated less favourably on grounds of her sex than a man would be treated. This involves consideration of the circumstances in which, and the purposes for which, the questions were asked.

Hurley v   **[1981] IRLR 208 EAT**
Mustoe
A policy not to employ women with children which is not applied to men with children is discrimination against women on grounds of sex contrary to s.1(1)(a) of the Sex Discrimination Act.

Noble v   **[1980] IRLR 252 CA**
David Gold & Son (Holdings) Ltd
An employer who allocated light work to women and heavier work to men had not discriminated on grounds of sex where the division of work was based on practical experience of organising the work and not on the assumption that no woman was capable of doing the heavier work. The Sex Discrimination Act provides that employers, when offering jobs, must not assume that women are less capable of doing them than men, and vice versa. This does not mean that a particular applicant for a job, whether male or female, can

do it. Much will depend upon the applicant's physical attributes. Whether a woman applicant for a job can physically do it is a matter of judgment for the employer, and he should base his judgment on his own assessment of the candidate, based upon her physique and his experience of what other women doing that kind of job have been able to do. What he must not do is assume that all women are incapable of doing a particular job.

Horsey v   **[1982] IRLR 395 EAT**
Dyfed County Council
The employers had unlawfully discriminated on grounds of sex against the complainant by refusing to second her from Wales to a training course in the London area where her husband was employed, because they assumed that she would remain in London when her course was completed and would not return to work with them in Wales.

Offer of employment

Anya v   **[2001] IRLR 377 CA**
University of Oxford
The choice between two comparably well-qualified candidates on the basis of how the panel viewed their personal and professional qualities is notoriously capable of being influenced, often not consciously, by idiosyncratic factors, especially where proper equal opportunity procedures have not been followed. If these are to any significant extent racial factors, it will in general be only from the surrounding circumstances and the previous history, not from the act of discrimination itself, that they will emerge.

Adekeye v   **[1997] IRLR 105 CA**
Post Office (No.2)
Section 4(1) of the Race Relations Act, which refers to discrimination "in relation to employment" by the employer, prohibits discrimination against applicants and does not cover a situation where an employee has been dismissed and is applying to be reinstated on appeal. The sidenote to s.4 accurately reflects its substance: subsection (1) relates to applicants seeking the offer of a job. A dismissed employee seeking reinstatement by an appeal against dismissal cannot be regarded as seeking an offer of employment. On the appeal, the appellant is not seeking an offer which can be accepted or refused; the appellant is seeking the reversal of a decision to dismiss.

Promotion, transfer or training

West Midlands Passenger Transport   **[1988] IRLR 186 CA**
  Executive v
Singh
Since the suitability of candidates can rarely be measured objectively and often requires subjective judgments, evidence of a high percentage rate of failure to achieve promotion at particular levels by members of a particular racial group may indicate that the real reason for refusal is a conscious or unconscious racial attitude which involves stereotyped assumptions about members of that group.

Mecca Leisure Group plc v   **[1993] IRLR 531 EAT**
Chatprachong
The employers did not discriminate against an Asian-born employee on grounds of race by failing to provide him with English language training in order to prepare him for promotion where there was no evidence to suggest that the employers would have given special speech training to any member of staff not of Asian origin who had difficulties.

Iske v   **[1997] IRLR 401 EAT**
P & O European Ferries (Dover) Ltd
An employer cannot avoid the effect of s.6(2) by contracting out a job to which the employee could be transferred.

Access to benefits

Clymo v   **[1989] IRLR 241 EAT**
London Borough of Wandsworth
Section 6(2)(a) of the Sex Discrimination Act refers to the employer's acts or omissions in affording access to "facilities" which already exist. Therefore, the appellant could not complain that her employer's refusal to allow her to share her job was contrary to s.6(2)(a) since employment in the appellant's job did not allow anyone to jobshare. It was just not available and therefore was not an existing facility.

Eke v   **[1981] IRLR 334 EAT**
Commissioners of Customs
  and Excise
A refusal to investigate complaints of unfair treatment, whether based on grounds of race or otherwise, may amount to a refusal of access to "any other benefits, facilities or services" within the meaning of s.4(2)(b) of the Race Relations Act. To be a breach of the Act, however, the refusal to investigate must be one which itself is "on racial grounds".

Wakeman v   **[1999] IRLR 424 CA**
Quick Corporation
Locally-recruited British managers were not discriminated against on racial grounds by being paid substantially less than managers seconded from Japan. The fact that locally-hired Japanese were paid on the same scale as other locally-hired nationals at their level indicated that locally-recruited staff were treated equally regardless of race, and that the secondees' pay depended on the place of their permanent employment rather than their racial origin.

Dismissal

(1) In this section a "relevant relationship" is a relationship during the course of which, by virtue of any provision referred to in section 1(1B), taken with section 1(1) or (1A), or (as the case may be) by virtue of section 3A –

(a) an act of discrimination by one party to the relationship ("the relevant party") against another party to the relationship, on grounds of race or ethnic or national origins, or

(b) harassment of another party to the relationship by the relevant party,

is unlawful.

(2) Where a relevant relationship has come to an end it is unlawful for the relevant party –

(a) to discriminate against another party, on grounds of race or ethnic or national origins, by subjecting him to a detriment, or

(b) to subject another party to harassment

where the discrimination or harassment arises out of and is closely connected to that relationship.

(3) In subsection (1) reference to an act of discrimination or harassment which is unlawful includes, in the case of a relationship which has come to an end before 19th July 2003, reference to such an act which would, after that date, be unlawful.

(4) For the purposes of any proceedings in respect of an unlawful act under subsection (2), that act shall be treated as falling within circumstances relevant for the purposes of such of the provisions, or Parts, referred to in subsection (1) as determine most closely the nature of the relevant relationship.

RACE RELATIONS ACT 1976 (as amended) – s.27A

(1) This section applies where –

(a) there has been a relevant relationship between a woman and another person ("the relevant person"), and

(b) the relationship has come to an end (whether before or after the commencement of this section).

(2) In this section, a "relevant relationship" is a relationship during the course of which an act of discrimination by one party to the relationship against the other party to it is unlawful under any preceding provision of this Part.

(3) It is unlawful for the relevant person to discriminate against the woman by subjecting her to a detriment where the discrimination arises out of and is closely connected to the relevant relationship.

SEX DISCRIMINATION ACT 1975 (as amended) – s.20A

Detrimental treatment

General principles

Shamoon v   **[2003] IRLR 285 HL**
Chief Constable of the Royal Ulster Constabulary
In order for a disadvantage to qualify as a "detriment", it must arise in the employment field in that the court or tribunal must find that by reason of the act or acts complained of a reasonable worker would or might take the view that he

had thereby been disadvantaged in the circumstances in which he had thereafter to work.

Shamoon v   **[2003] IRLR 285 HL**
Chief Constable of the Royal Ulster Constabulary
An unjustified sense of grievance cannot amount to "detriment".

Jiad v   **[2003] IRLR 232 CA**
Byford
Enduring physical or psychological injury can (depending on the facts) be capable of constituting detriment in the sense that a reasonable worker would regard it as a disadvantage, even though transitory hurt feelings may not (depending on the facts) suffice.

The Home Office v   **[1984] IRLR 299 EAT**
Holmes
The "detriment" referred to in s.6(2)(b) of the Sex Discrimination Act does not have to be a detriment of a different kind than that which must be shown under s.1(1)(b)(ii). It is entirely consistent with the scheme and language of the Act that the same disadvantage to a woman may be relied on to found the detriment of incapacity under s.1 as to qualify under the broad head of detriment under s.6.

Sexual harassment

Macdonald v   **[2003] IRLR 512 HL**
Advocate General for Scotland
Pearce v
Governing Body of Mayfield Secondary School
Sexual harassment is only prohibited by the Sex Discrimination Act if the claimant can show she was harassed because she was a woman. Section 1(1)(a) requires the employment tribunal to compare the way the alleged discriminator treats the woman with the way he treats or would treat a man. In any case where discrimination is established, this exercise must involve comparing two forms of treatment which are different, whether in kind or in degree. It also involves the tribunal in evaluating the differences and deciding which form of treatment is less favourable. The suggestion in some cases that if the form of the harassment is sexual or gender-specific, such as verbal abuse in explicitly sexual terms, that of itself constitutes less favourable treatment on the ground of sex, could not be reconciled with the language or the scheme of the statute. The fact that harassment is gender-specific in form cannot be regarded as of itself establishing conclusively that the reason for the harassment is gender-based, "on the ground of her sex". It will be evidence, whose weight will depend on the circumstances, that the reason for the harassment was the sex of the victim, although in some circumstances, the inference may readily be drawn that the reason for the harassment was gender-based, as where a male employee subjects a female colleague to persistent, unwanted sexual overtures. In such a case, the male employee's treatment

of the woman is compared with his treatment of men, even though the comparison may be self-evident.

Reed and Bull Information Systems Ltd v Stedman
[1999] IRLR 299 EAT

Sexual harassment is a type of "detriment" within the meaning of s.6 of the Sex Discrimination Act. The question in each case is whether the alleged victim has been subjected to a detriment, and was it on the grounds of sex. Lack of intent is not a defence.

British Telecommunications plc v Williams
[1997] IRLR 668 EAT

Sexual harassment is a particular form of discrimination on the grounds of sex which can best be defined as "unwanted conduct of a sexual nature or other conduct based on sex affecting the dignity of women and men at work".

Reed and Bull Information Systems Ltd v Stedman
[1999] IRLR 299 EAT

The essential characteristic of sexual harassment is that it is words or conduct which are unwelcome to the recipient and it is for the recipient to decide for themselves what is acceptable to them and what they regard as offensive.

Driskel v Peninsula Business Services Ltd
[2000] IRLR 151 EAT

That which in isolation may not amount to discriminatory detriment may become such if persisted in notwithstanding objection.

Bracebridge Engineering Ltd v Darby
[1990] IRLR 3 EAT

A single incident of sexual harassment, provided it is sufficiently serious, is a "detriment" to the complainant on grounds of sex.

Insitu Cleaning Co Ltd v Heads
[1995] IRLR 4 EAT

Whether a single act of verbal sexual harassment is sufficient to found a complaint is a matter of fact and degree. That the EC Code of Practice refers to "unwanted conduct" does not mean that a single act can never amount to harassment in that it cannot be said to be "unwanted" until it is done and rejected. The word "unwanted" is essentially the same as "unwelcome" or "uninvited".

Reed and Bull Information Systems Ltd v Stedman
[1999] IRLR 299 EAT

Some conduct, if not expressly invited, could properly be described as unwelcome. A woman does not have to make it clear in advance that she does not want to be touched in a sexual manner. At the lower end of the scale, a woman may appear, objectively, to be unduly sensitive to what might otherwise be regarded as unexceptional behaviour. But because it is for each person to define their own levels of acceptance, the question would then be whether by words or conduct she had made it clear that she found such conduct unwelcome. Provided that any reasonable person would understand her to be rejecting the conduct of which she was complaining, continuation of the conduct would, generally, be regarded as harassment.

Driskel v Peninsula Business Services Ltd
[2000] IRLR 151 EAT

In a complaint of sexual harassment, in hearing the evidence and finding the facts, a tribunal should not make judgments as to the discriminatory significance, if any, of individual incidents. If ad hoc assessments are made, there is the potential for ignoring the impact of the totality of successive incidents, individually trivial. Instead, the tribunal should judge whether the facts as found disclose apparent treatment of a female applicant in one or more of the respects identified in ss.6(2)(a) and (b) of the Sex Discrimination Act that was less favourable than the treatment, actual or potential, of a man. A tribunal should then consider any explanation put forward by the employers and in light of this determine whether the discrimination so far potentially identified is real or illusory.

British Telecommunications plc v Williams
[1997] IRLR 668 EAT

An employment tribunal erred in finding that an interview by a male manager of a female employee was sexually intimidating because there was no woman present and the interview took place in a confined space. It is neither required by law nor desirable in practice that employers should see that male managers are chaperoned when dealing with female staff.

De Souza v The Automobile Association
[1986] IRLR 103 CA

If sexual harassment was such that the putative reasonable employee could justifiably complain about his or her working conditions or environment, it could contravene the relevant statutory provisions whether or not the working conditions were so bad as to be able to amount to constructive dismissal or even if the employee was prepared to work on and put up with the harassment.

Stewart v Cleveland Guest (Engineering) Ltd
[1994] IRLR 440 EAT

An employment tribunal was entitled to decide that the employers had not discriminated against the appellant on the ground of her sex by allowing their male employees to display pictures of nude women in the workplace when they knew that the display was offensive to her, or by failing to deal with her complaints properly. The tribunal had not erred in law in finding that since the display of pictures of nude women was "neutral", in that a man might have found the display as offensive as did the appellant, the appellant had not established that she had been treated less favourably than a man was or would have been treated.

Insitu Cleaning Co Ltd v   **[1995] IRLR 4 EAT**
Heads
A remark by a man about a woman's breasts cannot sensibly be equated with a remark by a woman about a bald head or a beard. One is sexual, the other is not.

Driskel v   **[2000] IRLR 151 EAT**
Peninsula Business Services Ltd
A tribunal should not lose sight of the significance of the sex of both the complainant and the alleged discriminator. Sexual badinage of a heterosexual male by another man cannot be completely equated with like badinage by him of a woman. Prima facie the treatment is not equal, since in the latter circumstance it is the sex of the alleged discriminator that potentially adds a material element absent as between two heterosexual men.

Balgobin v   **[1987] IRLR 401 EAT**
London Borough of Tower Hamlets
Women were not treated less favourably than a man was, or would be treated on grounds of their sex by being required to work with an alleged harasser after they had made complaints, where the reason they were exposed to the risk of sexual harassment was not on account of their being women, but because the employers' inquiry into their complaints had been inconclusive and all the parties had returned to their previous employment. As the employers did not require the women to work with the harasser because of their sex, the detrimental treatment they suffered was not on grounds of their sex within the meaning of s.1(1)(a) of the Sex Discrimination Act.

Balgobin v   **[1987] IRLR 401 EAT**
London Borough of Tower Hamlets
Requiring women to continue to work with an alleged harasser after an employers' inquiry into their complaints of sexual harassment was inconclusive was not less favourable treatment on grounds of sex where it was accepted that if the victim had been a man to whom homosexual advances had been made it would have been dealt with in the same way, so that there was no evidence that the employers had treated the women less favourably than they would have treated a comparable man.

Smith v   **[1998] IRLR 520 CA**
Gardner Merchant Ltd
Discrimination stemming from the victim's sexual orientation may at the same time constitute discrimination on the ground of his or her sex. Where a male employee has been harassed and suffered less favourable treatment by reason of his homosexual orientation, to compare like with like, his treatment must be compared with that of a female homosexual. In such a case, homosexuality as such is the relevant circumstance which must remain the same for the purpose of the comparative analysis required by s.5(3). Therefore, if an applicant was subjected to sexual harassment, in the form of homophobic abuse, by his colleague, it is for the tribunal to determine whether that treatment was less favourable than would have been meted out to a homosexual woman in a

similar position to him. The applicant would also have to establish that it was the fact of his being male that caused his colleague to treat him in a way which was less favourable than the way she would have treated a female with the same personal characteristic of homosexual preference.

Macdonald v   **[2003] IRLR 512 HL**
Advocate General for Scotland
Pearce v
Governing Body of Mayfield Secondary School
The natural inference to be drawn from homophobic terms of abuse was that the reason for this treatment was sexual orientation, even though the form which the abuse took was gender-specific. The issue under s.1(1)(a) cannot turn on a minute examination of the precise terms of the abuse.

Snowball v   **[1987] IRLR 397 EAT**
Gardner Merchant Ltd
Evidence as to a complainant's attitude to matters of sexual behaviour was relevant and admissible for the purpose of determining the degree of injury to feelings that the complainant suffered as a result of sexual harassment. Compensation for sexual harassment must relate to the degree of detriment, and evidence as to whether she had talked freely to fellow employees about her attitude to sexual matters was relevant for determining whether the complainant was unlikely to be very upset by a degree of familiarity with a sexual connotation, so as to challenge the alleged detriment suffered and any hurt to feelings.

Wileman v   **[1988] IRLR 144 EAT**
Minilec Engineering Ltd
A person may be happy to accept the remarks of A or B in a sexual context, and wholly upset by similar remarks made by C. Therefore, the probative value in a sexual harassment case of the fact that the complainant posed for a newspaper in a flimsy costume was almost minimal since the fact that she was upset at remarks made by a director of the employers was not vitiated in any way or inconsistent with her being willing to pose for a newspaper.

Wileman v   **[1988] IRLR 144 EAT**
Minilec Engineering Ltd
Evidence of how a director was alleged to have harassed other women was correctly not admitted by an employment tribunal since sexual remarks made to a number of people have to be looked at in the context of each person. All the people to whom they are made may regard them as wholly inoffensive; everyone else may regard them as offensive. Each individual has the right, if the remarks are regarded as offensive, to treat them as an offence under the Sex Discrimination Act.

Leicester University v   **[1999] IRLR 352 EAT**
A
An employment tribunal has no power to make a restricted reporting order in a case of alleged sexual misconduct which prohibits identification of the employer.

Appearance

Schmidt v   **[1977] IRLR 360 EAT**
Austicks Bookshops Ltd

A rule prohibiting women from wearing trousers at work was not discriminatory where the employers treated both male and female staff alike in that there were rules restricting wearing apparel and governing appearance which applied to men and women, although the rules in the two cases were not the same given the difference of sexes. An employer is entitled to a large measure of discretion in controlling the image of his establishment, including the appearance of staff, especially when those staff, as a result of their duties, come into contact with the public.

Smith v   **[1996] IRLR 456 CA**
Safeway plc

An appearance code which applies a standard of what is conventional applies an even-handed approach between men and women, and not one which is discriminatory. The principle to be applied is that derived from *Schmidt v Austicks Bookshops Ltd*: Rules concerning appearance will not be discriminatory because their content is different for men and women if they enforce a common principle of smartness or conventionality, and taken as a whole and not garment by garment or item by item, neither gender is treated less favourably in enforcing that principle, for example, because of the impact on comfort or health.

Smith v   **[1996] IRLR 456 CA**
Safeway plc

A package approach to the effect of an appearance code necessarily follows once it is accepted that the code is not required to make provisions which apply identically to men and women. The requirement of one particular item of a code may have the effect that the code treats one sex less favourably than the other, but this has to be considered in the context of the code as a whole. This approach is to be applied both to dress and to more permanent characteristics such as hairstyle. That a restriction extends beyond the workplace is a factor to be taken into account in considering whether or not the rule is discriminatory and has been applied in a discriminatory fashion, but does not affect the test itself.

Smith v   **[1996] IRLR 456 CA**
Safeway plc

An appearance code can be challenged before an employment tribunal on the ground that it operates unfavourably towards the applicant on grounds of his or her sex, for example, because of the impact on comfort or health, or the degree of restriction imposed on the freedom to govern one's own appearance. A tribunal has to consider interrelated questions of whether the restriction, such as on the length of hair being worn by men, could properly be justified on the ground that it represents a requirement of conventional appearance, and whether the restriction, when considered in the context of the code as a whole, results in men being treated less favourably than women.

Department for Work and   **[2004] IRLR 348 EAT**
Pensions v
Thompson

If members of one sex are required to wear clothing of a particular kind, and members of the other sex are not, the former are not necessarily treated less favourably than the latter. In a case where men are required to wear a collar and tie at work, the question is whether, in the context of an overarching requirement for staff to dress in a professional and businesslike way, the level of smartness which the employers required, applying contemporary standards of conventional dresswear, could only be achieved for men by requiring them to wear a collar and tie. If that could be achieved by men dressing otherwise than in a collar and tie, the lack of flexibility in the dress code would suggest that men were being treated less favourably than women because it would not have been necessary to restrict men's choice of what to wear in order to achieve the standard of smartness required.

Burrett v   **[1994] IRLR 7 EAT**
West Birmingham Health Authority

A female nurse who was required to wear a cap was not treated less favourably on grounds of sex than male nurses who were not required to wear a cap, even though she considered the requirement demeaning, where the requirement to wear a uniform applied equally to male and female nurses, and it was merely the form of uniform that differed for men and women.

Smith v   **[1996] IRLR 456 CA**
Safeway plc

An employment tribunal was entitled to find that it was not discriminatory for an employer to ban unconventionally long hair for men when such length of hair for a woman was not unconventional.

Other examples

Jeremiah v   **[1979] IRLR 436 CA**
Ministry of Defence

Requiring a man to work in dirty conditions when women were not so required was a "detriment" to him within the meaning of s.6(2)(b) of the Sex Discrimination Act, notwithstanding that he was compensated for the working conditions by an additional payment. An employer cannot buy a right to discriminate by making an additional payment.

Automotive Products Ltd v   **[1977] IRLR 365 CA**
Peake

A complaint by a man under the Sex Discrimination Act objecting to a rule permitting women employees who ceased work at the same time as men to leave the factory premises five minutes earlier than men was subject to the maxim *de minimis non curat lex* and could not be upheld.

BL Cars Ltd v [1985] IRLR 193 EAT
Brown

The issuing of a written instruction to check the identity of black employees and the setting up of a regime under which black employees would have to undergo special investigation before they could have access to their place of work was capable of amounting to a "detriment" to those employees contrary to s.4(2)(c) of the Race Relations Act. It could not be accepted that the "detriment" could only arise when the instruction issued was implemented.

Garry v [2001] IRLR 681 CA
London Borough of Ealing

An employee was subjected to a "detriment" when, for reasons connected with her ethnic origin, an investigation by her employers into her activities was continued longer than an ordinary investigation would have been, even though she was unaware that the investigation was continuing.

Retirement

Bullock v [1992] IRLR 564 CA
Alice Ottley School

There is nothing in the Sex Discrimination Act which prevents an employer having a variety of retiring ages for different jobs, provided that there is no direct or indirect discrimination based on gender.

Racial harassment

---

(1) A person subjects another to harassment in any circumstances relevant for the purposes of any provision referred to in section 1(1B) where, on grounds of race or ethnic or national origins, he engages in unwanted conduct which has the purpose or effect of –
> *(a) violating that other person's dignity, or*
> *(b) creating an intimidating, hostile, degrading, humiliating or offensive environment for him.*

(2) Conduct shall be regarded as having the effect specified in paragraph (a) or (b) of subsection (1) only if, having regard to all the circumstances, including in particular the perception of that other person, it should reasonably be considered as having that effect.

RACE RELATONS ACT 1976 (as amended) – s.3A

(2A) It is unlawful for an employer, in relation to employment by him at an establishment in Great Britain, to subject to harassment a person whom he employs or who has applied to him for employment.

RACE RELATONS ACT 1976 (as amended) – s.4

"Detriment" does not include conduct of a nature such as to constitute harassment under s.3A

RACE RELATONS ACT 1976 (as amended) – s.78

INDIRECT DISCRIMINATION

(b) he applies to that other a requirement or condition which he applies or would apply equally to persons not of the same racial group as that other but –
> *(i) which is such that the proportion of persons of the same racial group as that other who can comply with it is considerably smaller than the proportion of persons not of that racial group who can comply with it, and*
> *(ii) which he cannot show to be justifiable irrespective of the colour, race, nationality or ethnic or national origins of the person to whom it is applied, and*
> *(iii) which is to the detriment of that other because he cannot comply with it.*

RACE RELATIONS ACT – s.1(1)

A person also discriminates against another if, in any circumstances relevant for the purposes of any provision referred to in subsection (1B), he applies to that other a provision, criterion or practice which he applies or would apply equally to persons not of the same race or ethnic or national origins as that other, but –
> *(a) which puts or would put persons of the same race or ethnic or national origins as that other at a particular disadvantage when compared with other persons,*
> *(b) which puts that other at that disadvantage, and*
> *(c) which he cannot show to be a proportionate means of achieving a legitimate aim.*

RACE RELATIONS ACT 1976 (as amended) – s.1A

(b) he applies to her a provision, criterion or practice which he applies or would apply equally to a man, but –
> *(i) which is such that it would be to the detriment of a considerably larger proportion of women than of men, and*
> *(ii) which he cannot show to be justifiable irrespective of the sex of the person to whom it is applied, and*
> *(iii) which is to her detriment.*

SEX DISCRIMINATION ACT as amended– s.1(2)

(3) A comparison of the cases of persons of different sex or marital status under s.1(1) or 3(1) must be such that the relevant circumstances in the one case are the same, or not materially different, in the other.

SEX DISCRIMINATION ACT – s.5

(4) A comparison of the case of a person of a particular racial group with that of a person not of that group under s.1(1) or (1A) must be such that the relevant circumstances in the one case are the same, or not materially different, in the other.

RACE RELATIONS ACT – s.3

General principles

James v [1990] IRLR 288 HL
Eastleigh Borough Council

Section 1(1)(b) cannot sensibly apply in the case of a

---

requirement or condition which is itself gender-based. The conditions for the application of s.1(1)(b) presuppose a requirement or condition which is of itself gender-neutral. Where the requirement or condition is gender-based, the question is whether or not there has been direct discrimination under s.1(1)(a).

Nelson v   **[2003] IRLR 428 CA**
Carillion Services Ltd
In a claim of indirect sex discrimination, the effect of the amendment made to the Sex Discrimination Act by the Burden of Proof Regulations is to codify rather than alter the pre-existing position established by the case law. The burden of proving indirect discrimination was always on the complainant, and there it remains. The complainant still has to prove facts from which the tribunal could conclude that he or she has been unlawfully discriminated against "in the absence of an adequate explanation" from the employer. Unless and until the complainant establishes that the condition in question has had a disproportionate adverse impact upon her sex, the tribunal could not, even without explanation from the employer, conclude that she has been unlawfully discriminated against.

Jones v   **[1990] IRLR 533 CA**
Chief Adjudication Officer
Per Mustill LJ: The "demographic" argument is one way in which indirect discrimination can be established. Where one qualification is being challenged, the process takes the following shape:
1. Identify the criterion for selection.
2. Identify the relevant population, comprising all those who satisfy the other criteria for selection.
3. Divide the relevant population into groups representing those who satisfy the criterion and those who do not.
4. Predict statistically what proportion of each group should consist of women.
5. Ascertain what are the actual male/female balances in the two groups.
6. Compare the actual with the predicted balances.
7. If women are found to be under-represented in the first group and over-represented in the second, it is proved that the criterion is discriminatory.

Clarke v   **[1982] IRLR 482 EAT**
Eley (IMI) Kynoch Ltd
The purpose of the legislature in introducing the concept of indirect discrimination was to seek to eliminate those practices which had a disproportionate impact on women and were not justifiable for other reasons. Although the policy lying behind the Act cannot be used to give the words any wider meaning than they naturally bear, it is a powerful argument against giving the words a narrower meaning thereby excluding cases which fall within the mischief with which the statute was meant to deal.

Disproportionate impact

Pool for comparison

Allonby v   **[2001] IRLR 364 CA**
Accrington & Rossendale College
The identification of the pool for comparison is a matter of logic rather than of discretion or fact-finding. Once the requirement or condition has been defined, there is likely to be only one pool which serves to test its effect.

Rutherford v   **[2004] IRLR 892 CA**
Secretary of State for Trade
   and Industry (No.2)
The sections of the Employment Rights Act which provide that an employee who has reached age 65 does not have the right either not to be unfairly dismissed or to receive a redundancy payment do not have a disparate impact on men. In assessing the disparate adverse impact of the upper age limit on male and female employees, the relevant pool should be defined by reference to the entire workforce to which the requirement of being under 65 applies, including those who are not adversely affected by the upper age limit because they are able to comply with the requirement at the relevant time (the advantaged group), rather than by reference only to those who were disadvantaged by the upper age limit. The respective proportions of men and women who could satisfy that requirement should then be compared. Taking that pool, the difference in the working population between the proportion of men aged under 65 who can comply and the proportion of women aged under 65 who can comply is very small.

Proportionate comparison

Rutherford v   **[2004] IRLR 892 CA**
Secretary of State for Trade and Industry (No.2)
The Burden of Proof Directive, which defines indirect discrimination as existing "where an apparently neutral provision, criterion or practice disadvantages a substantially higher proportion of the members of one sex", does not require the focus to be on the disadvantaged rather than the advantaged group. The definition describes when indirect discrimination exists. It does not prescribe the methodology for assessing the statistical evidence in order to determine whether or not that state of affairs exists. That has been left to the national courts and tribunals to work out. It is a matter of applying considerations of logic, relevance and common sense to the raw material of the statistical evidence in order to determine the existence or otherwise of the objectionable state of affairs.

Harvest Town Circle Ltd v   **[2001] IRLR 599 EAT**
Rutherford

The proper approach to statistics relating to disparate impact is as follows:

(i) There will be some cases where, on the statistics, a disparate impact is so obvious that a look at numbers alone or proportions alone, whether of the advantaged (qualifiers) or disadvantaged (non-qualifiers), will suffice beyond doubt to show that members of one sex are substantially or considerably disadvantaged in comparison with those of the other;

(ii) However, in less obvious cases it will be proper for an employment tribunal to use more than one form of comparison, no one of which is necessarily to be regarded as on its own decisive;

(iii) In such less obvious cases it will be proper for the employment tribunal to look not merely at proportions (as proportions alone can be misleading) but also at numbers, and to look at both disadvantaged and non-disadvantaged groups and even to the respective proportions in the disadvantaged groups expressed as a ratio of each other;

(iv) It will never be wrong for a tribunal to look at more than one form of comparison, if only to confirm that the case remains as obvious as it had first appeared. Moreover, if there is any doubt as to the obviousness of the case, the tendency should always be to look at a second or further form of comparison;

(v) As more cases of indirect discrimination are heard, a better feel, a more soundly based assessment of what is or is not properly to be regarded as a considerable or substantial disparity will develop.

(vi) No distinction is to be drawn between a considerable and a substantial disparity. That being so, it would be a mistake to conclude that anything that was merely not trivial or de minimis sufficed.

(vii) The employment tribunal, in such less obvious cases, after looking in detail at such figures as should have been laid before it, must then stand back and, assimilating all the figures then judge whether the apparently neutral provision, criterion or practice in issue has a disparate impact, be it on men or women, that could fairly be described as considerable or substantial.

Coker v   **[2002] IRLR 80 CA**
Lord Chancellor's Department

Making an appointment from within a circle of family, friends and personal acquaintances is seldom likely to constitute indirect discrimination since the requirement of personal knowledge will exclude the vast proportion of the pool, be they men, women, white or another racial group.

Whether to complainant's detriment

Raval v   **[1985] IRLR 370 EAT**
Department of Health and
    Social Security

Whether a complainant's inability to comply with a

requirement or condition operated to his or her detriment is a finding of fact.

Barclays Bank plc v   **[1995] IRLR 87 CA**
Kapur

An unjustified sense of grievance cannot amount to detriment.

Justifiable

Standard of proof

Hampson v   **[1989] IRLR 69 CA**
Department of Education and Science

Whether a requirement or condition is "justifiable" requires an objective balance to be struck between the discriminatory effect of the requirement or condition and the reasonable needs of the person who applies it. It is not sufficient for the employer to establish that he considered his reasons adequate.

Webb v   **[1993] IRLR 27 HL**
EMO Air Cargo (UK) Ltd

The test of what is "justifiable" formulated by Balcombe LJ in *Hampson v Department of Education and Science* must now be regarded as the appropriate one and as superseding that expressed by Eveleigh LJ in *Ojutiku v Manpower Services Commission.*

Orphanos v   **[1985] IRLR 349 HL**
Queen Mary College

"Justifiable" for the purposes of s.1(1)(b)(ii) means "capable of being justified", and "irrespective of" means "without regard to".

Whiffen v   **[2001] IRLR 468 CA**
Milham Ford Girls' School

It is not a sufficient justification of a condition that has operated in a discriminatory manner that the policy of which that condition is a part, or even the condition itself, may operate in a non-discriminatory manner in other cases. The fact that a policy on its face is gender-neutral and is not inherently sex discriminatory is the very fact that brings the indirect discrimination provisions into operation and that fact loses any conclusive nature once the policy is found to have a discriminatory effect.

Rainey v   **[1987] IRLR 26 HL**
Greater Glasgow Health Board

Per Lord Keith: There is no material difference in principle between the need to demonstrate objectively justified grounds of difference for the purposes of s.1(3) of the Equal Pay Act and the need to justify a requirement or condition under s.1(1)(b)(ii) of the Sex Discrimination Act.

Allonby v   **[2001] IRLR 364 CA**
Accrington & Rossendale College

Once a finding of a condition having a disparate impact on women has been made, what is required of the tribunal at a minimum is a critical evaluation of whether the employers' reasons demonstrate a real need; if there was such a need, consideration of the seriousness of the disparate impact on women including the applicant; and an evaluation of whether the former were sufficient to outweigh the latter.

Board of Governors of St Matthias Church of England School v Crizzle
[1993] IRLR 472 EAT

In determining whether a condition is justifiable, the approach of the employment tribunal should be to consider (a) Was the objective legitimate? (b) Were the means used to achieve the objective reasonable in themselves? and (c) Were they justified when balanced on the principles of proportionality between the discriminatory effect upon the applicant's racial group and the reasonable needs of those applying the condition?

Cobb v Secretary of State for Employment and Manpower Services Commission
[1989] IRLR 464 EAT

In a case of indirect discrimination, it is for the respondent to satisfy the tribunal that the decisions which he took were objectively justified for economic, administrative or other reasons. It is not for the respondent to show that he objectively balanced the adverse impact of the criteria against the need for them. It is for the tribunal to carry out the balancing exercise involved, taking into account all the surrounding circumstances and giving due emphasis to the degree of discrimination caused against the object or aim to be achieved – the principle of proportionality.

Greater Manchester Police Authority v Lea
[1990] IRLR 372 EAT

In order to carry out the objective balance between the discriminatory effect of a condition and the reasonable needs of the person who applies it, there has to be a nexus established between the function of the employer and the imposition of the condition. It is not enough for it to be shown that a condition was imposed in pursuance of an intrinsically laudable and otherwise reasonable policy if there is no relevant need of the employer in connection with the condition.

Cobb v Secretary of State for Employment and Manpower Services Commission
[1989] IRLR 464 EAT

The respondent is under no obligation to prove that there was no other possible way of achieving his objective however expensive and administratively complicated.

Cobb v Secretary of State for Employment and Manpower Services Commission
[1989] IRLR 464 EAT

If alternative criteria are thought to be reasonable, then those should be put forward by the complainant. If the tribunal finds that the respondent ought reasonably to have considered and adopted them, in carrying out the balancing exercise the tribunal might find that the defence is not proved.

Ojutiku v Manpower Services Commission
[1982] IRLR 418 CA

There is no rule of law which requires an employer to call independent evidence to establish the justifiability of a requirement.

Cobb v Secretary of State for Employment and Manpower Services Commission
[1989] IRLR 464 EAT

The production of a mass of statistics, or of sociological or other expert evidence, is not necessary to find that a respondent has established his defence. A respondent is entitled to take a broad and rational view provided that it is based on logic, and is in the view of the tribunal a tenable view.

Panesar v The Nestlé Co Ltd
[1980] IRLR 60 EAT

In order to show that a requirement or condition is justifiable, it is not enough merely for an employer to show that it was introduced as a matter of convenience.

Panesar v The Nestlé Co Ltd
[1980] IRLR 60 EAT

In determining whether a requirement is justifiable, the employment tribunal must be satisfied that it was genuinely introduced for the reason which was put forward.

Panesar v The Nestlé Co Ltd
[1980] IRLR 60 EAT

If a rule is applied to a particular individual in a particular case, it is for the employment tribunal to decide whether the employer has shown that the rule is justifiable in relation to the individual complaint. That the rule is not applied by most companies does not mean that the employer cannot establish that it is justifiable if, on its own merit, it is shown to be justifiable in the particular case.

Tribunal discretion

Mandla v Lee
[1983] IRLR 209 HL

Whether a requirement or condition is "justifiable" is a question of fact for the tribunal to discover, and if there is evidence for which it can find the condition to be justifiable, its finding is not liable to be disturbed on appeal.

Raval v Department of Health and Social Security
[1985] IRLR 370 EAT

The issue of justifiability, being a question of fact, is one that has been left by Parliament to the employment tribunals. Instances are bound to be rare in which a finding on justifiability is capable of being disturbed on appeal. A tribunal's finding on whether or not a requirement is justifiable cannot be disturbed if the conclusion was capable of having been reached by any reasonable tribunal, notwithstanding that another tribunal might perfectly reasonably have taken a contrary view.

Specific examples

The Home Office v Holmes
[1984] IRLR 299 EAT

An employment tribunal's conclusion that the employers had not shown that a requirement to work full time was justifiable could not be held to have been perverse. Whether such a requirement is justified or not is precisely the line of inquiry that Parliament intended to entrust to the employment tribunals. All such cases will turn upon their own particular facts.

Greater Glasgow Health Board v Carey
[1987] IRLR 484 EAT

An employment tribunal which concluded that an employer's requirement that a health visitor work a five-day week was not justifiable within the meaning of s.1(1)(b)(ii) of the Sex Discrimination Act had failed to have sufficient regard to the administrative "efficiency" of the service as referred to by the House of Lords in *Rainey v Greater Glasgow Health Board*.

London Underground Ltd v Edwards (No.2)
[1997] IRLR 157 EAT

The employment tribunal was entitled to find that the employers had not justified indirectly discriminatory rostering arrangements requiring employees to make an early start. There was good evidence that the employers could have made arrangements which would not have been damaging to their business plans but which would have accommodated the reasonable demands of their employees.

Bullock v Alice Ottley School
[1992] IRLR 564 CA

In order to justify a later retirement age for a group which in fact though not by design consists wholly or largely of men it is necessary for the employer to show a real and genuine need for this later retirement age. In this case, the employment tribunal was entitled to accept evidence that a later retirement age for gardeners and the maintenance staff was objectively justified in that it was necessary because of the difficulty of recruiting such staff and the need to retain them as long as possible.

Secretary of State for Trade and Industry v Rutherford and others (No.2)
[2003] IRLR 858 EAT

The Secretary of State objectively justified the default limitation on the right to claim unfair dismissal or redundancy payments to those under age 65. The policy arguments advanced by the Secretary of State in respect of the upper age limit for unfair dismissal and redundancy payments were legitimate aims of the State's social policy and were not related to any discrimination based on sex.

VICTIMISATION

(1) A person ("the discriminator") discriminates against another person ("the person victimised") in any circumstances relevant for the purposes of any provision of this Act if he treats the person victimised less favourably than in those circumstances he treats or would treat other persons, and does so by reason that the person victimised has –

(a) brought proceedings against the discriminator or any other person under this Act [or the Equal Pay Act 1970 – SDA], or

(b) given evidence or information in connection with proceedings brought by any person against the discriminator or any other person under this Act [or the Equal Pay Act 1970 – SDA], or

(c) otherwise done anything under or by reference to this Act [or the Equal Pay Act 1970 – SDA] in relation to the discriminator or any other person, or

(d) alleged that the discriminator or any other person has committed an act which (whether or not the allegation so states) would amount to a contravention of this Act [or give rise to a claim under the Equal Pay Act 1970 – SDA],

or by reason that the discriminator knows the person victimised intends to do any of those things, or suspects the person victimised has done, or intends to do, any of them.

(2) Subsection (1) does not apply to treatment of a person by reason of any allegation made by him if the allegation was false and not made in good faith.

SEX DISCRIMINATION ACT – s.4
RACE RELATIONS ACT – s.2

General principles

Chief Constable of West Yorkshire Police v Khan
[2001] IRLR 830 HL

Victimisation occurs when, in any circumstances relevant for the purposes of any provision of the Act, a person is treated less favourably than others because he has done one of the protected acts.

Aziz v Trinity Street Taxis Ltd
[1988] IRLR 204 CA

The categories of acts set out in s.2(1)(a)-(d) of the Race Relations Act may fairly be described as "protected acts" and the clear legislative purpose of s.2(1) is to ensure, so far as possible, that victims of racial discrimination shall not be deterred from doing any of the acts set out in paras (a)-(d) by the fear that they may be further victimised in one way or another.

Cornelius v University College of Swansea
[1987] IRLR 141 CA

The purpose of the "victimisation" provisions in s.4 of the Sex Discrimination Act is to protect those who seek to rely

---

on the Act or to promote its operation by word or deed. Discrimination under s.4 is not discrimination on the ground of sex but discrimination on the ground of conduct of the type described in that section. Thus the word "discriminate" as used in the Act bears both its meaning under s.1 and its meaning under s.4.

Nagarajan v   **[1994] IRLR 61 EAT**
Agnew

An infringement of the statutory provisions relating to victimisation can only constitute an unlawful act if there is a case established under one of the sections in Part II. There is no illegality involved in victimisation by itself without any repercussions. One cannot have an unlawful act if all there is is either discrimination under s.1 or discrimination by way of victimisation, unaccompanied by any event or action which fits into one of the sections in Part II.

Waters v   **[1997] IRLR 589 CA**
Commissioner of Police
   of the Metropolis

In the case of an act allegedly committed by an employee, s.4(1)(d) of the Sex Discrimination Act only applies where the act, if established, is one for which the employer would be vicariously liable and therefore treated as if the act of the employee had been done by the employer as well.

Standard of proof

Nagarajan v   **[1999] IRLR 572 HL**
London Regional Transport

Conscious motivation on the part of the discriminator is not a necessary ingredient of unlawful victimisation.

Chief Constable of West Yorkshire   **[2001] IRLR 830 HL**
   Police v
Khan

In order to determine whether there has been less favourable treatment, the statute calls for a simple comparison between the treatment afforded to the complainant who has done a protected act and the treatment which was or would be afforded to other employees who have not done the protected act.

Chief Constable of West Yorkshire   **[2001] IRLR 830 HL**
   Police v
Khan

Whether a complainant has been victimised "by reason" that he has done a protected act is not to be determined by application of a "but for" test.

Aziz v   **[1988] IRLR 204 CA**
Trinity Street Taxis Ltd

For the purpose of the requisite comparison, which requires

a claimant seeking to establish that there has been discrimination by victimisation to show that the respondent "in any circumstances relevant for the purposes of any provision of this Act" treated him "less favourably than in those circumstances it treats or would treat other persons", the relevant circumstances do not include the fact that the complainant has done a protected act. The treatment applied by the alleged discriminator to the complainant has to be compared with the treatment which has applied or would apply to persons who have not done the relevant protected act. If the doing of a protected act itself constituted part of the relevant circumstances, a complainant would necessarily fail to establish discrimination if the alleged discriminator could show that he treated or would treat all other persons who did the like protected act with equal intolerance.

St Helens Metropolitan Borough   **[2004] IRLR 851 EAT**
   Council v
Derbyshire

A direct threat of a disciplinary or other sanction made to the individual applicant is not a necessary element in order to show less favourable treatment for the purposes of the victimisation provisions.

Specific examples

Aziz v   **[1986] IRLR 435 EAT**
Trinity Street Taxis Ltd

Section 2(1)(b) of the Race Relations Act, which applies where the person victimised has "given evidence or information in connection with proceedings brought by any person against the discriminator or any other person under this Act", is intended to cover the situation where the person victimised is not a party but is a witness or provides information in connection with the proceedings.

Kirby v   **[1980] IRLR 229 EAT**
Manpower Services Commission

Although the giving of information prior to the commencement of proceedings may fall within s.2(1)(b) of the Race Relations Act, before an allegation of victimisation can be made it must be shown that the victimisation has occurred at a time when proceedings have actually been brought. If the proceedings had been brought, it does not matter whether the information was given before or after the commencement of proceedings so long as it is something which is relied upon by the discriminator as a reason for the victimisation.

Aziz v   **[1988] IRLR 204 CA**
Trinity Street Taxis Ltd

An act can properly be said to be done "by reference to" the Race Relations Act within the meaning of s.2(1)(c) – which applies where a person allegedly victimised has "otherwise done anything under or by reference to this Act in relation to the discriminator or any other person" – if it is done by reference to the race relations legislation in the broad sense, even though the doer does not focus his mind specifically on any provision of the Act. The phrase "by reference to" is a much wider one than "under" and should be read accordingly.

Kirby v   **[1980] IRLR 229 EAT**
Manpower Services Commission
Making a report of alleged discrimination is an act done "by reference to" the statute in relation to another person within the meaning of s.2(1)(c). If a report is made which states that facts are available which ought to be investigated, and which indicates a possible breach of the Race Relations Act, the making of that report is an act done by reference to the statute in relation to the person against whom it is said discrimination might have occurred.

Chief Constable of West Yorkshire   **[2001] IRLR 830 HL**
Police v
Khan
It was not unlawful victimisation to refuse to provide a reference in respect of an employee because the employee had a pending discrimination claim against the employer and the employer needed to preserve its position in the outstanding proceedings. In such a case, the reference was not withheld "by reason that" the applicant had brought discrimination proceedings, but rather because the employer temporarily needed to preserve his position, in that the evidence established that once the litigation had concluded, the request for a reference would have been complied with.

St Helens Metropolitan Borough   **[2004] IRLR 851 EAT**
Council v
Derbyshire
In writing letters to the applicants warning them of the consequences of continuing their equal pay claims, the employers had treated them less favourably within the meaning of the victimisation provisions in the Sex Discrimination Act, notwithstanding that there had been no direct threat to the applicants.

Kirby v   **[1980] IRLR 229 EAT**
Manpower Services Commission
What has to be considered under s.2(1)(d) is whether the allegation, which must be assumed for this purpose to be true, does amount to an act which would be a contravention of the statute.

Waters v   **[1995] IRLR 531 EAT**
Commissioner of Police
of the Metropolis
An employer cannot be liable for victimising an employee who alleged that she was sexually harassed by a work colleague, where the alleged harassment was not committed in the course of employment.

EMPLOYER LIABILITY

(1) Anything done by a person in the course of his employment shall be treated for the purposes of this Act [(except as regards offences thereunder) – RRA] as done by his employer as well as by him, whether or not it was done with the employer's knowledge or approval.

(2) Anything done by a person as agent for another person with the authority (whether express or implied, and whether precedent or subsequent) of that other person shall be treated for the purposes of this Act [(except as regards offences thereunder) – RRA] as done by that other person as well as by him.

(3) In proceedings brought under this Act against any person in respect of an act alleged to have been done by an employee of his it shall be a defence for that person to prove that he took such steps as were reasonably practicable to prevent the employee from doing that act, or from doing in the course of his employment acts of that description.

SEX DISCRIMINATION ACT – s.41
RACE RELATIONS ACT – s.32

Jones v   **[1997] IRLR 168 CA**
Tower Boot Co Ltd
In determining whether conduct complained of was done by a person "in the course of employment", for the purposes of s.32 of the Race Relations Act and the corresponding provisions in s.41 of the Sex Discrimination Act, the words "in the course of employment" should be interpreted in the sense in which they are employed in everyday speech and not restrictively by reference to the principles laid down by case law for establishing an employer's vicarious liability for the torts committed by an employee. The application of the phrase is a question of fact for each employment tribunal to resolve.

Liversidge v   **[2002] IRLR 651 CA**
Chief Constable of Bedfordshire Police
Section 32(1) of the Race Relations Act is not a provision making the employer vicariously liable for the acts of the employee, but one deeming the employer also to have done the employee's acts. The employer may also be liable directly for the discrimination if what was done by the employee was sufficiently under the control of the employer that he could have prevented what was done.

Liversidge v   **[2002] IRLR 651 CA**
Chief Constable of Bedfordshire Police
In the ordinary employment case, where employee A makes a remark racially abusive of employee B in the course of employment, the employer may be liable for an unlawful act under s.4(2)(c) of the Race Relations Act by virtue of s.32(1).

Kingston v   **[1982] IRLR 274 EAT**
British Railways Board
As a matter of law, an employer cannot say that it is not

liable for the unlawful discriminatory behaviour of one employee just because the detriment flowing from that unlawful conduct involves a step taken by another, innocent employee. In such circumstances, the detriment to the complainant would flow directly from the discriminatory conduct of an employee for whom the employer was responsible under s.32 of the Race Relations Act.

Waters v [1997] IRLR 589 CA
Commissioner of Police of the
    Metropolis
No tribunal applying the *Tower Boot* test could find that an alleged sexual assault by a male police constable on a female police constable was committed in the "course of employment", where both parties were off duty at the time of the alleged offence, and the man was a visitor to the woman's room at a time and in circumstances which placed them in no different position from that which would have applied if they had been social acquaintances only, with no working connection.

Chief Constable of the [1999] IRLR 81 EAT
    Lincolnshire Police v
Stubbs
A police officer was acting in the "course of his employment" when he subjected a female colleague to inappropriate sexual behaviour, even though the incidents occurred at social events away from the police station. When there is a social gathering of work colleagues, a tribunal should consider whether or not the circumstances show that what was occurring was an extension of their employment. In the present case, both incidents were at social gatherings involving officers from work and the applicant could not be thought to have been socialising with the male police officer on either occasion. It would have been different had the discriminatory acts occurred during a chance meeting.

Defence

Jones v [1997] IRLR 168 CA
Tower Boot Co Ltd
The policy of the statutory provisions on employer liability is to deter racial and sexual harassment in the workplace through a widening of the net of responsibility beyond the guilty employees themselves, by making all employers additionally liable for such harassment, and then supplying them with the reasonable steps defence, which will exonerate the conscientious employer who has used his best endeavours to prevent such harassment, and will encourage all employers who have not yet undertaken such endeavours to take the steps necessary to make the same defence available in their own workplace.

Croft v [2003] IRLR 592 CA
Royal Mail Group plc
In considering whether an action which it is submitted the employers should have taken is reasonably practicable, it is permissible to take into account the extent of the difference, if any, which the action is likely to make. The concept of reasonable practicability entitles the employer in this context to consider whether the time, effort and expense of the suggested measures are disproportionate to the result likely to be achieved.

Canniffe v [2000] IRLR 555 EAT
East Riding of Yorkshire Council
An employer does not satisfy the defence to liability for acts of their employee merely by showing that there was nothing it could have done to stop the discrimination from occurring. The proper approach to determining whether an employer has satisfied the defence is first to identify whether the employer took any steps at all to prevent the employee from doing the act or acts complained of in the course of his employment; and secondly, having identified what steps, if any, they took, to consider whether there were any further acts that they could have taken which were reasonably practicable. Whether taking any such steps would have been successful in preventing the acts of discrimination in question is not determinative. An employer will not be exculpated if it has not taken reasonably practicable steps simply because, if it had taken those steps, they would not have prevented anything from occurring.

Balgobin v [1987] IRLR 401 EAT
London Borough of Tower Hamlets
An employment tribunal was entitled to find that the employers had proved a defence under s.41(3) of the Sex Discrimination Act to acts of sexual harassment committed by their employee, by establishing that they "took such steps as were reasonably practicable to prevent the employee from doing" the acts complained of in circumstances in which the allegations had not been made known to management; that there was proper and adequate staff supervision; and that the employers had made known their policy of equal opportunities.

Direct liability

Macdonald v [2003] IRLR 512 HL
Advocate General for Scotland
Pearce v
Governing Body of Mayfield Secondary School
Burton v De Vere Hotels Ltd was wrongly decided in that it treated an employer's inadvertent failure to take reasonable steps to protect employees from racial or sexual abuse by third parties as discrimination even though the failure had nothing to do with the sex or race of the employees. The employment tribunal's finding that the hotel manager's failure to protect the waitresses from the offensive content of the comedian's speech was not connected with their ethnic origin, and that, by implication, the employer would have

treated white waitresses in the same way, negatived racial discrimination on the part of the employer. The approach of the EAT, that the tribunal should ask themselves whether the event in question was something which was sufficiently under the control of the employer that he could by the application of "good employment practice" have prevented the harassment or reduced the effect of it was not based on anything which is to be found in the statute.

Chessington World of	[1997] IRLR 556 EAT
Adventures Ltd v	
Reed	

The employers were directly liable for sex discrimination in circumstances in which it was clear that they were aware of a campaign of harassment by some of their employees directed towards the applicant, but took no adequate steps to prevent it, although it was plainly something over which they could exercise control.

Secondary liability

Lana v	[2001] IRLR 501 EAT
Positive Action Training in Housing	
(London) Ltd	

Section 41(2) of the Sex Discrimination Act is not restricted to situations in which the contract gives the agent authority to discriminate. The proper construction of s.41(2) is that the "authority" referred to is the authority to do an act which is capable of being done in a discriminatory manner just as it is capable of being done in a lawful manner.

Lana v	[2001] IRLR 501 EAT
Positive Action Training in Housing	
(London) Ltd	

The effect of the interaction of s.14 and s.41(2) is that where a person who agrees to provide or make arrangements for the provision of facilities for training discharges any obligation to make those arrangements by using another agency, he will be liable for any act of discrimination which falls within the scope of that agency. Accordingly, if it was within the authority of the agent to terminate the engagement of an applicant, and that act was done in circumstances in which it constituted discrimination, it falls within the scope of s.41(2). Thus, in such a case, the relevant question is why the agent terminated the engagement.

Nagarajan v	[1994] IRLR 61 EAT
Agnew	

An employee is liable for the actions of a fellow employee only if there is a relationship of principal and agent between them. Simply by making a request to a fellow employee one employee does not make himself the principal of the another employee if that employee complies with the request.

OTHER UNLAWFUL ACTS

Aiding unlawful acts

(1) A person who knowingly aids another person to do an act made unlawful by this Act shall be treated for the purposes of this Act as himself doing an unlawful act of the like description.

(2) For the purposes of subsection (1) an employee or agent for whose act the employer or principal is liable under s.41 [s.32] (or would be so liable but for s.41(3)) [s.32(3)] shall be deemed to aid the doing of the act by the employer or principal.

SEX DISCRIMINATION ACT – s.42
RACE RELATIONS ACT – s.33

Anyanwu v	[2001] IRLR 305 HL
South Bank Students' Union	

"Aids" is a familiar word in everyday use bearing no technical or special meaning in this context. A person aids another if he helps or assists, or co-operates or collaborates with him. He does so whether or not his help is substantial and productive, provided the help is not so insignificant as to be negligible. It does not matter who instigates or initiates the relationship, and it is not helpful to introduce "free agents" and "prime movers", which can only distract attention from the essentially simple test to be applied.

Hallam v	[2001] IRLR 312 HL
Cheltenham Borough Council	

Section 33(1) of the Race Relations Act requires more than a general attitude of helpfulness and co-operation. It is aid to another to do the unlawful act in question which must be shown. Where a party gives information to another on which that other relies in doing an unlawfully discriminatory act, whether the first party will be liable under s.33(1) will almost always turn on the facts.

Sinclair Roche & Temperley v	[2004] IRLR 763 EAT
Heard	

The element of knowledge is additional to the element of aid. Whereas discrimination can be, and very often is, unconscious, aiding cannot be.

Yeboah v	[2002] IRLR 634 CA
Crofton	

Even if an employer is not vicariously liable because it showed that it took such steps as were reasonably practicable to prevent its employee from doing the act in question within the meaning of s.32(3) of the Race Relations Act, an employee can be personally liable under s.33(1) for "knowingly" aiding the unlawful act by the employer.

Under s.33(2), the employee for whose acts the employer is liable under s.32 or would be so liable but for s.32(3), is deemed to aid the doing of the act by the employer.

Instructions to discriminate

It is unlawful for a person –
> *(a) who has authority over another person; or*
> *(b) in accordance with whose wishes that other person is accustomed to act,*
to instruct him to do any act which is unlawful by virtue of Part II or III [, s.76ZA or, where it renders an act unlawful on grounds of race or ethnic or national origins, s.76 – RRA], or procure or attempt to procure the doing by him of any such act.

SEX DISCRIMINATION ACT – s.39
RACE RELATIONS ACT – s.30

Commission for Racial Equality v   **[1983] IRLR 315 EAT**
Imperial Society of Teachers of
    Dancing

The words "procure" and "attempt to procure" in s.30 of the Race Relations Act have a wide meaning and include the use of words which bring about or attempt to bring about a certain course of action. Therefore, an expression of preference for applicants from a particular racial group is "an attempt to procure" within the meaning of s.30.

Commission for Racial Equality v   **[1983] IRLR 315 EAT**
Imperial Society of Teachers of
    Dancing

Section 30 of the Race Relations Act requires that there should be some relationship between the person giving the instructions or doing the procuring and the other person and that the other person is a person who is accustomed to act in accordance with the wishes of the first person. Since "person", by reason of the Interpretation Act, includes "a body of persons incorporate or unincorporate", if there is evidence that the other person is accustomed to act in accordance with the wishes of the employer, it would not matter that the other person had never before spoken to the particular person giving the instructions. However, it is not possible to construe s.30 as meaning that it is sufficient to show that the other person is accustomed to act with another employer in accordance with the wishes of persons in the same position as the person giving the instructions.

Pressure to discriminate

(1) It is unlawful to induce, or attempt to induce, a person to do any act which contravenes Part II or III, s.76ZA or, where it renders an act unlawful on grounds of race or ethnic or national origins, s.76 .

(2) An attempted inducement is not prevented from falling within subsection (1) because it is not made directly to the person in question, if it is made in such a way that he is likely to hear of it.

RACE RELATIONS ACT 1976 (as amended) – s.31

(1) It is unlawful to induce, or attempt to induce, a person to do any act which contravenes Part II or III by –
> *(a) providing or offering to provide him with any benefit; or*
> *(b) subjecting or threatening to subject him to any detriment.*

(2) An offer or threat is not prevented from falling within subsection (1) because it is not made directly to the person in question, if it is made in such a way that he is likely to hear of it.

SEX DISCRIMINATION ACT – s.40

Commission for Racial Equality v   **[1983] IRLR 315 EAT**
Imperial Society of Teachers of
    Dancing

The word "induce" in s.31 of the Race Relations Act covers a mere request to discriminate. It does not necessarily imply an offer of some benefit or the threat of some detriment. The ordinary meaning of the word "induce" is "to persuade or to prevail upon or to bring about" and there is no reason to construe the word narrowly or in a restricted sense. Therefore, a request by the respondents' secretary to a head of careers at a school that "she would rather the school did not send anyone coloured" to fill a job vacancy constituted an attempt to induce the head of careers not to send coloured applicants for interview in contravention of s.31.

DISCRIMINATION BY OTHERS THAN EMPLOYERS

Discrimination against contract workers

(1) This section applies to any work for a person ('the principal') which is available for doing by individuals ('contract workers') who are employed not by the principal himself but by another person, who supplies them under a contract made with the principal.

(2) It is unlawful for the principal, in relation to work to which this section applies, to discriminate against [a woman who is – SDA] a contract worker –

(a) in the terms on which he allows her [him – RRA] to do that work, or
(b) by not allowing her [him – RRA] to do it or continue to do it, or
(c) in the way he affords her [him – RRA] access to any benefits, facilities or services or by refusing or deliberately omitting to afford her [him – RRA] access to them, or
(d) by subjecting her [him – RRA] to any other detriment.

SEX DISCRIMINATION ACT – s.9
RACE RELATIONS ACT – s.7

Allonby v   **[2001] IRLR 364 CA**
Accrington & Rossendale College
The prohibition against discrimination against contract workers applies both between one contract worker and another and as between a contract worker and an employee so long as they are working for the same principal. Nothing in the section says that it is limited to discrimination between male and female contract workers supplied to a particular employer. It would be remarkable if it permitted an employer, by bringing in female workers on subcontract to work alongside a predominantly male employed workforce, to give them inferior conditions so long as they were all treated equally badly or (if differentially treated) were all of the same sex and so unable to complain.

Harrods Ltd v   **[1997] IRLR 583 CA**
Remick
The prohibition against discrimination against contract workers is not limited to cases where those doing the work are under the managerial power or control of the principal. Staff employed by concessionaires at Harrods department store were contract workers who worked "for" Harrods within the meaning of s.7 of the Race Relations Act and were therefore protected from being discriminated against by Harrods. It is implicit that the

"work" to which s.7(1) is referring will not only be work for the employer, in that it is work done pursuant to the contract of employment, but will also be work done for the principal. The fact that the applicants, as employees, also worked for their employer did not prevent the work which they did from being work "for" Harrods within the meaning of s.7.

Harrods Ltd v   **[1997] IRLR 583 CA**
Remick
The prohibition against discrimination against contract workers applies if there is a contractual obligation to supply individuals to do work that can properly be described as "work for" the principal. There is no requirement that the supply of workers should be the dominant purpose of the contract made between the principal and the employer.

Jones v   **[2004] IRLR 783 NICA**
Friends Provident Life Office
The statutory provisions relating to contract workers were designed to prevent an employer from escaping his responsibilities under anti-discrimination legislation by bringing in workers on sub-contract, and therefore should receive a broad construction which has the effect of providing the statutory protection to a wider range of workers. The purpose of the statutory provisions is to ensure that persons who are employed to perform work for someone other than their nominal employers receive the protection of the legislation forbidding discrimination by employers.

Jones v   **[2004] IRLR 783 NICA**
Friends Provident Life Office
It is implicit in the philosophy underlying the provision that the principal must be in a position to discriminate against the contract worker. The principal must therefore be in a position to influence or control the conditions under which the employee works. It is also inherent in the concept of supplying workers under a contract that it is contemplated by the employer and the principal that the former will provide the services of employees in the course of performance of the contract. It is necessary for both these conditions to be fulfilled to bring a case within the contract worker provisions. It is not sufficient, therefore, for an applicant to show that her employer had a contract with the principal to have certain work done for the latter and that the applicant did that work as an employee of the former.

BP Chemicals Ltd v   **[1995] IRLR 128 EAT**
Gillick
The prohibition on discrimination against a contract worker is not restricted to discrimination against a contract worker who is actually working. It prohibits discrimination in the selection by the principal from among workers supplied under an agency arrangement. Therefore, a complaint could be brought by a contract worker that she had been discriminated against by a principal by

not permitting her to return to work after absence due to maternity.

Patefield v   **[2000] IRLR 664 NICA**
Belfast City Council
A council discriminated against a contract worker on grounds of sex when it replaced her with a permanent employee when she went on maternity leave, in circumstances in which there was a job available for a contract worker when she went off work for maternity reasons and she would have been kept in her post indefinitely if she had not gone off work at that time. By replacing her with a permanent employee when it knew that she wanted to return to her post after the birth of her child, the council subjected her to a detriment at that time by effectively removing the possibility of her returning to her post. In so acting, the council treated her less favourably than they would have treated a man, who would not have become unavailable for work because of pregnancy.

Discrimination by trade unions

(1) This section applies to an organisation of workers, an organisation of employers, or any other organisation whose members carry on a particular profession or trade for the purposes of which the organisation exists.

(2) It is unlawful for an organisation to which this section applies, in the case of a person [woman – SDA] who is not a member of the organisation, to discriminate against him [her – SDA] –
> *(a) in the terms on which it is prepared to admit him [her – SDA] to membership; or*
> *(b) by refusing, or deliberately omitting to accept, his [her – SDA] application for membership.*

(3) It is unlawful for an organisation to which this section applies, in the case of a person [woman – SDA] who is a member of the organisation, to discriminate against him [her – SDA] –
> *(a) in the way it affords him [her – SDA] access to any benefits, facilities or services, or by refusing or deliberately omitting to afford him [her – SDA] access to them; or*
> *(b) by depriving him [her – SDA] of membership, or varying the terms on which he [she – SDA] is a member; or*
> *(c) by subjecting him [her – SDA] to any other detriment.*

[(4) This section does not apply to provision made in relation to the death or retirement from work of a member. – SDA]
SEX DISCRIMINATION ACT – s.12
RACE RELATIONS ACT – s.11

FTATU v   **[1980] IRLR 142 EAT**
Modgill
The task of an employment tribunal in a complaint of race discrimination against a union under s.11(3) of the Race Relations Act is to ask whether the complainants have shown that the union has treated them on racial grounds less favourably than the union treats or would treat other persons in the way it affords them access to benefits, facilities or ser-

vices, or by refusing or deliberately omitting to afford them access to such benefits or by subjecting them to any other detriment. That a union did not give sufficient support to Asian members, or dealt with them inefficiently, was not evidence that there had been less favourable treatment by the union of this particular group of workers than the treatment afforded to any other group of workers. Nor was it evidence that such acts were attributable to racial discrimination.

Fire Brigades Union v   **[1998] IRLR 697 CS**
Fraser
An employment tribunal erred in finding that a union discriminated against a member on grounds of sex by refusing to afford him access to representation or legal assistance for the purpose of disciplinary proceedings by his employer following a complaint of sexual harassment made against him by a woman member. Although the union might have treated those complaining of sexual harassment more favourably than alleged harassers, there was no material on which the tribunal could draw the inference that the decision not to provide representation was gender-related, rather than conduct-related. Therefore, the tribunal was not entitled to find that a woman accused of sexual harassment would have been treated differently.

National Federation of Self-Employed   **[1997] IRLR 340 EAT**
    and Small Businesses Ltd v
Philpott
The expression "organisation of employers" has to be given its ordinary and natural meaning in the context in which it appears, having regard to the characteristics of the organisation in question. On that basis, the National Federation of Self-Employed and Small Businesses is an "organisation of employers", notwithstanding that not all of its members are employers, since it represents its members, who are predominantly employers, specifically as employers, as well as across a range of other matters.

Discrimination by qualifying bodies

(1) It is unlawful for an authority or body which can confer an authorisation or qualification which is needed for, or facilitates, engagement in a particular profession or trade to discriminate against a woman [person – RRA] –
> *(a) in the terms on which it is prepared to confer on her [him – RRA] that authorisation or qualification; or*
> *(b) by refusing or deliberately omitting to grant her [his – RRA] application for it; or*
> *(c) by withdrawing it from her [him – RRA] or varying the terms on which she [he – RRA] holds it.*

[(2) Where an authority or body is required by law to satisfy itself as to his good character before conferring on a person an authorisation or qualification which is needed for, or facilitates, his engagement in any profession or trade then, without prejudice to any other duty to which it is subject, that requirement shall be taken to impose on the authority or body a duty to have regard to any evidence tending to

show that he, or any of his employees, or agents (whether past or present), has practised unlawful discrimination in, or in connection with, the carrying on of any profession or trade. – SDA]

(3) In this section –
>   *(a) "authorisation or qualification" includes recognition, registration, enrolment, approval and certification;*
>   *(b) "confer" includes renew or extend.*

SEX DISCRIMINATION ACT – s.13
RACE RELATIONS ACT – s.12

British Judo Association v   **[1981] IRLR 484 EAT**
Petty
The prohibition on discrimination by qualifying bodies covers all cases where a qualification in fact facilitates a woman's employment, whether or not it is intended by the authority or body which confers the authorisation or qualification so to do.

British Judo Association v   **[1981] IRLR 484 EAT**
Petty
The prohibition on discrimination by qualifying bodies renders unlawful all discriminatory conditions attached to qualifications affecting employment. There is no requirement that the discriminatory term (as opposed to the qualification itself) has any impact on the employment prospects of the person discriminated against or that they must show proof of actual damage. A complainant must show simply that the qualification facilitates his or her job prospects and that attached to such qualification is a term which is discriminatory against the sex or race of the complainant.

Tattari v   **[1997] IRLR 586 CA**
Private Patients Plan
The prohibition on discrimination by qualifying bodies applies to a body which has the power or authority to confer on a person a professional qualification or other approval needed to enable them to practice a profession, exercise a calling or take part in some other activity. It does not refer to a body like PPP which is not authorised to or empowered to confer such qualification or permission but which stipulates that a particular qualification is required for the purpose of its commercial agreements. Therefore, the applicant could not bring a complaint that PPP's failure to include her on their list of specialists because it did not recognise her EC certificate of higher specialist training was racially discriminatory.

Treisman v   **[2002] IRLR 489 CA**
Ali
In selecting a candidate for local government elections or allowing a person to be nominated to the pool from which prospective candidates are to be selected, the Labour Party is not a "body which can confer an authorisation or qualification which is needed for, or facilitates, engagement in a particular profession" within the meaning of s.12 of the Race Relations Act. Even if being a Labour councillor is being engaged in a profession for the purposes of s.12, the Labour Party in selecting a candidate or accepting a nomination for such candidacy is not conferring an "authorisation or qualification" such as is within the contemplation of the section. There is no conferment of approval by the Labour Party when a member who has been nominated as a local government candidate has his name go forward to the pool available for selection. It would be wholly artificial to treat s.12 as applying to such a case.

Patterson v   **[2004] IRLR 153 CA**
Legal Services Commission
When the Legal Services Commission grants a franchise to a solicitor, it is conferring an authorisation on the franchisee to perform publicly funded legal services for its clients. The franchise "facilitates" engagement in the profession of solicitor, in that it makes it easier or less difficult to carry on the profession.

Appeals

(1) A complaint by any person ("the complainant") that another person ("the respondent") –
>   *(a) has committed an act of discrimination against the complainant which is unlawful by virtue of Part II, or*
>   *(b) is by virtue of s.41 or 42 [32 or 33 – RRA] to be treated as having committed such an act of discrimination against the complainant,*
may be presented to an employment tribunal.

(2) Subsection (1) does not apply to a complaint under s.13(1) [12(1) – RRA] of an act in respect of which an appeal, or proceedings in the nature of an appeal, may be brought under any enactment [or to a complaint to which s.75(8) applies – RRA].

SEX DISCRIMINATION ACT – s.63
RACE RELATIONS ACT – s.54

Khan v   **[1994] IRLR 646 CA**
General Medical Council
The essence of what is meant by "proceedings in the nature of an appeal" is that the decision can be reversed by a differently constituted set of persons. The possibility of common membership of the original and appellate tribunals does not make the process any the less an appeal, though it might be a breach of natural justice if it were to happen.

Khan v   **[1994] IRLR 646 CA**
General Medical Council
The right to apply to a Review Board for a review of the General Medical Council's decision, conferred by s.29 of the Medical Act 1983, is a proceeding "in the nature of an appeal" within the meaning of s.54(2) of the Race Relations

Act, since the proceedings had the necessary characteristics of a two-stage decision to be in the nature of an appeal.

between men and women as regards the wearing of personal jewellery or other items of personal adornment.

Discrimination in provision of goods, facilities or services

(1) It is unlawful for any person concerned with the provision (for payment or not) of goods, facilities or services to the public or a section of the public to discriminate against a person [woman – SDA] who seeks to obtain or use those goods, facilities or services –

(a) by refusing or deliberately omitting to provide him [her – SDA] with any of them; or

(b) by refusing or deliberately omitting to provide him [her – SDA] with goods, facilities or services of the like quality, in the like manner and on the like terms as are normal in the first-mentioned person's [his – SDA] case in relation to other [male – SDA] members of the public or (where the person so seeking [she – SDA] belongs to a section of the public) to other [male – SDA] members of that section.

(2) The following are examples of the facilities and services mentioned in subsection (1) –

(a) access to and use of any place which members of the public [or a section of the public – SDA] are permitted to enter;

(b) accommodation in a hotel, boarding house or other similar establishment;

(c) facilities by way of banking or insurance or for grants, loans, credit or finance;

(d) facilities for education;

(e) facilities for entertainment, recreation or refreshment;

(f) facilities for transport or travel;

(g) the services of any profession or trade, or any local or other public authority.

SEX DISCRIMINATION ACT – s.29
RACE RELATIONS ACT – s.20

McConomy v   **[1992] IRLR 562 NIHC**
Croft Inns Ltd
A public house unlawfully discriminated on grounds of sex by adopting an admission policy under which men were not permitted to wear earrings where there was no objection to women being served while wearing earrings. Such less favourable treatment took the form of refusing to provide a man with refreshment facilities "in the like manner and on the like terms" as were normal in the case of women.

McConomy v   **[1992] IRLR 562 NIHC**
Croft Inns Ltd
In comparing like with like, account has to be taken of certain basic rules of human conduct, such as the ordinary rules of decency accepted in the community, which might permit or require different dress regulations as between men and women. In today's conditions, however, it is not possible to say that the circumstances are different as

Discrimination by public authorities

(1) It is unlawful for a public authority in carrying out any functions of the authority to do any act which constitutes discrimination.

RACE RELATIONS ACT 1976 (as amended) – s.19B

R (on the application of European   **[2003] IRLR 577 CA**
Roma Rights Centre) v
Immigration Officer at Prague Airport
Immigration officers at Prague airport did not treat Roma applicants for leave to enter the UK for non-asylum purposes less favourably on racial grounds than non-Roma by being more sceptical of a Roma applicant's true intentions than those of a non-Roma and therefore questioning Roma for longer and more intensively than non-Roma. The policy was not to refuse Roma as Roma. Rather, it was to refuse those who cannot satisfy the immigration officer that they will not claim asylum on arrival. An objection to the more rigorous questioning of some than others is not reconcilable with the exhortation repeatedly to be found throughout the case law that applications must be investigated individually, each applicant being given the opportunity to establish that he or she can satisfy whatever may be the legitimate requirements of the questioner.

INDIVIDUAL REMEDIES

(1) Where an employment tribunal finds that a complaint presented to it under [s.63 – SDA; s.54 – RRA] is well-founded the tribunal shall make such of the following as it considers just and equitable –

(a) an order declaring the rights of the complainant and the respondent in relation to the act to which the complaint relates;

(b) an order requiring the respondent to pay to the complainant compensation of an amount corresponding to any damages he could have been ordered by a county court or by a sheriff court to pay to the complainant if the complaint had fallen to be dealt with under [s.66 – SDA; s.57 – RRA];

(c) a recommendation that the respondent take within a specified period action appearing to the tribunal to be practicable for the purpose of obviating or reducing the adverse effect on the complainant of any act of discrimination to which the complaint relates.

SEX DISCRIMINATION ACT – s.65
RACE RELATIONS ACT – s.56

(1) A claim by any person ("the claimant") that another person ("the respondent") –

(a) has committed an act of discrimination against the claimant which is unlawful by virtue of Part III, or

(b) is by virtue of [s.41 – SDA; s.32 – RRA] or [s.42 – SDA; s.33 – RRA] to be treated as having committed such an act of discrimination against the claimant,

may be made the subject of civil proceedings in like manner as any other claim in tort or (in Scotland) in reparation for breach of statutory duty.

(3) As respects an unlawful act of discrimination falling within s.1(1)(b), no award of damages shall be made if the respondent proves that the requirement or condition in question was not applied with the intention of treating the claimant unfavourably on [racial grounds – RRA] [the ground of his sex – SDA].

(4) For the avoidance of doubt it is hereby declared that damages in respect of an unlawful act of discrimination may include compensation for injury to feelings whether or not they include compensation under any other head.

SEX DISCRIMINATION ACT – s.66
RACE RELATIONS ACT – s.57

(1A) In applying s.66 for the purposes of subsection (1)(b), no account shall be taken of subsection (3) of that section.

(1B) As respects an unlawful act of discrimination falling within s.1(1)(b) or s.3(1)(b), if the respondent proves that the requirement or condition in question was not applied with the intention of treating the complainant unfavourably on the ground of his sex or marital status as the case may be, an order may be made under subsection (1)(b) only if the employment tribunal –

(a) makes such an order under subsection (1)(a) and such recommendation under subsection (1)[c] (if any) as it would have made if it had no power to make an order under subsection (1)(b);

and

(b)(where it makes an order under subsection (1)(a) or a recommendation under subsection (1)[c] or both) considers that it is just and equitable to make an order under subsection (1)(b) as well.

SEX DISCRIMINATION ACT – s.65

Compensation

General principles

Ministry of Defence v   **[1998] IRLR 23 CA**
Wheeler
The general principle in assessing compensation is that, as far as possible, complainants should be placed in the same position as they would have been in but for the unlawful act.

Coleman v   **[1981] IRLR 398 CA**
Skyrail Oceanic Ltd
Compensation is to be awarded for foreseeable damage arising directly from an unlawful act of discrimination. It follows that an applicant can claim for any pecuniary loss properly attributable to an unlawful act of discrimination.

Sheriff v   **[1999] IRLR 481 CA**
Klyne Tugs (Lowestoft) Ltd
An employment tribunal has jurisdiction to award compensation by way of damages for personal injury, including both physical and psychiatric injury, caused by the statutory tort of unlawful discrimination.

Essa v   **[2004] IRLR 313 CA**
Laing Ltd
A claimant who is the victim of direct discrimination in the form of racial abuse is entitled to be compensated for the loss which arises naturally and directly from the wrong. It is not necessary for the claimant to show that the particular type of loss was reasonably foreseeable.

Ministry of Defence v   **[1998] IRLR 23 CA**
Wheeler
The correct approach in calculating compensation to women dismissed on grounds of pregnancy is to take the sum they would have earned had they remained in the job, deduct from that the amount which they had, or should have, earned elsewhere, and then discount the net loss by a percentage to reflect the chance that they might have left the job in any event.

Abbey National plc v   **[1999] IRLR 222 EAT**
Formoso
The correct approach in awarding compensation for a discriminatory dismissal is to ask what were the chances, in percentage terms, that the employer would have dismissed the applicant had she not been pregnant and had a fair procedure been followed, rather than what a "reasonable

employer" would have done. The "reasonable employer" approach is appropriate when considering the fairness of a dismissal, but not when assessing the loss flowing from a discriminatory dismissal.

Ministry of Defence v   **[1994] IRLR 509 EAT**
Cannock
There is no separate head of damage for loss of career prospects. The financial consequences of being deprived of the opportunity of promotion should be compensated for under damages for loss of employment. The award for injury to feelings should include a sum for the injury to feelings sustained as a result of the loss of chosen career.

Alexander v   **[1988] IRLR 190 CA**
The Home Office
The mere fact that a defendant is guilty of discrimination is not in itself a factor affecting damages. Although in the substantial majority of discrimination cases the unlawful conduct will cause personal hurt, in the sense of injury to feelings, or of preventing the complainant from obtaining a better, more remunerative job, the court must feel it right to draw an inference that the discrimination will cause a plaintiff "hurt" of a particular kind.

Coleman v   **[1981] IRLR 398 CA**
Skyrail Oceanic Ltd
An appellate court is entitled to interfere with the assessment of compensation by an employment tribunal where the tribunal has acted on a wrong principle of law or has misapprehended the facts, or for other reasons has made a wholly erroneous estimate of the damage suffered.

Orthet Ltd v   **[2004] IRLR 857 EAT**
Vince-Cain
In a case where the period of loss is likely to be more than two years, the correct method of calculating future pension loss is the "substantial loss approach" as suggested in the guidelines to employment tribunal chairmen on *Compensation for Loss of Pension Rights*.

Harvey v   **[1995] IRLR 416 EAT**
Institute of the Motor Industry (No.2)
The removal of statutory limit on compensation for sex discrimination took effect in relation to all awards made from the date of commencement of the Sex Discrimination and Equal Pay (Remedies) Regulations 1993, 22 November 1993.

London Borough of Lambeth v   **[1999] IRLR 240 CA**
D'Souza
The Race Relations (Remedies) Act 1994, which removed the upper limit on compensation, only applied to cases where compensation was awarded for race discrimination after that Act came into force on 3 July 1994.

Aggravated damages

Alexander v   **[1988] IRLR 190 CA**
The Home Office
Compensatory damages may, and in some instances should, include an element of aggravated damages where, for example, the defendant may have behaved in a high-handed, malicious, insulting or oppressive manner in committing the act of discrimination.

(1) Armitage, (2) Marsden and   **[1997] IRLR 162 EAT**
(3) HM Prison Service v
Johnson
As a matter of principle, aggravated damages should be available to applicants for the statutory torts of race and sex discrimination. The torts may be sufficiently intentional as to enable the applicant to rely upon malice or the respondent's manner of committing the tort or other conduct as aggravating the injury to feelings.

Scott v   **[2004] IRLR 713 CA**
Commissioners of Inland Revenue
Aggravated damages are intended to deal with cases where the injury was inflicted by conduct which was high-handed, malicious, insulting or oppressive. Aggravated damages, therefore, should not be aggregated with and treated as part of the damages for injury to feelings.

Ministry of Defence v   **[1995] IRLR 539 EAT**
Meredith
In order for aggravated damages to be granted, there must be a causal connection between the exceptional or contumelious conduct or motive in committing the wrong and the intangible loss, such as injury to feelings, suffered by the plaintiff. Thus, in order for the plaintiff's feelings to have suffered an aggravated hurt, he or she must have had some knowledge or suspicion of the conduct or motive which caused that increase.

Zaiwalla & Co v   **[2002] IRLR 697 EAT**
Walia
There is no reason in law why aggravated damages should not be awarded by reference to conduct in the defence of proceedings in a discrimination case.

City of Bradford Metropolitan   **[1989] IRLR 442 EAT**
Council v
Arora
In considering an award of aggravated damages for injury to feelings, an employment tribunal is entitled to take into account unsatisfactory answers to a questionnaire issued under s.74 of the Sex Discrimination Act or s.65 of the Race Relations Act. The answers to a questionnaire are part of the conduct of the proceedings and may in some cases merit consideration.

HM Prison Service v   **[2001] IRLR 425 EAT**
Salmon

An employment tribunal did not err in awarding aggravated damages to reflect its view that the manner in which the employers dealt with an incident in which offensive and sexually degrading comments were written about the applicant by one of her colleagues suggested that the employers perceived the entire incident as trivial and that the way the incident was dealt with communicated that perception to the applicant. The tribunal was entitled to find that conduct aggravated the injury to the applicant's feelings.

British Telecommuncations plc v   **[2004] IRLR 327 CA**
Reid

A complainant having to undergo a totally unjustified disciplinary investigation into his own conduct could be an indignity which exacerbates his wounded feelings arising from the act of discrimination itself.

British Telecommuncations plc v   **[2004] IRLR 327 CA**
Reid

Although there is no principle that an employer cannot promote an employee whilst disciplinary proceedings are hanging over his or her head, on the particular facts and circumstances of a particular case it can be a material factor demonstrating the high-handedness of the employer.

Exemplary damages

Deane v   **[1993] IRLR 209 EAT**
London Borough of Ealing

Exemplary damages cannot be awarded under the Race Relations Act 1976. In accordance with the binding decision of the Court of Appeal in *Gibbons v South West Water Services*, exemplary damages can only be awarded in respect of torts for which exemplary damages had been awarded prior to the decision of the House of Lords in *Rookes v Barnard* in 1964.

Ministry of Defence v   **[1995] IRLR 539 EAT**
Meredith

Exemplary damages are not available for breach of the Equal Treatment Directive.

Psychiatric injury

HM Prison Service v   **[2001] IRLR 425 EAT**
Salmon

The assessment of damages for psychiatric injury caused by an act of unlawful discrimination is a matter of fact to be determined by the employment tribunal, which can only be overturned on appeal if the tribunal has made an error of principle or arrived at a figure which is so high or so low as to be perverse.

HM Prison Service v   **[2001] IRLR 425 EAT**
Salmon

In principle, injury to feelings and psychiatric injury are distinct. In practice, however, the two types of injury are not always easily separable, giving rise to a risk of double recovery. In a given case, it may be impossible to say with any certainty or precision when the distress and humiliation that may be inflicted on the victim of discrimination becomes a recognised psychiatric illness such as depression. Injury to feelings can cover a very wide range. At the lower end are comparatively minor instances of upset or distress, typically caused by one-off acts or episodes of discrimination. At the upper end, the victim is likely to be suffering from serious and prolonged feelings of humiliation, low self-esteem and depression; and in these cases it may be fairly arbitrary whether the symptoms are put before the tribunal as a psychiatric illness, supported by a formal diagnosis and/or expert evidence.

Injury to feelings

(1) Armitage, (2) Marsden and   **[1997] IRLR 162 EAT**
(3) HM Prison Service v
Johnson

The relevant principles for assessing awards for injury to feelings for unlawful discrimination can be summarised as follows:

(i) Awards for injury to feelings are compensatory. They should be just to both parties. They should compensate fully without punishing the tortfeasor. Feelings of indignation at the tortfeasor's conduct should not be allowed to inflate the award.

(ii) Awards should not be too low as that would diminish respect for the policy of the anti-discrimination legislation. Society has condemned discrimination and awards must ensure that it is seen to be wrong. On the other hand, awards should be restrained, as excessive awards could be seen as the way to untaxed riches.

(iii) Awards should bear some broad general similarity to the range of awards in personal injury cases. This should be done by reference to the whole range of such awards, rather than to any particular type of award.

(iv) In exercising their discretion in assessing a sum, tribunals should remind themselves of the value in everyday life of the sum they have in mind. This may be done by reference to purchasing power or by reference to earnings.

(v) Tribunals should bear in mind the need for public respect for the level of awards made.

Vento v   **[2003] IRLR 102 CA**
Chief Constable of West Yorkshire Police (No.2)

Subjective feelings of upset, frustration, worry, anxiety, mental distress, fear, grief, anguish, humiliation, stress, depression etc and the degree of their intensity are incapable of objective proof or of measurement in monetary terms. Translating hurt feelings into hard currency is bound to be an artificial exercise. Nevertheless, employment tribunals have to do the best they can on the available material to make a sensible assessment. In carrying out this exercise, they should have in mind the summary of the general principles on compensation for non-pecuniary loss by Smith J in *Armitage v Johnson.*

Ministry of Defence v   **[1994] IRLR 509 EAT**
Cannock
An award for injury to feelings is not automatically to be made whenever unlawful discrimination is proved or admitted. Injury must be proved, though it will often be easy to prove in the sense that no tribunal will take much persuasion that the anger, distress and affront caused by the act of discrimination has injured the applicant's feelings.

Murray v   **[1992] IRLR 257 EAT**
Powertech (Scotland) Ltd
A claim for hurt feelings is so fundamental to a sex discrimination case that it is almost inevitable. All that is required is that the matter of hurt feelings be simply stated. It is then for the employment tribunal to consider what degree of hurt feelings had been sustained and to make an award accordingly.

Coleman v   **[1981] IRLR 398 CA**
Skyrail Oceanic Ltd
Injury to feelings unrelated to sex discrimination is not properly attributable to an unlawful act of sex discrimination and therefore must be disregarded in the assessment of compensation.

Alexander v   **[1988] IRLR 190 CA**
The Home Office
The injury to feelings for which compensation is sought must have resulted from knowledge of the discrimination. If the plaintiff knows of the discrimination and that he has thereby been held up to "hatred, ridicule or contempt", then the injury to his feelings will be an important element in the damages.

ICTS (UK) Ltd v   **[2000] IRLR 643 EAT**
Tchoula
A global approach to assessing compensation for injury to feelings is preferable to making separate awards in respect of each of three acts of discrimination, since it would be unrealistic to seek to ascribe to each act of discrimination a proportion of the overall injury to feelings suffered.

O'Donoghue v   **[2001] IRLR 615 CA**
Redcar & Cleveland Borough Council
That an applicant would notionally have been fairly dismissed within a relatively short period is properly to be taken into account as a cut-off point in respect of any claim based on future loss of earnings in respect of a discriminatory dismissal but is not grounds for discounting an award for injury to feelings.

Alexander v   **[1988] IRLR 190 CA**
The Home Office
Damages for injury to feelings, humiliation and insult in respect of unlawful discrimination should not be minimal since this would tend to trivialise or diminish respect for the public policy to which the statute gives effect. On the other hand, awards should be restrained. To award sums which are generally felt to be excessive would do almost as much harm to the policy, and the results which it seeks to achieve, as nominal awards.

Vento v   **[2003] IRLR 102 CA**
Chief Constable of West Yorkshire Police (No.2)
An award of £74,000 for non-pecuniary loss, made up of £50,000 for injury to feelings, £15,000 aggravated damages and £9,000 for psychiatric injury, was so excessive as to constitute an error of law in that it was seriously out of line with the majority of awards made and approved on appeal in reported EAT cases, with the guidelines compiled for the Judicial Studies Board and with cases reported in the personal injury field where general damages have been awarded for pain, suffering, disability and loss of amenity. The fair, reasonable and just award for non-pecuniary loss was a total of £32,000, made up as to £18,000 for injury to feelings, £5,000 aggravated damages and £9,000 for psychiatric damage.

Vento v   **[2003] IRLR 102 CA**
Chief Constable of West Yorkshire Police (No.2)
Observed: Three broad bands of compensation for injury to feelings, as distinct from compensation for psychiatric or similar personal injury, can be identified:
1. The top band should normally be between £15,000 and £25,000. Sums in this range should be awarded in the most serious cases, such as where there has been a lengthy campaign of discriminatory harassment on the ground of sex or race. Only in the most exceptional case should an award of compensation for injury to feelings exceed £25,000.
2. The middle band of between £5,000 and £15,000 should be used for serious cases, which do not merit an award in the highest band.
3. Awards of between £500 and £5,000 are appropriate for less serious cases, such as where the act of discrimination is an isolated or one off occurrence. In general, awards of less than £500 are to be avoided altogether, as they risk being regarded as so low as not to be a proper recognition of injury to feelings.

Orlando v   **[1996] IRLR 262 EAT**
Didcot Power Station
  Sports & Social Club
In assessing injury to feelings, the willingness of the employer to admit that it has acted in breach of the discrimination legislation may help to reduce the hurt which is felt, in that it can spare the complainant the indignity and further hurt of having to rehearse the nature of her treatment.

Snowball v   **[1987] IRLR 397 EAT**
Gardner Merchant Ltd
Compensation for sexual harassment must relate to the degree of detriment suffered and, in that context, there has to be an assessment of the injury to the woman's feelings, which must be looked at both objectively, with reference to what any ordinary reasonable female employee would feel, and subjectively, with reference to her as an individual.

Wileman v   **[1988] IRLR 144 EAT**
Minilec Engineering Ltd
In awarding compensation for injury to feelings resulting from sexual harassment, an employment tribunal is entitled to take into account the fact that on occasions the complainant wore clothes at work which were scanty and provocative as an element in deciding whether the harassment to which she was subjected constituted a detriment.

Wileman v   **[1988] IRLR 144 EAT**
Minilec Engineering Ltd
In determining the detriment caused by sexual harassment for the purpose of awarding compensation for injury to feelings, employment tribunals have to be very careful to ensure that the situation is not one in which no complaint has been made and the matter was borne with increasing irritation and distress because the applicant was frightened of her boss or frightened of losing her job.

Orlando v   **[1996] IRLR 262 EAT**
Didcot Power Station
  Sports & Social Club
The nature of lost employment, including the fact that the position was part time, is relevant in making an award for injury to feelings. A person who unlawfully loses an evening job may be expected to be less hurt and humiliated by the discriminatory treatment than a person who loses their entire professional career.

Ministry of Defence v   **[1994] IRLR 509 EAT**
Cannock
There is sufficient overlap between compensation for injury to feelings and loss of congenial employment due to discrimination for employment tribunals to confine themselves to making an award for injury to feelings, where such has been proved, which will include compensation for the hurt caused by the loss of a chosen career which gave job satisfaction.

HM Prison Service v   **[2001] IRLR 425 EAT**
Salmon
There is nothing wrong in principle in a tribunal treating "stress and depression" as part of the injury to be compensated for under the heading "injury to feelings", provided it clearly identifies the main elements in the victim's condition which the award is intended to reflect (including any psychiatric injury) and the findings in relation to them. But where separate awards are made, tribunals must be alert to

the risk that what is essentially the same suffering may be being compensated twice under different heads.

Orthet Ltd v   **[2004] IRLR 857 EAT**
Vince-Cain
An award of compensation for injury to feelings should be made without regard to the tax implications of the award, and therefore should not be grossed-up.

Unintentional indirect discrimination

Orphanos v   **[1985] IRLR 349 HL**
Queen Mary College
Whereas s.1(1)(b)(ii) of the Race Relations Act is looking at the objective possibility of justifying the discrimination without reference to racial grounds, s.57(3) is looking at the subjective intention of the discriminator. Therefore, where indirect discrimination is unintentional and not intended to discriminate on any racial ground, compensation will not be awarded.

London Underground Ltd v   **[1995] IRLR 355 EAT**
Edwards
The relevant question under s.66(3) of the Sex Discrimination Act relates to the intention with which the requirement or condition was applied, rather than to the more generalised intention relating to the introduction of the requirement or condition. It is open to a tribunal to infer that a requirement was applied with the knowledge of its unfavourable consequences for a complainant as a woman, and an intention to produce those consequences thus can be inferred.

J H Walker Ltd v   **[1996] IRLR 11 EAT**
Hussain
"Intention", for the purpose of s.57(3), is concerned with the state of mind of the respondent in relation to the consequences of his acts. He intended those consequences to follow from his acts if he knew when he did them that those consequences would follow and if he wanted those consequences to follow. Accordingly, a requirement or condition resulting in indirect discrimination is applied with the "intention of treating the claimant unfavourably on racial grounds" if, at the time the relevant act is done, the person (a) wants to bring about the state of affairs which constitutes the prohibited result of unfavourable treatment on racial grounds; and (b) knows that that prohibited result will follow from his acts. Section 57(3) is not concerned with the motivation of a respondent, ie the reason why he did what he did.

J H Walker Ltd v   **[1996] IRLR 11 EAT**
Hussain
A tribunal may infer that a person wanted to produce cer-

tain consequences from the fact that he acted knowing what those consequences would be. For example, if an employer continued to apply an indirectly discriminatory requirement or condition after it had been declared unlawful, it would not be difficult for a tribunal to infer that he intended to treat an employee unfavourably on racial grounds, even though his reason or motive for persisting in the action was business efficiency.

Mitigation

Ministry of Defence v   **[1996] IRLR 139 EAT**
Hunt

The burden of proving a failure to mitigate loss is on the person who asserts it. If a tribunal is to be invited to consider whether or not there has been a failure to mitigate or, if there has been such a failure, the quantification of any reduction in the value of the claim, it must be provided with the evidence with which to perform its task, either arising from cross-examination or from evidence called. It is not for the employment tribunal, as an industrial jury, to fill an evidential vacuum itself.

Ministry of Defence v   **[1996] IRLR 139 EAT**
Hunt

In a case where an employment tribunal has assessed a percentage chance of completing a certain number of years service and has also found some failure to mitigate on the part of the applicant, in the final calculation of compensation the tribunal should deduct the failure to mitigate figure before, rather than after, applying the percentage chance figure.

Interest

4. (1) In this regulation and regulations 5 and 6, "day of calculation" means the day on which the amount of interest is calculated by the tribunal;

(2) In reg. 6, "mid-point date" means the day which falls halfway through the period mentioned in para. 3 or, where the number of days in that period is even, the first day of the second half of the period.

(3) The period referred to in para. 2 is the period beginning on the date, in the case of an award under the 1970 Act, of the contravention and, in other cases, of the act of discrimination complained of, and ending on the day of calculation.

5. No interest shall be included in respect of any sum awarded for a loss or matter which will occur after the day of calculation or in respect of any time before the contravention or act of discrimination complained of.

6. (1) Subject to the following paragraphs of this regulation –

(a) in the case of any sum for injury to feelings, interest shall be for the period beginning on the date of the contravention or act of discrimination complained of and ending on the day of calculation;

(b) in the case of all other sums of damages or compensation in the award (other than any sum referred to in reg. 5) and all arrears of remuneration, interest shall be for the period beginning on the mid-point date and ending on the day of calculation.

(2) Where any payment has been made before the day of calculation to the complainant by or on behalf of the respondent in respect of the subject matter of the award, interest in respect of that part of the award covered by the payment shall be calculated as if the references in para. 1, and in the definition of "mid-point date" in reg. 4, to the day of calculation were to the date on which the payment was made.

(3) Where the tribunal considers that in the circumstances, whether relating to the case as a whole or to a particular sum in an award, serious injustice would be caused if interest were to be awarded in respect of paras. 1 or 2, it may –

(a) calculate interest, or as the case may be interest on the particular sum, for such different period, or

(b) calculate interest for such different periods in respect of various sums in the award,

as it considers appropriate in the circumstances, having regard to the provisions of these Regulations.

EMPLOYMENT TRIBUNALS (INTEREST ON AWARDS IN DISCRIMINATION CASES) REGULATIONS 1996

Ministry of Defence v   **[1994] IRLR 509 EAT**
Cannock

An employment tribunal is entitled to exercise its powers to depart from the normal procedure of awarding interest from the mid-point date between the act of discrimination and the date of the employment tribunal hearing and to award interest over a different and longer period by reason of the fact that the whole of the loss was incurred many years ago. The statutory provisions expressly cater for the exceptional case and what is exceptional is a matter for the employment tribunal.

Derby Specialist Fabrication Ltd v   **[2001] IRLR 69 EAT**
Burton

It is clear that Parliament intended that, unlike interest on other awards where the midpoint was to be taken, interest on an award for injury to feelings should normally be from the date of the discriminatory act. That must be taken to allow for the fact that injury to feelings is not a one-off event but something which will often persist over a period of time.

Ministry of Defence v   **[1994] IRLR 509 EAT**
Cannock

An employment tribunal is not entitled to award interest in respect of pension losses. [Regulation 5 of the Interest on Awards in Discrimination Cases Regulations] precludes interest "in respect of a sum awarded for a loss or matter which will occur after the day of calculation".

Action recommendation

Chief Constable of West   **[2002] IRLR 177 EAT**
   Yorkshire Police v
Vento (No.2)
The statutory provisions on action recommendations give the employment tribunal an extremely wide discretion.

Ministry of Defence v   **[1978] IRLR 402 EAT**
Jeremiah
Employment tribunals have no power under s.65 of the Sex Discrimination Act to order an employer to discontinue a discriminatory practice. The tribunal's powers are limited to making a recommendation, an order declaratory of the rights of the complainant, and an order requiring the respondent to pay compensation.

Irvine v   **[1981] IRLR 281 CA**
Prestcold Ltd
An employment tribunal's power to make a recommendation for the taking of action under s.65(1)(c) of the Sex Discrimination Act does not include the power to make a recommendation as to payment of remuneration. Monetary compensation for loss of remuneration is fully provided for by s.65(1)(b).

Noone v   **[1988] IRLR 530 CA**
North West Thames Regional Health
   Authority (No.2)
An employment tribunal exceeded its powers under s.56(1)(c) of the Race Relations Act to make a recommendation that an employer take action for the purpose of obviating or reducing the adverse effect on a complainant of any act of discrimination to which a complaint relates by recommending that a hospital authority seek the authority of the Secretary of State to dispense with its statutory obligations governing the appointment of consultants by not advertising its next vacancy for a consultant's post similar to that for which the complainant unsuccessfully applied. Such a recommendation would set at nought the statutory procedure for making consultant appointments set out for the benefit of the NHS, the public and the professions concerned.

British Gas plc v   **[1991] IRLR 101 EAT**
Sharma
An employment tribunal does not have the power to make a recommendation that the employers promote a successful complainant to the next suitable vacancy. The Act does not allow positive discrimination, and to promote a complainant without considering other applicants who might have superior qualifications for the vacancy could amount to direct discrimination against those other applicants on grounds of race.

Chief Constable of West   **[2002] IRLR 177 EAT**
   Yorkshire Police v
Vento (No.2)
An employment tribunal did not err in making a recommen-
dation that the Deputy Chief Constable should interview named police officers and discuss with them relevant parts of the decisions of the employment tribunal and the EAT on liability for sex discrimination.

Other statutory redress

R v   **[1991] IRLR 425 DC**
Army Board of the Defence Council
   ex parte Anderson
The Army Board, in exercising its statutory function of dealing with a complaint of racial discrimination, is obliged to give full effect to the substantive provisions of the Race Relations Act. It is thus necessary for the Board to give specific consideration to the relevant provisions of the Act, to consider whether there had been unlawful discrimination within the terms of the Act, and to give proper consideration to whether compensation or other redress should be granted. Moreover, as the forum of last resort dealing with an individual's fundamental statutory rights, the Army Board must by its procedures achieve a high standard of fairness.

R v   **[1991] IRLR 431 DC**
Department of Health
   ex parte Gandhi
In hearing an appeal under the National Health Service Act against a decision by a Medical Practices Committee not to appoint a doctor to a vacancy, where it is alleged that the decision was on racial grounds, the Secretary of State is not under a duty to pronounce separately on the complaint of racial discrimination, or grant any specific redress in respect of it. However, although the Secretary of State is not required to determine a race discrimination complaint discretely, he is required to consider it in determining the appeal and in doing so must apply the provisions of the Race Relations Act. Moreover, the procedures followed by the Secretary of State in exercising his appellate function must be fair to the appellant.

Formal investigations

(1) Without prejudice to their general power to do anything requisite for the performance of their duties under section [53(1) – SDA; 43(1) – RRA] the Commission may if they think fit, and shall if required by the Secretary of State, conduct a formal investigation for any purpose connected with the carrying out of these duties.

(2) The Commission may, with the approval of the Secretary of State, appoint, on a full-time or part-time basis, one or more individuals as additional Commissioners for the purposes of a formal investigation.

(3) The Commission may nominate one or more Commissioners, with or without one or more additional Commissioners, to conduct a formal investigation on their behalf, and may delegate any of their functions in relation to the investigation to the persons so nominated.

SEX DISCRIMINATION ACT – s.57
RACE RELATIONS ACT – s.48

(1) The Commission shall not embark on a formal investigation unless the requirements of this section have been complied with.

(2) Terms of reference for the investigation shall be drawn up by the Commission or, if the Commission were required by the Secretary of State to conduct the investigation, by the Secretary of State after consulting the Commission.

(3) It shall be the duty of the Commission to give general notice of the holding of the investigation unless the terms of reference confine it to activities of persons named in them, but in such a case the Commission shall in the prescribed manner give those persons notice of the holding of the investigation.

(4) [3A – SDA] Where the terms of reference of the investigation confine it to activities of persons named in them and the Commission in the course of it propose to investigate any act made unlawful by this Act which they believe that a person so named may have done, the Commission shall –

  (a) inform that person of their belief and of their proposal to investigate the act in question; and
  (b) offer him an opportunity of making oral or written representations with regard to it (or both oral and written representations if he thinks fit);
and a person so named who avails himself of an opportunity under this subsection of making oral representations may be represented –
    (i) by counsel or a solicitor, or
    (ii) by some other person of his choice, not being a person to whom the Commission object on the ground that he is unsuitable.

(5) The Commission or, if the Commission were required by the Secretary of State to conduct the investigation, the Secretary of State after consulting the Commission may from time to time revise the terms of reference; and subsections (1), (3) and (4) [3A – SDA] shall apply to the revised investigation and terms of reference as they applied to the original.

SEX DISCRIMINATION ACT – s.58
RACE RELATIONS ACT – s.49

Launching an investigation

London Borough of Hillingdon v   **[1982] IRLR 424 HL**
Commission for Racial Equality
To enable the Commission to embark upon a formal investigation, it is enough that there should be material before the Commission sufficient to raise in the minds of reasonable men, possessed of the experience of covert racial discrimination that has been acquired by the Commission, a suspicion that the person named may have carried out acts of racial discrimination of the kind which it is proposed to investigate. It is not necessary for there to be something which causes the Commission to believe that it is more likely than not that there may have been an act of discrimination. That state of mind, which corresponds with the civil burden of proof, is one which must be reached by the Commission in the course of the full investigation in order to justify the service of a Non-discrimination Notice under s.58.

In re Prestige Group plc   **[1984] IRLR 166 HL**
On a proper construction of s.49(4) and s.50(2)(b) of the Race Relations Act, it is a condition precedent to the exercise by the CRE of its power to conduct a formal investigation into the activities of named persons that the CRE should in fact have already formed a suspicion that the person named may have committed some unlawful act of discrimination and have had at any rate some grounds for so suspecting, albeit that the grounds upon which such suspicion was based might, at that stage, be no more than tenuous because they had not yet been tested. Therefore, it is an error of law for the CRE to embark upon a formal investigation under s.49(1) into the activities of a named employer in the absence of any belief that that employer might have committed some acts of unlawful racial discrimination.

Terms of reference

London Borough of Hillingdon v   **[1982] IRLR 424 HL**
Commission for Racial Equality
In a formal investigation into the activities of named persons, it is a condition precedent that the CRE should have formed the belief, and should so state in the terms of reference, that the named persons may have done or may be doing discriminatory acts, made unlawful by the Act, of a kind specified in the terms of reference. The Commission's belief as stated in the terms of reference defines and limits the scope of the full investigation. Having regard to the wide variety of acts that are made unlawful by the Act, fairness requires that the statement in the terms of reference as to the kind of acts which the Commission believes the persons named may have done or may be doing should not be expressed in any wider language than is justified by the genuine extent of the Commission's belief.

London Borough of Hillingdon v   **[1982] IRLR 424 HL**
Commission for Racial Equality

Where the Commission are of the opinion that from individual acts which raise a suspicion that they may have been influenced by racial discrimination an inference can be drawn that the persons doing those acts were also following a more general policy of racial discrimination, they are entitled to draw up terms of reference wide enough to enable them to ascertain whether such inference is justified.

London Borough of Hillingdon v   **[1982] IRLR 424 HL**
Commission for Racial Equality

It was an error of law for the Commission for Racial Equality to embark upon a general and unlimited form of investigation on the basis of a belief that there may have been a limited category of acts, which would justify an investigation confined to those acts.

Preliminary inquiry

In re Prestige Group plc   **[1982] IRLR 166 HL**

It was an error of law for the Commission for Racial Equality to embark upon a formal investigation into a company under s.49(1) of the Race Relations Act without holding a preliminary inquiry as required by s.49(4). The purpose of the preliminary inquiry provided for by s.49(4) is to give to any employer, against whom the CRE are minded to launch a named-person investigation, notice of what are the unlawful acts which are to form the subject of a formal investigation as to whether or not he has done them, and give to him the opportunity to make representations to the CRE with a view to persuading them either not to embark upon the proposed named-person investigation at all, or before issuing definitive terms of reference, to amend them so as to exclude from the matters proposed to be investigated questions as to whether or not the employer has done particular kinds of unlawful acts which he denies ever committing.

London Borough of Hillingdon v   **[1982] IRLR 424 HL**
Commission for Racial Equality

The requirement at the preliminary inquiry stage to inform the persons named of any act which the Commission propose to investigate applies to every such act and serves to inform such persons that what the Commission propose shall be the kinds of acts to which the full investigation should be limited. The right of a person to be heard in support of his objection to a proposal to embark upon an investigation of his activities cannot be exercised effectively unless that person is informed with reasonable specificity what are the kinds of acts to which the proposed investigation is to be directed and confined. The Commission cannot "throw the book at him". They cannot, without further particularisation of the kinds of acts of which he is suspected, tell him no more than that they believe that he may have done or may be doing *some* acts that are capable of amounting to unlawful discrimination under the Race Relations Act or some very broadly drafted sections of it, if their

real belief is confined to a belief that he may have done or may be doing only acts of one or more particularised kinds that fall within the general definition of unlawful acts contained in some broadly drafted section. However, the expression "act" in s.49(4) is not limited to individual acts rather than kinds of acts. If the Commission discover what they believe to be prima facie evidence of even one or two instances of racial discrimination by a particular person, the circumstances may be such that they may not unreasonably suspect that these are but instances of a more widespread discrimination of a similar kind that has not yet been uncovered.

Non-discrimination Notice

(1) This section applies to –
     (a) an unlawful [act of discrimination or harassment – RRA; discriminatory act – SDA]; and
     (b) an act contravening [a contravention of s.37 – SDA] s.28 [– RRA]; and
     (c) an act contravening [a contravention of s.38, 39 or 40 – SDA] s.29, 30 or 31 [– RRA];
     [(d) an act in breach of a term modified or included by virtue of an equality clause – SDA]
and so applies whether or not proceedings have been brought in respect of the act.

(2) If in the course of a formal investigation the Commission become satisfied that a person is committing, or has committed, any such acts, the Commission may in the prescribed manner serve on him a notice in the prescribed form ("a non-discrimination notice") requiring him –
     (a) not to commit any such acts; and
     (b) where compliance with paragraph (a) involves changes in any of his practices or other arrangements –
         (i) to inform the Commission that he has effected those changes and what those changes are, and
         (ii) to take such steps as may be reasonably required by the notice for the purpose of affording that information to other persons concerned.

(3) A non-discrimination notice may also require the person on whom it is served to furnish the Commission with such other information as may be reasonably required by the notice in order to verify that the notice has been complied with.

(4) The notice may specify the time at which, and the manner and form in which, any information is to be furnished to the Commission, but the time at which any information is to be furnished in compliance with the notice shall not be later than five years after the notice has become final.

(5) The Commission shall not serve a non-discrimination notice in respect off any person unless they have first –
     (a) given him notice that they are minded to issue a non-discrimination notice in his case, specifying the grounds on which they contemplate doing so; and
     (b) offered him an opportunity of making oral or written representations in the matter (or both oral and written representations if he thinks fit) within a period of not less than 28 days specified in the notice; and
     (c) taken account of any representations so made by him.

                        SEX DISCRIMINATION ACT – s.67
                        RACE RELATIONS ACT – s.58

R v [1980] IRLR 279 HC
Commission for Racial Equality
  ex parte Cottrell & Rothon

The CRE had not failed to act in accordance with the rules of natural justice at a hearing during which representations were made in respect of its decision to issue a Non-discrimination Notice against the applicant firm by not permitting the applicants to cross-examine witnesses upon whose evidence the Commission relied in reaching its decision. Compliance with s.58(5) of the Race Relations Act does not require in the name of fairness the formalities of a right to be able to cross-examine witnesses whom the Commission had seen and from whom statements had been taken.

R v [1984] IRLR 230 HC
Commission for Racial Equality
  ex parte Westminster City Council

Since an appeal against a Non-discrimination Notice can be made to an employment tribunal, courts will not ordinarily intervene by way of judicial review of the Notice until the employment tribunal has had an opportunity to adjudicate on the matter.

Appeal against
Non-discrimination Notice

---

(1) Not later than six weeks after a non-discrimination notice is served on any person he may appeal against any requirement of the notice –

    (a) to an employment tribunal, so far as the requirement relates to acts which are within the jurisdiction of the tribunal;

    (b) to a [designated – RRA] county court or a sheriff court, so far as the requirement relates to acts which are within the jurisdiction of the court and are not within the jurisdiction of an employment tribunal.

(2) Where the tribunal or court considers a requirement in respect of which an appeal is brought under subsection (1) to be unreasonable because it is based on an incorrect finding of fact or for any other reason, the tribunal or court shall quash the requirement.

            RACE RELATIONS ACT – s.59

Commission for Racial Equality v [1982] IRLR 252 CA
Amari Plastics Ltd

On an appeal under s.59 of the Race Relations Act against the requirements contained in a Non-discrimination Notice, all issues of fact on the basis of which the requirements were made are open for consideration, including findings of fact as to whether in the past the employers have been guilty of the unlawful conduct which has led the CRE to make the requirements for the future. The Commission's argument that an appeal against the requirements of a Non-discrimination Notice is limited to an appeal as to the reasonableness of the requirements as they relate to implementation of the Notice in the future could not be accepted. A requirement in a Non-discrimination Notice may only contain a requirement not to commit an unlawful act if the Commission has made a finding of fact that an act of that kind has been committed in the past. Section 59(2) specifically provides that the tribunal is to quash the requirement in the

Notice if it considers it to be unreasonable "because it is based on an incorrect finding of fact". It is unreasonable to require someone to stop doing something that he has never done. It follows that it is open to an appellant to challenge the Commission's findings of fact relating to past unlawful discrimination, because it was upon those findings of fact that the Commission must have based the requirement set out in the Notice.

Commission for Racial Equality v [1982] IRLR 252 CA
Amari Plastics Ltd

Where there is an appeal against a Non-discrimination Notice, the Commission should state the facts on which they relied as the basis of their requirements and then the appellants, in answer, should say which of those findings of fact they challenge.

Judicial review

R v [1994] IRLR 176 HL
Secretary of State for Employment
  ex parte Equal Opportunities Commission

Judicial review is available in the Divisional Court for the purpose of securing a declaration that UK primary legislation is incompatible with European Community law. The Court has power to make a declaratory judgment in judicial review proceedings brought by a plaintiff who has locus standi, whether or not the Court can also make a prerogative order.

R v [1994] IRLR 176 HL
Secretary of State for Employment
  ex parte Equal Opportunities Commission

The EOC had legal standing to bring judicial review proceedings against the Secretary of State in respect of the discriminatory hours per week qualifying thresholds for redundancy pay and unfair dismissal compensation in the Employment Protection (Consolidation) Act, since it had sufficient interest in the matter to which the complaint related, whether the relevant provisions of the 1978 Act were compatible with European Community law regarding equal pay and equal treatment.

R v [1997] IRLR 315 HL
Secretary of State for Employment
  ex parte Seymour-Smith

A person claiming to be entitled as a matter of private law to compensation from their employer should ordinarily bring proceedings in the employment tribunal, even if they will raise an issue of incompatibility between domestic and Community law, rather than by way of judicial review.

R v [1994] IRLR 176 HL
Secretary of State for Employment
  ex parte Equal Opportunities Commission

Since Article 141 prevails over the discriminatory provisions of the Employment Protection (Consolidation) Act, an employment tribunal was the appropriate forum for an employee's claim against her employers for a redundancy payment directly under Article 141.

SCOPE OF EC LAW

Each Member State shall during the first stage ensure and subsequently maintain the application of the principle that men and women should receive equal pay for equal work.

For the purpose of this Article, "pay" means the ordinary basic or minimum wage or salary and any other consideration, whether in cash or in kind, which the worker receives, directly or indirectly, in respect of his employment from his employer.

Equal pay without discrimination based on sex means:

(a) that pay for the same work at piece rates shall be calculated on the basis of the same unit of measurement;

(b) that pay for work at time rates shall be the same for the same job.

EC TREATY – Article 141

The principle of equal pay for men and women outlined in Article 141 of the Treaty, hereinafter called "principle of equal pay", means, for the same work or for work to which equal value is attributed, the elimination of all discrimination on grounds of sex with regard to all aspects and conditions of remuneration.

In particular, where a job classification system is used for determining pay, it must be based on the same criteria for both men and women and so drawn up as to exclude any discrimination on grounds of sex.

EQUAL PAY DIRECTIVE – Article 1

Member States shall introduce into their national legal systems such measures as are necessary to enable all employees who consider themselves wronged by failure to apply the principle of equal pay to pursue their claims by judicial process after possible recourse to other competent authorities.

EQUAL PAY DIRECTIVE – Article 2

Member States shall, in accordance with their national circumstances and legal systems, take the measures necessary to ensure that the principle of equal pay is applied. They shall see that effective means are available to take care that this principle is observed.

EQUAL PAY DIRECTIVE – Article 6

Remedies under EC law

Worringham v   **[1981] IRLR 178 ECJ**
Lloyds Bank Ltd
Article 141 applies directly in Member States, so as to confer enforceable Community rights upon individuals, to all forms of discrimination which may be identified solely with the aid of the criteria of equal work and equal pay referred to by that Article, without national or Community measures being required to define them with greater precision in order to permit of their application. In such a situation the court is in a position to establish all the facts enabling it to decide whether a woman receives less pay than a man engaged in the same work, or work of equal value.

Allonby v   **[2004] IRLR 224 ECJ**
Accrington & Rossendale College
The term "worker" used in Article 141 has a Community meaning and cannot be defined by reference to the legislation of Member States. A "worker" for the purposes of Article 141 is a person who, for a certain period of time, performs services for and under the direction of another person for which they receive remuneration. The term "worker" does not include independent providers of services who are not in a relationship of subordination with the person who receives the services. However, provided that a person is a "worker" within the meaning of Article 141, the nature of their legal relationship with the other party to the employment relationship is of no consequence in regard to the application of that Article.

Gerster v   **[1997] IRLR 699 ECJ**
Freistaat Bayern
Article 141 applies to employment relationships arising in the public service.

Jenkins v   **[1981] IRLR 228 ECJ**
Kingsgate (Clothing Productions) Ltd
Article 1 of the EC Equal Pay Directive, which is principally designed to facilitate the practical application of the principle of equal pay outlined in Article 141 of the EC Treaty, in no way alters the content or the scope of that principle as defined in the Treaty.

Worringham v   **[1981] IRLR 178 ECJ**
Lloyds Bank Ltd
National courts have a duty to ensure the protection of the rights which Article 141 vests in individuals.

Barber v   **[1996] IRLR 209 CA**
Staffordshire County Council
Article 141 can be relied upon by an applicant to disapply barriers to a claim which are incompatible with Community law.

Perceval-Price v   **[2000] IRLR 380 NICA**
Department of Economic Development
In applying the statutory provisions on equal pay and sex discrimination, the phrase "other than service of a person holding a statutory office" should be disregarded as inconsistent with the requirements of Article 141 and the Equal Pay and Equal Treatment Directives, and the legislation read as if that exception were deleted.

Smith v   **[1994] IRLR 602 ECJ**
Avdel Systems Ltd
Application of the principle of equal treatment between men and women in relation to pay by employers must be immediate and full. Achievement of equality cannot be made progressive on a basis that still maintains discrimination, even if only temporarily.

Pickstone v   **[1988] IRLR 357 HL**
Freemans plc
The Equal Pay (Amendment) Regulations 1983 were enacted for the express purpose of giving full effect to the UK's obligations under Article 141 of the EC Treaty and the EC Equal

Pay Directive. In order to give effect to the purpose for which the Regulations were enacted, s.1(2)(c) should be construed in a way which gives effect to the declared intention of the UK Government responsible for drafting the Regulations and which was consistent with the objects of the EC Treaty, the provisions of the Equal Pay Directive and the rulings of the European Court. As the draft Regulations were not subject to any process of amendment by Parliament as a Bill would have been, and as a statute which is passed in order to give effect to the UK's obligations under the EC Treaty falls into a special category because, by virtue of s.2 of the European Communities Act, those obligations have, in effect, been incorporated into English law, it was legitimate for the purpose of ascertaining the intention of Parliament to take into account the terms in which the draft was presented by the responsible Minister and which formed the basis of its acceptance.

Claim in time

Biggs v   **[1996] IRLR 203 CA**
Somerset County Council
UK domestic law time limits apply to a claim relying on Article 141 of the Treaty, unless it can be shown that they are less favourable than those relating to similar actions of a domestic nature or are such as to make it impossible in practice to exercise the rights under Article 141.

Magorrian v   **[1998] IRLR 86 ECJ**
Eastern Health and Social Services Board
EC law precludes the application, to a claim based on Article 141, of a national rule, such as that in the Occupational Pensions Regulations, which limits the entitlement of a claimant to join an occupational pension scheme to a period which starts to run from two years prior to the date proceedings were commenced. The rule was such as to render any action by individuals relying on Community law impossible in practice, in that its application in the present case would deprive the applicants of the additional benefits under the scheme to which they were entitled, since those benefits could be calculated only by reference to periods of service completed by them as from two years prior to commencement of proceedings.

Barber v   **[1996] IRLR 209 CA**
Staffordshire County Council
Article 141 does not confer any right to a redundancy payment or to unfair dismissal compensation. Community law does not create rights of action which have an existence apart from domestic law.

Setiya v   **[1995] IRLR 348 EAT**
East Yorkshire Health Authority
It would not be just to grant an employee, whose unfair dismissal complaint was dismissed by an employment tribunal in 1992 on grounds that he worked less than eight hours per week, an extension of time for appealing to the EAT against the tribunal's decision, in light of the decision of the House of Lords in 1994 that the hours per week qualification contravened EC law. To be granted an extension of time, it is not sufficient for the appellant simply to point to a subsequent decision of a higher court to the effect that the decision sought to be appealed against was wrongly decided.

Same work

Brunnhofer v   **[2001] IRLR 571 ECJ**
Bank der österreichischen Postsparkasse
In order to determine whether employees perform the same work or work to which equal value can be attributed, it is necessary to ascertain whether, taking account of a number of factors such as the nature of the activities actually entrusted to each of the employees, the training requirements for carrying them out and the working conditions, those persons are in fact performing the same or comparable work.

Angestelltenbetriebsrat der Wiener   **[1999] IRLR 804 ECJ**
    Gebietskrankenkasse v
Wiener Gebietskrankenkasse
Two groups of employees who have different professional qualifications cannot be regarded as employed on "the same work" for the purpose of Article 141, even where the same activities are performed over a considerable length of time, if the different groups cannot be considered to be in a comparable situation. Professional training is not merely one of the factors that may be an objective justification for giving different pay for doing the same work; it is also one of the possible criteria for determining whether or not the same work is being performed.

Brunnhofer v   **[2001] IRLR 571 ECJ**
Bank der österreichischen Postsparkasse
The fact that the employees concerned are classified in the same job category under a collective agreement is not in itself sufficient for concluding that they perform the same work or work of equal value. The general indications provided in a collective agreement are only one indication amongst others and must, as a matter of evidence, be corroborated by precise and concrete factors based on the activities actually performed by the employees concerned.

Burden of proof

Brunnhofer v   **[2001] IRLR 571 ECJ**
Bank der österreichischen Postsparkasse
The burden is normally on the employee to establish that the conditions giving rise to a presumption that there is unequal pay are fulfilled by proving by evidence that the pay she receives is less than that of her chosen comparator, and that she does the same work or work of equal value, comparable to that performed by him.

Enderby v   **[1993] IRLR 591 ECJ**
Frenchay Health Authority and
  Secretary of State for Health
There is a prima facie case of sex discrimination where valid statistics disclose an appreciable difference in pay between two jobs of equal value, one of which is carried out almost exclusively by women and other predominantly by men. It is for the national court to assess whether the statistics appear to be significant in that they cover enough individuals and do not illustrate purely fortuitous or short-term phenomena.

Brunnhofer v   **[2001] IRLR 571 ECJ**
Bank der österreichischen Postsparkasse
In comparing the pay of men and women in order to determine whether the principle of equal pay is being complied with, genuine transparency, permitting an effective review, is assured only if each aspect of remuneration is compared, rather than any general overall assessment of all the consideration paid to the workers.

Jämställdhetsombudsmannen v   **[2000] IRLR 421 ECJ**
Örebro Läns Landsting
Where the work of two groups can be regarded as of equal value, the national court must verify whether there is a substantially higher proportion of women than men in the disadvantaged group. If so, Article 141 requires the employer to justify the difference by showing that there are objective reasons for the difference in pay which are unrelated to any discrimination on grounds of sex.

Handels- og Kontorfunktionærernes   **[1989] IRLR 532 ECJ**
  Forbund i Danmark v
Dansk Arbejdsgiverforening
  (acting for Danfoss)
Pursuant to Article 6 of the Equal Pay Directive, Member States, in accordance with their national circumstances and their legal systems, must take the measures necessary in order to guarantee the application of the principle of equal pay and to ensure the existence of effective means to see to it that this principle is observed. The concern for effectiveness which therefore underlies the Directive must lead to an interpretation requiring adjustments to national rules relating to the burden of proof in specific situations where such adjustments are essential for the effective implementation of the principle of equality.

Handels- og Kontorfunktionaerernes   **[1989] IRLR 532 ECJ**
  Forbund i Danmark v
Dansk Arbejdsgiverforening
  (acting for Danfoss)
The EC Equal Pay Directive must be interpreted as meaning that when an undertaking applies a pay system which is characterised by a total lack of transparency, the burden of proof is on the employer to show that his pay practice is not discriminatory where a female worker establishes, by comparison with a relatively large number of employees, that the average pay of female workers is lower than that of male workers.

Specialarbejderforbundet   **[1995] IRLR 648 ECJ**
  i Danmark v
Dansk Industri, acting for
  Royal Copenhagen
The mere finding that in a piecework pay scheme the average pay of a group of workers consisting predominantly of women carrying out one type of work is appreciably lower than the average pay of a group of workers consisting predominantly of men carrying out another type of work to which equal value is attributed does not suffice to establish that there is discrimination with regard to pay, since that difference may be due to differences in individual output of the workers constituting the two groups. However, in a piecework pay system where individual pay includes a variable element depending on each worker's output and it is not possible to identify the factors which determined the rates or units of measurement used to calculate the variable element in the pay, the burden of proving that the differences found are not due to sex discrimination may shift to the employer in order to avoid depriving the workers concerned of any effective means of enforcing the principle of equal pay.

Specialarbejderforbundet   **[1995] IRLR 648 ECJ**
  i Danmark v
Dansk Industri, acting for
  Royal Copenhagen
Where a comparison between workers of different sexes for work to which equal value is attributed involves the average pay of two groups paid by the piece, the national court must satisfy itself that the two groups each encompass all the workers who, taking account of factors such as the nature of the work, the training requirements and the working conditions, can be considered to be in a comparable situation. A comparison is not relevant where it involves groups formed in an arbitrary manner so that one comprises predominantly women and the other predominantly men with a view to carrying out successive comparisons. The comparison must also cover a relatively large number of workers in order to ensure that the differences found are not due to purely fortuitous or short-term factors or to differences in the individual output of the workers concerned.

Meaning of "pay"

Garland v   **[1982] IRLR 111 ECJ**
British Rail Engineering Ltd
"Pay", for the purposes of Article 141, comprises any consideration, whether in cash or in kind, whether immediate or future, that the worker receives, albeit indirectly, in respect of his employment from his employer.

Barber v   **[1990] IRLR 240 ECJ**
Guardian Royal Exchange
  Assurance Group
Although many advantages granted by an employer also

reflect considerations of social policy, the fact that a benefit is in the nature of pay cannot be called in question where the worker is entitled to receive it from his employer by reason of the existence of the employment relationship. Therefore, a redundancy payment made by an employer cannot cease to constitute a form of pay on the sole ground that, rather than deriving from the contract of employment, it is a statutory or ex gratia payment.

Barber v   **[1990] IRLR 240 ECJ**
Guardian Royal Exchange
    Assurance Group
Since Article 141 applies to discrimination arising directly from legislative provisions, benefits provided for by law may come within the concept of "pay".

Hill v   **[1998] IRLR 466 ECJ**
Revenue Commissioners
A system for classifying workers converting from job-sharing to full-time employment comes within the concept of "pay" for the purposes of Article 141, since it determines the progression of pay due to those workers.

Lewen v   **[2000] IRLR 67 ECJ**
Denda
A Christmas bonus constitutes "pay" within the meaning of Article 141, even if it is paid voluntarily by the employer as an exceptional allowance.

Jämställdhetsombudsmannen v   **[2000] IRLR 421 ECJ**
Örebro Läns Landsting
Differences in normal working time relate to working conditions and therefore fall under the Equal Treatment Directive rather than Article 141. The fact that the fixing of certain working conditions may have pecuniary consequences is not sufficient to bring such conditions within the scope of Article 141. However, any differences that might exist in the hours worked by two groups whose pay is being compared may constitute objective reasons unrelated to any discrimination on grounds of sex such as to justify a difference in pay.

Lommers v   **[2002] IRLR 430 ECJ**
Minister van Landbouw, Natuurbeheer en Visserij
A scheme under which an employer makes nursery places available to employees is to be regarded as a "working condition" within the meaning of the Equal Treatment Directive rather than as "pay" within the meaning of Article 141, notwithstanding that the cost of the nursery places was partly borne by the employer.

Gerster v   **[1997] IRLR 699 ECJ**
Freistaat Bayern
Rules concerning access to career advancement do not fall within the scope of Article 141, even though they are indirectly linked to pay. Such a rule is primarily designed to lay down conditions for inclusion on a list of persons eligible for promotion and only indirectly affects the level of pay to which the person concerned is entitled upon completion of the promotions procedure.

Legislation

Rinner-Kühn v   **[1989] IRLR 493 ECJ**
FWW Spezial-Gebäudereinigung GmbH
A legislative provision which results in practice in discrimination between male and female workers is, in principle, to be regarded as contrary to the objective pursued by Article 141. It would only be otherwise if the different treatment between the two categories of workers was justified by objective factors unrelated to any discrimination on grounds of sex.

Rinner-Kühn v   **[1989] IRLR 493 ECJ**
FWW Spezial-Gebäudereinigung GmbH
The mere fact that a legislative provision affects a considerably greater number of female than of male workers cannot be regarded as an infringement of Article 141 if a Member State can establish before the national court that the means selected correspond to an objective necessary for its social policy and are appropriate and necessary to the attainment of that objective.

Allonby v   **[2004] IRLR 224 ECJ**
Accrington & Rossendale College
Where State legislation is at issue, the applicability of Article 141 to an undertaking is not subject to a condition that the worker concerned can be compared with a worker of the other sex who is or has been employed by the same employer and has received higher pay for equal work or work of equal value. A woman may rely on statistics to show that a clause in State legislation is contrary to Article 141 because it discriminates against female workers, and may invoke Article 141 against the employer concerned.

KB v   **[2004] IRLR 240 ECJ**
National Health Service Pensions Agency
Legislation which, in breach of the European Convention on Human Rights, prevents transsexuals from fulfilling a marriage requirement which must be met for one of them to be able to have the benefit of a survivor's pension, must be regarded as being in principle incompatible with the requirements of Article 141 of the EC Treaty.

Collective agreements

Kowalska v   **[1990] IRLR 447 ECJ**
Freie und Hansestadt Hamburg
Article 141 is sufficiently precise to be relied upon by an individual before a national court in order to have any

national provision, including a collective agreement, contrary to Article 141 set aside.

Kowalska v   **[1990] IRLR 447 ECJ**
Freie und Hansestadt Hamburg
Article 141 precludes the application of a provision of a collective agreement under which part-time workers are excluded from a benefit where a considerably smaller percentage of men than of women work part time, unless the employer shows that the provision is justified by objective factors unrelated to any discrimination on grounds of sex. It is for the national court to determine whether and to what extent a provision of a collective agreement which in practice affects more women than men is justified on objective grounds unrelated to any discrimination based on sex.

Kowalska v   **[1990] IRLR 447 ECJ**
Freie und Hansestadt Hamburg
Where there is indirect discrimination in a provision of a collective agreement, the members of the group which is disadvantaged because of that discrimination must be treated in the same way and have the same system applied to them as the other workers, in proportion to their hours of work.

Nimz v   **[1991] IRLR 222 ECJ**
Freie und Hansestadt Hamburg
Where there is indirect discrimination in a provision of a collective agreement, the national court is required to disapply that provision, without requesting or awaiting its prior removal by collective negotiation or any other procedure. It would be incompatible with the nature of Community law for a judge to refuse to do all that is necessary, at the time when Community law is applied, to set aside any provisions of a collective agreement which might prevent Community standards from attaining their full effect.

Piecework

Specialarbejderforbundet   **[1995] IRLR 648 ECJ**
  i Danmark v
Dansk Industri, acting for
  Royal Copenhagen
Article 141 and the Equal Pay Directive apply to piecework pay schemes in which pay depends entirely or in large measure on the individual output of each worker.

Overtime

Stadt Lengerich v   **[1995] IRLR 216 ECJ**
Helmig
It is compatible with Article 141 and with the Equal Pay Directive for a collective agreement to provide for the pay-

ment of overtime supplements only for hours worked in excess of the normal working hours for full-time employees fixed by the agreement and to exclude any overtime supplement for part-time employees for hours worked in excess of their individual working hours if those hours do not exceed the number determined by the agreement. There was no unequal treatment as between part-time and full-time employees, since the overall pay was the same for the same number of hours worked, and therefore no discrimination incompatible with Article 141 and the Directive.

Sick pay

Rinner-Kühn v   **[1989] IRLR 493 ECJ**
FWW Spezial-Gebäudereinigung GmbH
The continued payment of wages to a worker in the event of illness falls within the definition of "pay" within the meaning of Article 141.

Rinner-Kühn v   **[1989] IRLR 493 ECJ**
FWW Spezial-Gebäudereinigung GmbH
Article 141 of the EC Treaty precludes national legislation which permits employers to exclude employees whose normal working hours do not exceed 10 hours a week or 45 hours a month from the continued payment of wages in the event of illness, where that measure affects a considerably greater number of women than men, unless the Member State shows that that legislation is justified by objective factors unrelated to any discrimination on grounds of sex.

Rinner-Kühn v   **[1989] IRLR 493 ECJ**
FWW Spezial-Gebäudereinigung GmbH
A submission that workers who work less than 10 hours a week or 45 hours a month are not integrated in and connected with the undertaking in a way comparable to that of other workers only represented generalised statements concerning categories of workers and could not be regarded as objective criteria unrelated to any discrimination on grounds of sex.

Pregnancy

HK (acting on behalf of   **[1999] IRLR 55 ECJ**
  Hoj Pedersen) v
Fællesforeningen for Danmarks Brugsforeninger
  (acting on behalf of Kvickly Skive)
It is contrary to Article 141 and the Equal Pay Directive to deprive a woman of her full pay when she is unfit for work before the beginning of her maternity leave as a result of a pregnancy-related condition, when a worker is in principle entitled to receive full pay in the event of incapacity for work on grounds of illness.

Maternity pay

Gillespie v   [1996] IRLR 214 ECJ
Northern Health and Social Services Board
The principle of equal pay does not require that women should continue to receive full pay during maternity leave. Women taking maternity leave are in a special position, which requires them to be afforded special protection, but which is not comparable with that of a man or a woman actually at work. Although the benefit paid by an employer to a woman on maternity leave constitutes "pay" within the meaning of Article 141 and the Equal Pay Directive, discrimination involves the application of different rules to comparable situations or the application of the same rule to different situations. Therefore, neither Article 141 or the Directive requires that women should continue to receive full pay during maternity leave.

Todd v   [1997] IRLR 410 NICA
Eastern Health and Social Services Board
Gillespie v
Northern Health and Social Services Board (No.2)
A healthy pregnancy did not come within the contractual provisions relating to sickness and disability. Pregnancy cannot be compared with sickness.

Clark v   [1996] IRLR 578 CA
Secretary of State for Employment
Special provisions which are made for women who are absent from work because of pregnancy or confinement are a separate code. The code provides pregnant women with special protection, but when in receipt of payments under the code their position cannot be "compared" with that of a man or with that of a woman in work.

Gillespie v   [1996] IRLR 214 ECJ
Northern Health and Social Services Board
A woman on maternity leave must receive a pay rise awarded before or during maternity leave.

Alabaster v   [2004] IRLR 486 ECJ
Woolwich plc
The principle of non-discrimination requires that a woman who still has a contract of employment or employment relationship during maternity leave must, like any other worker, benefit from any pay rise which is awarded between the beginning of the reference period and the end of maternity leave. To deny such an increase to a woman on maternity leave would discriminate against her since, had she not been pregnant, she would have received the pay rise. Therefore, a woman who receives a pay increase before the start of her maternity leave is entitled, in accordance with Article 141 of the EC Treaty and the judgment in *Gillespie v Northern Health and Social Services Board*, to have the increase taken into consideration in the calculation of the earnings-related element of her statutory maternity pay, even though the pay rise was not backdated to the relevant reference period for calculating her entitlement under the Statutory Maternity Pay (General) Regulations.

Gillespie v   [1996] IRLR 214 ECJ
Northern Health and Social Services Board
It is for national legislature to set the amount of maternity pay, provided the amount is not so low as to undermine the purpose of maternity leave, namely the protection of women before and after giving birth. In order to assess the adequacy of the amount payable, the national court must take account of other forms of social protection afforded by national law in the case of justified absence from work, as well as the length of maternity leave.

Abdoulaye v   [1999] IRLR 811 ECJ
Régie Nationale des Usines Renault
The principle of equal pay presupposes that male and female workers whom it covers are in comparable situations. Women on maternity leave are in a different situation than men since there are occupational disadvantages, inherent in maternity leave, which arise as a result of being away from work. Therefore, it is not contrary to Article 141 to make a lump-sum payment to female workers who take maternity leave, and not to men who become fathers, notwithstanding women on maternity leave receive full pay, where the lump-sum payment is designed to offset the occupational disadvantages which arise for those workers as a result of their being away from work.

Todd v   [1997] IRLR 410 NICA
Eastern Health and Social Services Board
Gillespie v
Northern Health and Social Services Board (No.2)
Contractual maternity pay which was at a higher level than statutory sickness benefit could not be held to be inadequate, or such as to undermine the purpose of maternity leave, so as to fall within the proviso to the ruling of the European Court in the *Gillespie* case.

Parental leave

Lewen v   [2000] IRLR 67 ECJ
Denda
Article 141 of the EC Treaty precludes an employer from entirely excluding women on parental leave from the benefit of a Christmas bonus without taking account of the work done in the year in which the bonus is paid or of periods of maternity leave during which they were prohibited from working, where that bonus is awarded retroactively as pay for work performed in the course of that year. If the Christmas bonus is retroactive pay for work performed, refusal to award a bonus, even one reduced proportionately, to workers on parental leave who worked during the year in which the bonus was granted, on the sole ground that their contract of employment is suspended when the bonus is granted, places them at a disadvantage as compared with those whose con-

tract is not suspended at the time of the award. Such a refusal constitutes discrimination within the meaning of Article 141, since female workers are far more likely to be on parental leave when the bonus is awarded than male workers.

Time off

Arbeiterwohlfahrt der Stadt   **[1992] IRLR 423 ECJ**
  Berlin eV v
Bötel
Compensation in the form of paid leave or overtime pay for participation in training courses given by an employer to staff committee members in accordance with statutory provisions falls within the concept of "pay" within the meaning of Article 141 of the EC Treaty and Equal Pay Directive 75/117. Although such compensation does not arise from the contract of employment, it is nevertheless paid by the employer by virtue of legislative provisions and by reason of the existence of an employment relationship with an employee.

Kuratorium für Dialyse und   **[1996] IRLR 637 ECJ**
  Nierentransplantation e V v
Lewark
National legislation which causes indirect discrimination against women by limiting to their individual working hours the compensation which staff council members employed on a part-time basis receive from their employer for attending training courses held during full-time working hours but which exceed their individual part-time working hours, when staff council members employed full-time receive compensation for attendance at the same courses on the basis of their full-time working hours, can be justified by objective factors unrelated to any discrimination based on sex. The mere fact that a legislative provision affects far more women workers than men cannot be regarded as a breach of Article 141 if the Member State is able to show that the measures chosen reflect a legitimate aim of its social policy, are appropriate to achieve that aim and are necessary in order to do so.

Arbeiterwohlfahrt der Stadt   **[1992] IRLR 423 ECJ**
  Berlin eV v
Bötel
Article 141 and the Equal Pay Directive preclude national legislation which applies to a considerably greater number of women than men limiting to their individual working hours the compensation which members of staff committees employed part-time should receive from their employer in the form of paid leave or overtime pay, in respect of their participation in training courses providing the knowledge and skills required for the running of staff committees and which are organised during the full-time working hours applicable in the undertaking but exceeding their own working hours as part-time employees, whereas the members of staff committees participating in the same courses who are full-time employees are paid compensation up to the limit of the full-time working

hours. It remains open to the Member State to establish that the said legislation is justified by objective factors unrelated to any discrimination on grounds of sex.

Davies v   **[1999] IRLR 769 EAT**
Neath Port Talbot County Borough Council
Part-time workers have a right under Article 141 to be paid on the same basis as their full-time counterparts when attending union-run training courses away from work.

Pension schemes

Scope of Article 141

Barber v   **[1990] IRLR 240 ECJ**
Guardian Royal Exchange
  Assurance Group
A pension paid under a contracted-out private occupational scheme constitutes consideration paid by the employer to the worker in respect of his employment and consequently falls within the scope of the definition of "pay" in Article 141.

Bestuur van het Algemeen   **[1995] IRLR 103 ECJ**
  Burgerlijk Pensioenfonds v
Beune
In order to determine whether the benefits provided by a pension scheme are within the scope of Article 141, the only possible decisive criterion is whether the pension is paid to the worker by reason of the employment relationship between him and his former employer.

Barber v   **[1990] IRLR 240 ECJ**
Guardian Royal Exchange
  Assurance Group
It is contrary to Article 141 to impose an age condition which differs according to sex in respect of pensions paid under a contracted-out scheme, even if the difference between the pensionable age for men and that for women is based on the one provided for by the national statutory scheme.

Coloroll Pension Trustees Ltd v   **[1994] IRLR 586 ECJ**
Russell
The principles laid down in the *Barber* judgment, and the limitation of its effects in time, concern not only contracted-out occupational schemes but also non-contracted-out occupational schemes.

Bestuur van het Algemeen   **[1995] IRLR 103 ECJ**
  Burgerlijk Pensioenfonds v
Beune
A civil service pension scheme, which essentially relates to the employment of the person concerned, forms part of the pay received by that person and comes within the scope of Article 141. If the pension paid by the public employer concerns only a particular category of workers, if it is directly related to the

period of service, and if its amount is calculated by reference to the civil servant's last salary, it is entirely comparable to the pension paid by a private employer to its former employees.

Bestuur van het Algemeen Burgerlijk Pensioenfonds v Beune
[1995] IRLR 103 ECJ

Article 141 precludes national legislation which applies different rules for calculating the occupational pension of married men and married women. Married men placed at a disadvantage by the discrimination are entitled to be treated in the same way and have the same scheme applied to them as is applied to married women.

Ten Oever v Stichting Bedrijfspensioenfonds voor het Glazenwassers- en Schoonmaakbedrijf
[1993] IRLR 601 ECJ

A survivor's pension provided by an occupational pension scheme, whose rules were agreed between both sides of the industry concerned and which was funded by the industry's employees and employers to the exclusion of any financial contribution from the public purse, falls within the concept of "pay" within the meaning of Article 141 of the EC Treaty, notwithstanding that, by definition, a survivor's pension is not paid to the employee.

Coloroll Pension Trustees Ltd v Russell
[1994] IRLR 586 ECJ

Article 141 may be relied upon by an employee's dependants.

Coloroll Pension Trustees Ltd v Russell
[1994] IRLR 586 ECJ

Article 141 may be relied upon against the trustees of an occupational pension scheme. Since the trustees are required to pay benefits which are "pay" within the meaning of Article 141, they are bound, in so doing, to do everything within the scope of their powers to ensure compliance with the principle of equal treatment.

Coloroll Pension Trustees Ltd v Russell
[1994] IRLR 586 ECJ

Employers and trustees cannot rely on the rules of their pension scheme, or those contained in the trust deed, in order to evade their obligation under Article 141 to ensure equal treatment in the matter of pay. In so far as the rules of national law prohibit them from acting beyond the scope of their powers or in disregard of the provisions of the trust deed, employers and trustees are bound to use all the means available under domestic law to ensure compliance with the principle of equal treatment, such as recourse to the national courts to amend the provisions of the pension scheme or of the trust deed.

Worringham v Lloyds Bank Ltd
[1981] IRLR 178 ECJ

A contribution to a retirement benefits scheme which is paid by an employer in the name of male employees only, by means of an addition to gross salary, is discrimination in the form of unequal pay for men and women contrary to Article 141, even though the salary of men after deduction of the contributions is comparable with that of women who do not pay contributions, since the amount of the gross salary determined the amount of certain benefits and social advantages to which workers of both sexes are entitled.

Barber v Guardian Royal Exchange Assurance Group
[1990] IRLR 240 ECJ

It is contrary to Article 141 for a man made compulsorily redundant to be entitled to claim only a deferred pension payable at the normal pension age, when a woman in the same position is entitled to an immediate retirement pension as a result of the application of an age condition that varies according to sex in the same way as is provided for by the national statutory pension scheme.

Neath v Hugh Steeper Ltd
[1994] IRLR 91 ECJ

The use of actuarial factors differing according to sex in funded defined-benefit occupational pension schemes to take account of the fact that women live on average longer than men does not fall within the scope of Article 141. Therefore, inequality of employers' contributions to funded defined-benefit pension schemes, which is due to the use of actuarial factors differing according to sex, is not prohibited by Article 141. Unlike periodic payment of pensions, the funding arrangement chosen to secure the adequacy of the funds necessary to cover the cost of the pensions promised is outside the concept of "pay" in Article 141 as it not a consequence of the employer's commitment to pay employees defined benefits or to grant them specific advantages and therefore does not come within the corresponding expectations of the employees as to the benefits which will be paid by the employer or the advantages with which they will be provided.

Coloroll Pension Trustees Ltd v Russell
[1994] IRLR 586 ECJ

Transfer benefits and capital-sum benefits, whose value depends on the funding arrangements chosen, do not constitute "pay". Consequently, Article 141 does not cover an inequality where a reduced pension is paid when the employer opts for early retirement or in the amount of a reversionary pension payable to a dependant in return for the surrender of part of the annual pension.

Coloroll Pension Trustees Ltd v Russell
[1994] IRLR 586 ECJ

Article 141 does not cover additional benefits stemming from additional voluntary contributions by employees, where the pension scheme does no more than provide the membership with the necessary arrangements for management.

Smith v Avdel Systems Ltd
[1994] IRLR 602 ECJ

Article 141 does not preclude an employer from raising the

retirement age for women to that for men in order to comply with the *Barber* judgment. Article 141 does not preclude measures which achieve equal treatment by reducing the advantages of the persons previously favoured. It merely requires that men and women should receive the same pay for the same work without imposing any specific level of pay. However, once discrimination in pay has been found to exist, so long as measures for bringing about equal treatment have not been adopted by the scheme, the only proper way of complying with Article 141 is to grant the persons in the disadvantaged class the same advantages as those enjoyed by the persons in the favoured class. In the present case, that meant that, as regards the period between the date of the Barber judgment and the date on which the scheme adopted measures to achieve equality, the pension rights of men must be calculated on the basis of the same retirement age as that for women.

Smith v   [1994] IRLR 602 ECJ
Avdel Systems Ltd
Where the retirement age for women is raised to that of men in order to remove discrimination in relation to occupational pensions, Article 141 does not allow transitional measures designed to limit the adverse consequences for women as regards benefits payable in respect of future periods of service.

Van Den Akker v   [1994] IRLR 616 ECJ
Stichting Shell Pensioenfonds
Article 141 does not allow an occupational pension scheme to maintain in force after the date of the *Barber* judgment a condition as to retirement age differing according to sex, even where that difference is due to giving female employees an option before the *Barber* judgment to maintain a retirement age lower than that for men.

Smith v   [1994] IRLR 602 ECJ
Avdel Systems Ltd
Article 141 precludes an occupational pension scheme, even where there are objectively justifiable considerations relating to the needs of the undertaking or of the scheme concerned, from retrospectively raising the retirement age for women in relation to periods of service between the date of the *Barber* judgment and the date of entry into force of the measures designed to achieve equal treatment.

Coloroll Pension Trustees Ltd v   [1994] IRLR 586 ECJ
Russell
The national court is bound to ensure correct implementation of Article 141 and, in order to do so, may make use of all means available to it under domestic law, such as by ordering the employer to pay additional sums into the scheme, ordering that any sum payable by virtue of Article 141 must be paid out of surplus funds or out of the scheme's assets. Any problems arising because the funds held by the trustee are insufficient or the employer cannot provide sufficient funds to equalise benefits must be resolved on the basis of national law in accordance with the principle of equal pay.

Coloroll Pension Trustees Ltd v   [1994] IRLR 586 ECJ
Russell
The rights accruing to a worker from Article 141 cannot be affected by the fact that he changes his job and has to join a new pension scheme, with his acquired pension rights being transferred to the new scheme. A worker entering retirement is entitled to expect the scheme of which he is then a member to pay him a pension calculated in accordance with the principle of equal treatment, and to increase benefits accordingly, even where the capital transferred is inadequate due to the discriminatory treatment under the first scheme. However, in accordance with the *Barber* judgment, neither the scheme which transferred rights nor the scheme which accepted them is required to take the financial steps necessary to bring about equality in relation to periods of service prior to 17 May 1990.

Bilka-Kaufhaus GmbH v   [1986] IRLR 317 ECJ
Weber von Hartz
Article 141 is restricted to pay discrimination and therefore does not have the effect of requiring an employer to organise an occupational pension scheme in such a manner as to take into account the particular difficulties faced by persons with family responsibilities in meeting the conditions for entitlement to such a pension.

Coloroll Pension Trustees Ltd v   [1994] IRLR 586 ECJ
Russell
Article 141 is not applicable to pension schemes which at all times have had members of only one sex.

Moroni v   [1994] IRLR 130 ECJ
Firma Collo GmbH
The provisions of EC Occupational Social Security Directive 86/378 cannot limit the scope of Article 141.

Temporal limitation

Barber v   [1990] IRLR 240 ECJ
Guardian Royal Exchange
Assurance Group
The direct effect of Article 141 may not be relied upon in order to claim entitlement to a pension with effect from a date prior to that of the judgment in this case (17 May 1990), except in the case of those who have before that date initiated legal proceedings or raised an equivalent claim under the applicable national law.

Ten Oever v   [1993] IRLR 601 ECJ
Stichting Bedrijfspensioenfonds voor
het Glazenwassers- en Schoonmaakbedrijf
The direct effect of Article 141 may be relied upon, for the purpose of claiming equal treatment in the matter of occupational pensions, only in relation to benefits payable in respect of periods of employment subsequent to 17 May 1990, the date of the *Barber* decision, subject to the exception in favour

of those who before that date initiated legal proceedings or raised an equivalent claim under the applicable national law.

Coloroll Pension Trustees Ltd v   **[1994] IRLR 586 ECJ**
Russell
Where a benefit is not linked to the actual length of service, such as a lump-sum payment in the event of the employee's death during employment, the limitation of the effects in time of the *Barber* judgment applies only where the operative event occurred before 17 May 1990. After that date, such benefits must be granted in accordance with the principle of equal treatment without distinguishing between periods of service prior to and subsequent to the *Barber* judgment.

Vroege v   **[1994] IRLR 651 ECJ**
NCIV Instituut voor
Volkshuisvesting BV
The temporal limitation of the *Barber* judgment concerns only those kinds of discrimination which employers and occupational pension schemes could reasonably have considered to be permissible owing to the transitional derogations provided by Community law in respect of equal treatment with regard to the determination of pensionable age

Quirk v   **[2002] IRLR 353 CA**
Burton Hospitals NHS Trust
The decisions of the European Court of Justice reveal a difference in the treatment of "access cases" relating to the right to join or to be fully admitted to a pension scheme and its benefits, and claims relating to the calculation of the level of benefits under a pension scheme. The Court of Justice has applied the temporal limitation to level of benefit cases but not to access cases.

Quirk v   **[2002] IRLR 353 CA**
Burton Hospitals NHS Trust
The provision in the NHS Pension Scheme Regulations allowing a woman retiring before age 60 to receive benefits calculated by reference to all of her pensionable service, whereas the pension payable to men before age 60 is calculated only by reference to service from 17 May 1990, the date of the *Barber* decision, did not discriminate against a man contrary to Article 141 since the claim was caught by the temporal limitation contained in the European Court's decision in the *Barber* case and in the *Barber* Protocol to the EC Treaty, in that it was a complaint about the level of benefit payable, rather than a complaint relating to access to benefits under a pension scheme. The essence of the complaint was not that the applicant was denied the right to be a member of the pension scheme, but that, unlike the case of a female nurse, the calculation of pension benefits on his retirement at age 55 would not take account of his years of pensionable service prior to 17 May 1990.

Howard v   **[1995] IRLR 570 EAT**
Ministry of Defence
The exclusion from the temporal limitation imposed by the European Court on the *Barber* decision for those who had made a claim "equivalent" to legal proceedings in national law, is restricted to where a dispute has been raised before an independent third party with power to determine the dispute conclusively, such as an administrative or arbitration tribunal, and does not extend to a person who only asserts a claim.

Admission

Bilka-Kaufhaus GmbH v   **[1986] IRLR 317 ECJ**
Weber von Hartz
The conditions for admission to an occupational pension scheme, where the benefits paid to employees constitute consideration received by the worker from the employer in respect of employment, fall within the scope of the definition of "pay" in Article 141 of the EC Treaty; such a scheme does not constitute a social security scheme governed directly by statute, which would be outside the scope of Article 141.

Vroege v   **[1994] IRLR 651 ECJ**
NCIV Instituut voor
   Volkshuisvesting BV
Article 141 of the EC Treaty covers the right to join an occupational pension scheme, as well as entitlement to benefits paid by an occupational pension scheme. Therefore, an occupational pension scheme which excludes part-time workers will contravene Article 141 if the exclusion affects a much greater number of women than men, unless the employer shows that it may be explained by objectively justified factors unrelated to any discrimination on grounds of sex.

Trustees of Uppingham School   **[2002] IRLR 792 CA**
   Retirement Benefit Scheme for
   Non-Teaching Staff v
Shillcock
Exclusion of the claimant part-time employee from membership of the appellant's occupational pension scheme on grounds that she earned less than the lower earnings limit for Class I national insurance contributions was not indirectly discriminatory on grounds of sex against women contrary to Article 141. Subtracting the lower earnings limit from the earnings of every employee for the purpose of assessing pensionable salary involved a consistent, and not a discriminatory, approach to all categories of employee.

Allonby v   **[2004] IRLR 224 ECJ**
Accrington & Rossendale College
A requirement of being employed under a contract of employment as a precondition for membership of a pension scheme for teachers, set up by State legislation, must be disapplied unless it is objectively justified, where it is shown that among the teachers who are "workers" within the meaning of Article 141 there is a much higher percentage of women than of men who fulfil all the conditions for membership of the scheme except that of being employed under a contract of employment as defined by national law.

Preston v   **[2004] IRLR 96 EAT**
Wolverhampton Healthcare
   NHS Trust (No.3)

There is a breach of the Equal Pay Act where pension scheme membership is compulsory for full-time staff but part-time staff are excluded, regardless of whether an employee joined the scheme when it became open to them. However, there is no breach of the Equal Pay Act where pension scheme membership is compulsory for full-time staff and optional for part-time staff.

Schröder v   **[2000] IRLR 353 ECJ**
Deutsche Telekom AG

Where the exclusion of part-time workers from an occupational pension scheme has been found to constitute indirect discrimination prohibited by Article 141, the only limitation in time on the possibility of relying on the direct effect of Article 141 in relation to membership of the scheme and the subsequent payment of a pension is that resulting from *Defrenne (No.2)*, that periods of service of such workers are to be taken into account only from 8 April 1976 onwards. The limitation in time of the *Barber* decision and the *Barber* Protocol concerns only those kinds of discrimination which employers and pension schemes could reasonably have considered to be permissible under Community law. Since it has been clear since the judgment in *Bilka* that any discrimination, based on sex, in the right to join an occupational pension scheme infringes Article 41, there was no reason to suppose that those concerned could have been mistaken as to the applicability of Article 41 to the right to join an occupational scheme.

Vroege v   **[1994] IRLR 651 ECJ**
NCIV Instituut voor
   Volkshuisvesting BV

The *Barber* Protocol to Article 141, which provides that benefits under occupational social security schemes shall not be considered as remuneration if and in so far as they are attributable to periods of employment prior to 17 May 1990, does not affect the right to join an occupational pension scheme. The Protocol is applicable to benefits paid under an occupational pension scheme, since that is all that is mentioned in the Protocol. Neither the Protocol, nor the *Barber* judgment, dealt with, or made any provision for, the conditions of membership of occupational schemes, which continues to be governed by the *Bilka* judgment.

Dietz v   **[1996] IRLR 692 ECJ**
Stichting Thuiszorg Rotterdam

The *Barber* Protocol to the Treaty on European Union does not affect the right to payment of a retirement pension where the worker was excluded from membership of an occupational pension scheme in breach of Article 141.

Fisscher v   **[1994] IRLR 662 ECJ**
Voorhuis Hengelo BV

National rules relating to time limits for bringing actions under national law may be relied on against workers who assert their right under Community law to join an occupational pension scheme, provided that they are not less favourable for that type of action than for similar actions of a domestic nature and that they do not render the exercise of rights conferred by Community law impossible in practice.

Fisscher v   **[1994] IRLR 662 ECJ**
Voorhuis Hengelo BV

The fact that a worker can claim retroactively to join an occupational pension scheme does not allow the worker to avoid paying the contributions relating to the period of membership concerned. The worker cannot claim more favourable treatment, particularly in financial terms, than if the worker had been duly accepted as a member.

Bridging pensions

Birds Eye Walls Ltd v   **[1994] IRLR 29 ECJ**
Roberts

It is not contrary to Article 141 for an employer to reduce the amount of a bridging pension to take account of the amount of the State pension which the employee will receive, even though, in the case of men and women aged between 60 and 65, the result is that a female ex-employee receives a smaller bridging pension than that paid to her male counterpart.

Birds Eye Walls Ltd v   **[1994] IRLR 29 ECJ**
Roberts

It is not contrary to Article 141 for an employer, when calculating a bridging pension, to take account of the full State pension which a married woman would have received if she had not opted in favour of paying contributions at a reduced rate. Nor is it contrary to Article 141 for an employer to take account of the widow's pension which may be drawn by the woman concerned.

Notice payment

Clark v   **[1995] IRLR 421 EAT**
Secretary of State for Employment

Sums payable by an employer to an employee for failing to give notice to which the employee is entitled are "pay" within the meaning of Article 141, because such payment is in respect of the employee's employment.

Clark v   **[1996] IRLR 578 CA**
Secretary of State for Employment

The exclusion of women absent from work because of pregnancy from the categories specified in para.2 of Schedule 3 to the Employment Protection (Consolidation) Act, which determines the liability of an employer for the statutory minimum notice period, did not amount to discrimination on the ground of sex contrary to Article 141. Discrimination on grounds of sex means either that different rules are applied to men and women in comparable situations or that the same rule is applied to men and women in different situations. Women taking maternity leave, however, are in a special position, since men are never in a "comparable situation".

Redundancy payment

Barber v   **[1990] IRLR 240 ECJ**
Guardian Royal Exchange
   Assurance Group
Benefits paid by an employer to a worker in connection with the latter's compulsory redundancy fall within the scope of Article 141 of the EC Treaty, whether they are paid under a contract of employment, by virtue of legislative provisions or on a voluntary basis.

McKechnie v   **[1991] IRLR 283 EAT**
UBM Building Supplies (Southern) Ltd
The decision of the European Court in *Barber v Guardian Royal Exchange Assurance Group Ltd* removed any possible doubt that both a statutory redundancy payment and an ex-gratia payment based on the statutory payment provided by a collective agreement are properly to be regarded as coming within the definition of "pay" in Article 141.

Commission of the European   **[1993] IRLR 404 ECJ**
   Communities v
Kingdom of Belgium
Payments in addition to unemployment benefit provided under Belgian law to men who are made redundant between ages 60 and 65 constitute "pay" within the scope of Article 141 of the EC Treaty, rather than a social security benefit falling outside Article 141, since the payment is the responsibility of the last employer of the employee dismissed, is due by reason of the employment relationship which existed, and has its origins in an agreement between the social partners.

Rankin v   **[1993] IRLR 69 EAT**
British Coal Corporation
The general policy in legislation, concerned not only with redundancy but with similar statutory claims such as equal pay and racial and sexual discrimination provisions, suggests that a period for bringing claims directly under Article 141 in the region of three to six months could not properly be stigmatised as unreasonable, given that the starting date for the running of the period is also reasonable.

Rankin v   **[1993] IRLR 69 EAT**
British Coal Corporation
Balancing the requirements of certainty and the protection of rights under the Treaty, a claim in respect of a discriminatory statutory redundancy payment brought within a reasonable period of time after the coming into force of the amending legislation which removed the discrimination should be regarded as timeous.

Severance pay

Barry v   **[1999] IRLR 581 HL**
Midland Bank plc
A security of employment agreement, whereby severance pay was calculated on the basis of the employee's current pay at the date of termination, was not indirectly discriminatory against women contrary to Article 141, even though the scheme made no allowance for employees whose hours of work fluctuated, thereby disadvantaging part-time workers by not taking into account any full-time service they may have had. The scheme did not have a discriminatory effect and thus did not infringe the principle of equal pay for equal work, since the same rules applied to women and men, to both full-time and part-time workers.

Unfair dismissal compensation

R v   **[1999] IRLR 253 ECJ**
Secretary of State for Employment
   ex parte Seymour-Smith
An award of unfair dismissal compensation constitutes "pay" within the meaning of Article 141, since it is paid to the employee by reason of his employment, which would have continued but for the unfair dismissal.

R v   **[1999] IRLR 253 ECJ**
Secretary of State for Employment
   ex parte Seymour-Smith
The conditions determining whether an unfairly dismissed employee is entitled to compensation fall within the scope of Article 141 rather than the Equal Treatment Directive, since the condition concerns access to a form of pay. However, where a dismissed employee seeks reinstatement or re-engagement, the conditions laid down by national law concern working conditions or the right to take up employment and would therefore fall under the Equal Treatment Directive.

Travel facilities

Garland v   **[1982] IRLR 111 ECJ**
British Rail Engineering Ltd
Travel facilities accorded to employees after retirement are "pay" within the meaning of Article 141, so that an employer who provided special travel facilities for former male employees to enjoy after their retirement discriminated within the meaning of Article 141 against former female employees who did not receive the same facilities.

PRELIMINARY ISSUES

Definition of "employed"

(6) Subject to the following subsections, for purposes of this section –

> *(a) "employed" means employed under a contract of service or of apprenticeship or a contract personally to execute any work or labour, and related expressions shall be construed accordingly;*

EQUAL PAY ACT – s.1

Quinnen v Hovells   **[1984] IRLR 227 EAT**

The definition of "employed" in s.1(6)(a) of the Equal Pay Act covering employment under "a contract personally to execute any work or labour" is a wide and flexible concept and was intended to enlarge upon the ordinary connotation of "employment" so as to include persons outside the master-servant relationship. It covers a self-employed person engaged by the respondent on activity amounting to work or labour, who was engaged personally and was discharging such functions under terms which were contractual.

Claim in time

(1) Any claim in respect of the contravention of a term modified or included by virtue of an equality clause, including a claim for arrears of remuneration or damages in respect of the contravention, may be presented by way of a complaint to an industrial tribunal.

EQUAL PAY ACT – s.2

2(1) The following provisions –
> *(a) paragraph (2) of regulation 3, and*
> *(b) regulation 4,*

apply for the purpose of determining whether an employment tribunal may make a determination in proceedings instituted on or after the commencement date (subject to para. (2) below).

(2) Those provisions do not so apply if the last day on which the woman was employed in the employment falls more than six months before the commencement date.

(3) If those provisions do so apply so as to enable an employment tribunal to make a determination in proceedings in a stable employment case (within the meaning given by virtue of regulation 4), the determination may not relate to any non-qualifying contract of employment forming part of the stable employment relationship.

(4) For the purposes of para. (3) above a contract of employment is a non-qualifying contract of employment if it ended more than six months before the commencement date.

(5) The following provisions –
> *(a) paragraph (3) of regulation 3,*
> *(b) regulation 5,*

> *(c) paragraph (4) of regulation 6, and*
> *(d) regulation 8,*

apply in relation to proceedings instituted on or after the commencement date.

(6) The following provisions –
> *(a) para. (3) of regulation 6, and*
> *(b) regulation 7,*

apply for the purpose of determining whether an employment tribunal may make a determination on a complaint presented to it on or after the commencement date (subject to para.(7) below).

(7) Those provisions do not so apply if the last day of the woman's period of service falls more than nine months before the commencement date.

EQUAL PAY ACT 1970 (AMENDMENT) REGULATIONS 2003: Reg.2

(4) No determination may be made by an employment tribunal in the following proceedings –
> *(a) on a complaint under subsection (1) above,*
> *(b) on an application under subsection (1A) above, or*
> *(c) on a reference under subsection (2) above,*

unless the proceedings are instituted on or before the qualifying date (determined in accordance with section 2ZA below).

EQUAL PAY ACT (as amended) – s.2

(1) This section applies for the purpose of determining the qualifying date, in relation to proceedings in respect of a woman's employment, for the purposes of section 2(4) above.

(2) In this section –

"concealment case" means a case where –
> *(a) the employer deliberately concealed from the woman any fact (referred to in this section as a "qualifying fact") –*
> > *(i) which is relevant to the contravention to which the proceedings relate, and*
> > *(ii) without knowledge of which the woman could not reasonably have been expected to institute the proceedings, and*
> *(b) the woman did not discover the qualifying fact (or could not with reasonable diligence have discovered it) until after –*
> > *(i) the last day on which she was employed in the employment, or*
> > *(ii) the day on which the stable employment relationship between her and the employer ended,*
> *(as the case may be);*

"disability case" means a case where the woman was under a disability at any time during the six months after –
> *(a) the last day on which she was employed in the employment,*
> *(b) the day on which the stable employment relationship between her and the employer ended, or*
> *(c) the day on which she discovered (or could with reasonable diligence have discovered) the qualifying fact deliberately concealed from her by the employer (if that day falls after the day referred to in paragraph (a) or (b) above, as the case may be),*

"stable employment case" means a case where the proceedings relate to a period during which a stable employment relationship subsists between the woman and the employer, notwithstanding that the period includes any time after the ending of a contract of employment when no further contract of employment is in force;

"standard case" means a case which is not –

(a) a stable employment case,

(b) a concealment case,

(c) a disability case, or

(d) both a concealment and a disability case.

(3) In a standard case, the qualifying date is the date falling six months after the last day on which the woman was employed in the employment.

(4) In a case which is a stable employment case (but not also a concealment or a disability case or both), the qualifying date is the date falling six months after the day on which the stable employment relationship ended.

(5) In a case which is a concealment case (but not also a disability case), the qualifying date is the date falling six months after the day on which the woman discovered the qualifying fact in question (or could with reasonable diligence have discovered it).

(6) In a case which is a disability case (but not also a concealment case), the qualifying date is the date falling six months after the day on which the woman ceased to be under a disability.

(7) In a case which is both a concealment and a disability case, the qualifying date is the later of the dates referred to in subsections (5) and (6) above."

EQUAL PAY ACT (as amended) – s.2ZA

Preston v   **[2000] IRLR 506 ECJ**
Wolverhampton Healthcare NHS Trust
Community law does not preclude a national procedural rule, such as that contained in s.2(4) of the Equal Pay Act, which requires that a claim for membership of an occupational pension scheme must be brought within six months of the end of the employment to which the claim relates, provided that that limitation period is not less favourable for actions based on Community law than for those based on domestic law. The setting of reasonable limitation periods for bringing proceedings satisfies the Community law principle of effectiveness, inasmuch as it constitutes an application of the fundamental principle of legal certainty, even if expiry of the limitation period results in the dismissal of the claimant's action.

Preston v   **[2001] IRLR 237 HL**
Wolverhampton Healthcare
  NHS Trust (No.2)
The limitation under s.2(4) requiring a claim to be brought within six months of the end of the employment to which the claim relates, is not less favourable than the time limit of six years for bringing a claim for breach of contract. Therefore, s.2(4) does not breach the principle of equivalence.

Preston v   **[2004] IRLR 96 EAT**
Wolverhampton Healthcare NHS Trust (No.3)
The features that characterise a "stable employment relationship" are that there is (1) a succession of short-term contracts, meaning three or more contacts for an academic year or shorter; (2) concluded at regular intervals, in that they are clearly predictable and can be calculated precisely, or where the employee is called upon frequently whenever a need

arises; (3) relating to the same employment; and (4) to which the same pension scheme applies. A stable employment relationship ceases for this purpose when a succession of short-term contracts is superseded by a permanent contract.

Powerhouse Retail Ltd v   **[2004] IRLR 979 CA**
Burroughs
Where there has been a relevant transfer under the Transfer of Undertakings Regulations, time begins to run under s.2(4) of the Equal Pay Act, for the purposes of an equal pay claim against a transferor, from the date of the relevant TUPE transfer rather than from the end of an employee's employment with the transferee.

Kells v   **[2002] IRLR 693 EAT**
Pilkington plc
There is no rule of law restricting the period of events in respect of which an equal pay comparison can be made to six years before the date of the application.

Preston v   **[2000] IRLR 506 ECJ**
Wolverhampton Healthcare NHS Trust
Where there has been a stable employment relationship resulting from a succession of short-term contracts concluded at regular intervals in respect of the same employment to which the same pension scheme applies, Community law precludes a procedural rule, such as that contained in s.2(4) of the Equal Pay Act, which has the effect of requiring a claim for membership of an occupational pension scheme to be brought within six months of the end of each contract of employment to which the claim relates.

National Power plc v   **[2001] IRLR 32 CA**
Young
The word "employment" in s.2(4) does not relate to the particular job on which the woman bases her claim to an equality clause. "Employed in the employment" means employed under a contract of service.

Choice of comparator

Ainsworth v   **[1977] IRLR 74 EAT**
Glass Tubes & Components Ltd
An employment tribunal cannot substitute its own choice of comparator for the comparator selected by the applicant.

Thomas v   **[1978] IRLR 451 EAT**
National Coal Board
There is no requirement that the comparator selected by the applicant should be representative of a group.

Macarthys Ltd v   **[1980] IRLR 210 ECJ**
Smith
The principle of equal pay in Article 141 is not confined to situations in which men and women are contemporaneously

doing equal work and therefore applies where it is established that, having regard to the nature of her services, a woman has received less pay than a man who was employed prior to her employment and who did equal work for the employer.

Diocese of Hallam Trustee v Connaughton
[1996] IRLR 505 EAT

The scope of Article 141 includes equal pay complaints based upon the use of an immediate successor as a notional contemporaneous comparator. The decision in *Macarthys Ltd v Smith* that Article 141 is not confined to situations in which men and women are employed contemporaneously supports the view that an applicant is entitled to contend that the male successor's contract is so proximate to her own as to render him an effective comparator.

Pointon v The University of Sussex
[1979] IRLR 119 CA

A complaint under the Equal Pay Act must relate to a term in the applicant's contract of employment that is less favourable than the equivalent term in the contract of the man with whom she is comparing herself. The Equal Pay Act cannot be used to establish a claim that an applicant should have been paid more than her comparator.

Macarthys Ltd v Smith
[1980] IRLR 210 ECJ

Comparisons under Article 141 are confined to parallels which may be drawn on the basis of concrete appraisals of the work actually performed by employees of different sex within the same establishment or service.

Allonby v Accrington & Rossendale College
[2004] IRLR 224 ECJ

Although Article 141 is not limited to situations in which men and women work for the same employer and may be invoked in cases of discrimination arising directly from legislative provisions or collective agreements, as well as in cases in which work is carried out in the same establishment or service, where the differences identified in the pay conditions of workers performing equal work or work of equal value cannot be attributed to a single source, there is no body which is responsible for the inequality and which could restore equal treatment. Such a situation does not come within the scope of Article 141. Therefore, a woman whose contract of employment was not renewed and who was immediately made available to her previous employer through another undertaking to provide the same services was not entitled to rely on Article 141 in a claim against the new employer, using as a basis for comparison the remuneration received for equal work or work of the same value by a man employed by the woman's previous employer.

Scullard v Knowles
[1996] IRLR 344 EAT

The class of comparators under Article 141, as interpreted by the European Court of Justice, is broader than defined under s.1(6) of the Equal Pay Act. The crucial question for the purpose of Article 141, in accordance with the decision of the European Court in *Defrenne (No.2)*, is whether the applicant and her comparators are employed "in the same establishment or service". No distinction was drawn by the European Court between work carried out in the same establishment or service of limited companies and of other employers. To the extent that that is a wider class of comparators than is contained in s.1(6), s.1(6) is displaced and must yield to the paramount force of Article 141, which has direct effect as between individuals.

South Ayrshire Council v Morton
[2002] IRLR 256 CS

In determining whether men and women receive unequal pay for equal work, the scope of the inquiry is not always confined to the claimant's own workplace or to the claimant's own employer. If a case falls within para.21 of the decision in *Defrenne (No.2)*, as being direct discrimination having its origin in legislative provisions or in a collective agreement, a comparison is admissible and there is no need to apply the further test in para.22 of *Defrenne (No.2)* as to whether the work of the applicant and the work of the comparator is carried out in the same establishment or service.

South Ayrshire Council v Morton
[2002] IRLR 256 CS

An applicant and her comparator who are in the same branch of public service and who are subject to a uniform system of national pay and conditions set by a statutory body whose decision is binding on their employers are engaged in the same "service" in the sense in which that expression is used in *Defrenne (No.2)*. Therefore, a female headteacher employed by a local education authority in Scotland was entitled to bring an equal pay claim relying on Article 141 to compare herself with a male headteacher employed by a different education authority in Scotland.

South Ayrshire Council v Milligan
[2003] IRLR 153 CS

A comparator who is earning the same or less than the applicant is a valid comparator in a contingent equal pay claim, founded on the case of a comparator whose success in her own claim could result in discrimination against the applicant. Therefore, a male primary school headteacher was entitled to present his equal pay claim on a contingent basis, by naming as a comparator a female primary school headteacher whose pay currently was the same as his or less, and to have his case adjourned pending resolution of the comparator's equal pay claim comparing her work to that of male secondary school headteachers.

McLoughlin v Gordons (Stockport) Ltd
[1978] IRLR 127 EAT

A comparison, once made and adjudicated upon under the Equal Pay Act, is *res judicata* and cannot be heard again unless there can be shown to be some appreciable difference in the facts.

Common terms and conditions

(6)(c) two employers are to be treated as associated if one is a company of which the other (directly or indirectly) has control or if both are companies of which a third person (directly or indirectly) has control,

[and men shall be treated as in the same employment with a woman if they are men employed by her employer or any associated employer at the same establishment or at establishments in Great Britain which include that one and at which common terms and conditions of employment are observed either generally or for employees of the relevant classes . . .]

EQUAL PAY ACT – s.1

Lawson v   **[1988] IRLR 53 EAT**
Britfish Ltd
The phrase "and at which common terms and conditions of employment are observed" in s.1(6) of the Equal Pay Act does not relate to employment at the same establishment. It relates to other establishments outside the establishment at which the applicant is employed. Once it is found that the applicants and the comparator are employed at the same establishment, whether there are common terms and conditions does not arise.

Leverton v   **[1989] IRLR 28 HL**
Clwyd County Council
The comparison called for by s.1(6) is between the terms and conditions of employment observed at the establishment at which the woman is employed and the establishment at which the men are employed, and applicable either generally, ie to all the employees at the relevant establishments, or to a particular class or classes of employees to which both the woman and the men belong. The comparison is not between the terms and conditions of employment of the complainant on the one hand and of the comparators on the other. The concept of common terms and conditions of employment observed generally at different establishments necessarily contemplates terms and conditions applicable to a wide range of employees whose individual terms will vary greatly as between each other.

British Coal Corporation v   **[1996] IRLR 404 HL**
Smith
"Common terms and conditions of employment" within the meaning of s.1(6) of the Equal Pay Act means terms and conditions which are substantially comparable on a broad basis, rather than the same terms and conditions subject only to de minimis differences. It is sufficient for the applicant to show that her comparator at another establishment and at her establishment were or would be employed on broadly similar terms.

Leverton v   **[1989] IRLR 28 HL**
Clwyd County Council
Terms and conditions of employment governed by the same collective agreement represent the paradigm, though not necessarily the only example, of the common terms and conditions of employment contemplated by s.1(6). Therefore, a nursery nurse was entitled to bring an equal value complaint comparing her work with that of male clerical workers employed by the respondents in different establishments where she and her comparators were employed on terms and conditions derived from the same collective agreement, notwithstanding that there were differences between her hours of work and holiday entitlement and those of her comparators.

Thomas v   **[1987] IRLR 451 EAT**
National Coal Board
There were "common terms and conditions of employment" between establishments for the relevant employees, notwithstanding that locally negotiated and varying bonus payments and concessionary entitlements formed a substantial part of remuneration, where the entitlement to bonuses and concessions was negotiated nationally, and it was only the amount which varied locally, so that the basic similarity of terms and conditions was not affected.

Associated employers

Hasley v   **[1989] IRLR 106 NICA**
Fair Employment Agency
The first limb of the statutory definition of associated employers, correctly interpreted, means that two employers are to be treated as associated if one employer is a company of which the other employer (not necessarily a company) has control. The second limb covers where both employers are companies of which a third person (not necessarily a company) has control.

Hasley v   **[1989] IRLR 106 NICA**
Fair Employment Agency
A statutory body corporate is not a "company" within the meaning of the statutory definition of associated employers.

Discovery and further particulars

Byrne v   **[1991] IRLR 417 EAT**
The Financial Times Ltd
An employment tribunal chairman did not err in refusing to order the employers to supply, by way of further and better particulars of their material factor defence, a breakdown of the difference between the applicants' salaries and those of their comparators and an allocation of a specific sum to a particular fact in the work record or history of each comparator since, in reality, it is often impossible to attribute a particular percentage or amount to a specific part of the variation.

LIKE WORK

(4) A woman is to be regarded as employed on like work with men if, but only if, her work and theirs is of the same or a broadly similar nature, and the differences (if any) between the things she does and the things they do are not of practical importance in relation to terms and conditions of employment; and accordingly in comparing her work with theirs regard shall be had to the frequency or otherwise with which any such differences occur in practice as well as to the nature and extent of the differences.

EQUAL PAY ACT – s.1

General principles

Capper Pass Ltd v   **[1976] IRLR 366 EAT**
Lawton
Section 1(4) requires the determination of whether a man and a woman are employed on like work to be approached in two stages. First, is the work which she does and the work which he does of the same or of a broadly similar nature? This can be answered by a general consideration of the type of work involved and the skill and knowledge required to do it. Second, if it is work of a broadly similar nature, are the differences between the things she does and the things he does of practical importance in relation to terms and conditions of employment? Once it is determined that work is of a broadly similar nature, it should be regarded as being "like work" unless the differences are plainly of a kind which the employment tribunal in its experience would expect to find reflected in the terms and conditions of employment. Trivial differences, or differences not likely in the real world to be reflected in terms and conditions of employment, ought to be disregarded.

Capper Pass Ltd v   **[1976] IRLR 366 EAT**
Lawton
In deciding whether the work done by a woman and the work done by a man is "like work", the employment tribunal has to make a broad judgment. The intention is that the employment tribunal should not be required to undertake too minute an examination, nor be constrained to find that work is not like work, merely because of insubstantial differences.

Maidment and Hardacre v   **[1978] IRLR 462 EAT**
Cooper & Co (Birmingham) Ltd
The Equal Pay Act does not allow for a gap in remuneration to be narrowed so that it truly reflects the difference in the value of the work done by a claimant and her comparator. If the complainant and her comparator are not employed on like work, it is irrelevant that the gap in remuneration between them is in no way commensurate to the difference in the work which they do.

Differences of practical importance

E Coomes (Holdings) Ltd v   **[1978] IRLR 263 CA**
Shields
Section 1(4) requires a comparison to be made between the things that the woman and the man actually do and the frequency with which they are done, rather than between their respective contractual obligations.

Electrolux Ltd v   **[1976] IRLR 410 EAT**
Hutchinson
For differences in contractual obligations to amount to a difference of practical importance in relation to terms and conditions within the meaning of s.1(4), it must be shown that, as well as being contractually obliged to do additional different duties, the duties are performed to some significant extent.

British Leyland Ltd v   **[1978] IRLR 57 EAT**
Powell
In determining under s.1(4) whether differences in the things done by a man and those done by a woman are of "practical importance in relation to terms and conditions of employment", a practical guide is whether the differences (which ex hypothesi are not sufficient to make the work not of the same or a broadly similar nature) are such as to put the two employments into different categories or grades in an evaluation study.

Responsibility

Eaton Ltd v   **[1977] IRLR 71 EAT**
Nuttall
In considering whether there is like work, the circumstances in which the man and the woman do their work should not be disregarded. One of the circumstances properly to be taken into account is the degree of responsibility involved in carrying out the job. A factor such as responsibility may be decisive where it can be seen to put one employee into a different grade from another with whom comparisons are being made.

Waddington v   **[1977] IRLR 32 EAT**
Leicester Council for Voluntary
  Services
An obligation to supervise, to take responsibility or to control, if it is discharged, falls within the words "the things she does and the things they do".

Thomas v   **[1987] IRLR 451 EAT**
National Coal Board
The additional responsibility entailed in working permanently at night, alone and without supervision can amount to a "difference of practical importance in relation to terms and conditions of employment".

Time of work

Dugdale v   **[1976] IRLR 368 EAT**
Kraft Foods Ltd
In determining whether men and women are employed on like work, the mere time at which the work is performed should be disregarded when considering for the purposes of s.1(4), the differences between the things that the women do and the things which the men do.

Electrolux Ltd v   **[1976] IRLR 410 EAT**
Hutchinson
If the basic rate payable to the men, unlike that payable to the women, reflects some additional element of remuneration attributable to an obligation to work at nights or on Sundays (over and above any shift or Sunday shift premium payable), that fact can be reflected in the way in which the equality clause is applied – ie, it can be discounted so that the equality clause is applied not to produce equality, but so that the woman is not treated less favourably.

National Coal Board v   **[1978] IRLR 122 EAT**
Sherwin
If the man and the woman do the same work, the mere fact that they do it at different times is of no importance. The disadvantage of working at night, or at other inconvenient times, can be compensated by an additional night shift premium or other appropriate arrangement, but there is no reason why the man should receive by way of remuneration a sum which is greater than necessary to recognise the fact that he works at night, or at other inconvenient times, and if he does there is no reason why the woman should not be remunerated to the extent of the excess. An employment tribunal is entitled to adjust the woman's remuneration upon a claim by her so that it is at the same rate as the man's, discounting for the fact that he works at inconvenient hours, and she does not.

Maidment and Hardacre v   **[1978] IRLR 462 EAT**
Cooper & Co (Birmingham) Ltd
In applying the test of like work, it is not permissible to ignore some part of the work which the man actually does on the ground that his pay includes an additional element in respect of that work, which can be discounted. There is no warrant for the exclusion or hiving-off of some part of the activities of the comparator. There can be no question of discounting, or of applying the equality clause, until it has been established that the man and the woman are employed on like work, so that it cannot be right in order to determine that question to pray in aid a result which could only be arrived at after deciding that they were engaged on like work.

WORK RATED AS EQUIVALENT

(5) A woman is to be regarded as employed on work rated as equivalent with that of any men if, but only if, her job and their job have been given an equal value, in terms of the demand made on a worker under various headings (for instance effort, skill, decision), on a study undertaken with a view to evaluating in those terms the jobs to be done by all or any of the employees in an undertaking or group of undertakings, or would have been given an equal value but for the evaluation being made on a system setting different values for men and women on the same demand under any heading.

                EQUAL PAY ACT – s.1

Bromley v   **[1988] IRLR 249 CA**
H & J Quick Ltd
A job evaluation scheme must be "analytical" in order to comply with the provisions of s.1(5). The word "analytical" indicates conveniently the general nature of what is required by the section, viz that the jobs of each worker covered by the study must have been valued in terms of the demand made on the worker under various headings. It is not enough that benchmark jobs have been evaluated on a factor demand basis as required by s.1(5) if the jobs of the applicants and their comparators were not.

Bromley v   **[1988] IRLR 249 CA**
H & J Quick Ltd
Per Woolf LJ: In order to comply with s.1(5), employers can identify a group of jobs which when evaluated under the headings have no material difference. Then one of that group of jobs can be evaluated under headings and slotted into the rank in the appropriate position, having taken into account the factor value, and that job can then represent the other jobs within the group. If, however, a system of choosing a representative job for a group of jobs is adopted, then in relation to a job which has not been evaluated under headings it will be open to an employee to contend that his or her job is materially different from the alleged representative job and, if this is the case, the study will not comply with s.1(5).

Eaton Ltd v   **[1977] IRLR 71 EAT**
Nuttall
Section 1(5) can only apply to a valid evaluation study – that is, a study satisfying the test of being thorough in analysis and capable of impartial application. It should be possible by applying the study to arrive at the position of a particular employee at a particular point in a particular salary grade without taking other matters into account, except those unconnected with the nature of the work. An evaluation study which does not satisfy that test, and which requires the management to make a subjective judgment concerning the nature of the work before the employee can be fitted in at the appropriate place in the appropriate salary grade would not be a valid study for the purposes of s.1(5).

Arnold v   **[1982] IRLR 307 EAT**
Beecham Group Ltd

Before s.1(5) can be applied, there must be a completed job evaluation study, and there is no complete job evaluation study unless and until the parties who have agreed to carry out the study have accepted its validity. However, it is not the stage of implementing the study by using it as the basis of the payment of remuneration that makes it complete; it is the stage at which it is accepted as a study.

O'Brien v   **[1980] IRLR 373 HL**
Sim-Chem Ltd

Once a job evaluation study has been undertaken and has resulted in a conclusion that the job of a woman is of equal value with that of a man, then a comparison of their respective terms and conditions is made feasible and, subject to s.1(3), the equality clause can take effect. It is not necessary for the pay structure to have been adjusted as a result of the conclusions of the job evaluation study.

Springboard Sunderland Trust v   **[1992] IRLR 261 EAT**
Robson

In determining whether two jobs have been given an equal value within the meaning of s.1(5), so as to be work rated as equivalent, it is necessary to have regard to the full results of the job evaluation scheme, including the allocation to grade or scale at the end of the evaluation process.

Eaton Ltd v   **[1977] IRLR 71 EAT**
Nuttall

It is the duty of employers in Equal Pay Act cases to come to the employment tribunal hearing with the relevant information prepared in a comprehensive and readily assimilable form, including adequate details of any job evaluation system or other payment method in use.

EQUAL VALUE

(2) An equality clause is a provision which relates to terms (whether concerned with pay or not) of a contract under which a woman is employed (the "woman's contract"), and has the effect that –

[(c) where a woman is employed on work which, not being work in relation to which paragraph (a) or (b) above applies, is, in terms of the demands made on her (for instance under such headings as effort, skill and decision), of equal value to that of a man in the same employment –

(i) if (apart from the equality clause) any term of the woman's contract is or becomes less favourable to the woman than a term of a similar kind in the contract under which that man is employed, that term of the woman's contract shall be treated as so modified as not to be less favourable, and

(ii) if (apart from the equality clause) at any time the woman's contract does not include a term corresponding to a term benefiting that man included in the contract under which he is employed, the woman's contract shall be treated as including such a term.]

                       EQUAL PAY ACT – s.1

Commission of the European   **[1982] IRLR 333 ECJ**
   Communities v
United Kingdom of Great Britain
   and Northern Ireland

Implementation of the EC Equal Pay Directive's principle of equal pay for work of equal value requires that where there is disagreement as to the application of that concept a worker must be entitled to claim before an appropriate authority that his work has the same value as other work and, if that is found to be the case, to have his rights under the EC Treaty and the Directive acknowledged by a binding decision. Any method which excludes that option prevents the aims of the Directive from being achieved.

Scope for comparison

Pickstone v   **[1988] IRLR 357 HL**
Freemans plc

Section 1(2)(c) of the Equal Pay Act as amended does not preclude a woman employed on like work or work rated as equivalent with one man within the meaning of s.1(2)(a) or (b) of the Act from claiming that she is employed on work of equal value to that of another man. The words "not being work to which para. (a) or (b) above applies" in s.1(2)(c) have effect only where the particular man with whom the woman seeks to compare herself is employed on like work or work rated as equivalent.

Murphy v   **[1988] IRLR 267 ECJ**
Bord Telecom Eireann

Article 141 of the EC Treaty must be interpreted as covering the case where a worker who relies on that provision to obtain equal pay within the meaning thereof is engaged in work of higher value than that of the person with whom a comparison is to be made.

Job evaluation

(2) Subsection (2A) below applies in a case where –
(a) a tribunal is required to determine whether any work is of equal value as mentioned in s.1(2)(c) above, and
(b) the work of the woman and that of the man in question have been given different values on a study such as is mentioned in s.1(5) above.

(2A) The tribunal shall determine that the work of the woman and that of the man are not of equal value unless the tribunal has reasonable grounds for suspecting that the evaluation contained in the study –
(a) was (within the meaning of subsection (3) below) made on a system which discriminates on grounds of sex, or
(b) is otherwise unsuitable to be relied upon.

(3) An evaluation contained in a study such as is mentioned in s.1(5) above is made on a system which discriminates on grounds of sex where a difference, or coincidence, between values set by that system on different demands under the same or different headings is not justifiable irrespective of the sex of the person on whom those demands are made.

EQUAL PAY ACT (as amended) – s.2A

The principle of equal pay for men and women outlined in Article 141 of the Treaty, hereinafter called "principle of equal pay", means, for the same work or for work to which equal value is attributed, the elimination of all discrimination on grounds of sex with regard to all aspects and conditions of remuneration.

In particular, where a job classification system is used for determining pay, it must be based on the same criteria for both men and women and so drawn up as to exclude any discrimination on grounds of sex.

EQUAL PAY DIRECTIVE – Article 1

Burden of proof

Dibro Ltd v　　　　　　　　　　**[1990] IRLR 129 EAT**
Hore
Provided that a job evaluation scheme is analytical and a valid one within s.1(5) and relates to facts and circumstances existing at the time when the equal value proceedings were instituted, it does not matter that it came into existence after the initiation of proceedings. It is open to an employer to utilise such a scheme as evidence at any stage up to the final hearing, after the independent expert's report has been admitted, at which the tribunal gives its decision on the whole of the evidence.

Work rated unequal

Bromley v　　　　　　　　　　**[1988] IRLR 249 CA**
H & J Quick Ltd
Section 1(5) requires a study undertaken with a view to evaluating jobs in terms of the demand made on a worker under various headings (for instance effort, skill, decision). It is necessary that both the work of the woman complainant and the work of her male comparator should have been valued in such terms of demand made on the worker under various headings.

Dibro Ltd v　　　　　　　　　　**[1990] IRLR 129 EAT**
Hore
A job evaluation scheme advanced by the employer must compare the jobs as they were being carried out at the date the proceedings were issued and not compare a job or jobs which may have been changed since the initiation of proceedings.

McAuley v　　　　　　　　　　**[1991] IRLR 467 NICA**
Eastern Health and Social
　Services Board
Per Sir Brian Hutton LCJ: A job evaluation study does not apply to employees unless they are employees in the undertaking or group of undertakings in respect of which the study was undertaken.

Bromley v　　　　　　　　　　**[1988] IRLR 249 CA**
H & J Quick Ltd
There was not "a study such as is mentioned in s.1(5)" where the jobs of the women and their comparators were slotted into the structure on a "whole job" basis and no comparison was made by reference to the selected factors between the demands made on the individual workers under the selected headings. That at an appeal stage two of the women's jobs were evaluated in terms of their demands under the selected factors made no difference to the outcome in their cases, since there was never any appeal by their comparator. Nor was it sufficient that every worker covered by the study had a right of appeal which if exercised would have led to an analysis of their jobs.

Bromley v　　　　　　　　　　**[1988] IRLR 249 CA**
H & J Quick Ltd
The good intentions of the parties to a job evaluation to avoid sex discrimination are of relatively minor importance when the question is whether the procedures followed in a job evaluation study matched up to the requirements of the Act as amended.

Avon County Council v　　　　　　**[1989] IRLR 435 EAT**
Foxall
An employment tribunal has a discretion whether or not to grant a stay of proceedings pending implementation of a job evaluation scheme. However, a claimant has a

prima facie right to prosecute her claim under the Act and there was not much force in the argument that there was a risk of a job evaluation scheme being undermined if the results of the independent expert's report were more favourable to the claimant than the result of the job evaluation.

Discriminatory evaluation

Rummler v   **[1987] IRLR 32 ECJ**
Dato-Druck GmbH

Article 1(2) of the EC Equal Pay Directive, which provides that a job classification system "must be based on the same criteria for both men and women and so drawn up as to exclude any discrimination on grounds of sex", requires that the system must be based on criteria which do not differ according to whether the work is carried out by a man or by a woman and must not be organised, as a whole, in such a manner that it has the practical effect of discriminating generally against workers of one sex.

Rummler v   **[1987] IRLR 32 ECJ**
Dato-Druck GmbH

In determining rates of pay, it is consistent with the principle of non-discrimination to use a criterion based on the objectively measurable expenditure of effort necessary in carrying out the work or the degree to which, viewed objectively, the work is physically heavy, even where the criterion may in fact tend to favour male workers. A job classification system is not discriminatory within the meaning of Article 1(2) of the EC Equal Pay Directive solely because one of its criteria is based on characteristics more commonly found among men than among women. However, if a job classification system is not to be discriminatory overall, it must be so designed, if the nature of the work so permits, as to take into account other criteria for which female employees may show particular aptitude.

Rummler v   **[1987] IRLR 32 ECJ**
Dato-Druck GmbH

The use of values reflecting the average performance of workers of one sex as a basis for determining the extent to which work makes demands or requires effort, or whether it is heavy, constitutes a form of discrimination on grounds of sex contrary to the Equal Pay Directive.

INDEPENDENT EXPERT'S REPORT

Leverton v   **[1989] IRLR 28 HL**
Clwyd County Council

An independent expert has to carry out what is, in effect, an ad hoc job evaluation study as between a complainant and her comparators and assess the demands of the job on a qualitative, rather than a quantitative, basis.

Leverton v   **[1989] IRLR 28 HL**
Clwyd County Council

Per Lord Bridge: Differences in hours of work and holidays between a complainant and her comparators are not a matter for assessment by the independent expert when considering the "demands" made upon them by their respective jobs.

Tennants Textile Colours Ltd v   **[1989] IRLR 3 NICA**
Todd

The burden of proving a claim under the Equal Pay Act is on the applicant. The burden of proof is not transferred to the employer if the independent expert's report is in favour of the applicant.

[(3) An equality clause shall not operate in relation to a variation between the woman's contract and the man's contract if the employer proves that the variation is genuinely due to a material factor which is not the difference of sex and that factor –

> *(a) in the case of an equality clause falling within subsection (2)(a) or (b) above, must be a material difference between the woman's case and the man's; and*
> *(b) in the case of an equality clause falling within subsection (2)(c) above, may be such a material difference.]*

EQUAL PAY ACT – s.1

Burden of proof

Enderby v   **[1993] IRLR 591 ECJ**
Frenchay Health Authority and
   Secretary of State for Health
Where there is a prima facie case of discrimination, Article 141 of the EC Treaty requires the employer to show that the difference in pay is based on objectively justified factors unrelated to any discrimination on grounds of sex. Workers would be unable to enforce the principle of equal pay before national courts if evidence of a prima facie case did not shift to the employer the onus of showing that the pay differential is not in fact discriminatory.

Brunnhofer v   **[2001] IRLR 571 ECJ**
Bank der österreichischen Postsparkasse
If the employee adduces evidence to show that the criteria for establishing the existence of a difference in pay between a woman and a man and for identifying comparable work are satisfied, a prima facie case of discrimination would exist, and it is then for the employer to prove that there was no breach of the principle of equal pay. To do this, the employer could deny that the conditions for the application of the principle were met, by establishing that the activities actually performed by the two employees were not in fact comparable. The employer could also justify the difference in pay by objective factors, by proving that there was a difference unrelated to sex to explain the comparator's higher pay.

Glasgow City Council v   **[2000] IRLR 272 HL**
Marshall
An employer who proves the absence of sex discrimination, direct or indirect, is under no obligation to prove a "good" reason for the pay disparity.

Strathclyde Regional Council v   **[1998] IRLR 146 HL**
Wallace
Section 1(3) provides a defence if the employer shows that the variation between the woman's contract and the man's contract is "genuinely" due to a factor which is (a) material and (b) not the difference of sex. The requirement of genuineness is satisfied if the tribunal comes to the conclusion that the reason put forward was not a sham or pretence. For the matters relied upon to constitute "material factors", it has to be shown that they were in fact causally relevant to the difference in pay, ie that they were significant factors. This is a test which looks to the reason why there is a disparity in pay and not to whether there is an excuse for such disparity. Finally, the employer has to show that the disparity in pay is due to a factor "which is not the difference of sex", ie is not directly or indirectly sexually discriminatory.

Glasgow City Council v   **[2000] IRLR 272 HL**
Marshall
If there is any evidence of sex discrimination, such as evidence that the difference in pay has a disparately adverse impact on women, the employer will be called upon to satisfy the tribunal that the difference in pay is objectively justifiable.

Barry v   **[1999] IRLR 581 HL**
Midland Bank plc
A claim of indirect discrimination contrary to Article 141 requires the applicant to show that she belongs to a group of employees which is differently and less well-treated than others, and that that difference affects considerably more women than men. If she can, the employer must show that the difference in treatment is objectively justified.

Nelson v   **[2003] IRLR 428 CA**
Carillion Services Ltd
In a case of alleged indirect discrimination under s.1(3), the complainant has the burden of proving on the balance of probabilities that the matter complained of has had a disproportionate adverse impact. It is for the claimant to provide the necessary statistics, seeking if necessary the relevant information from the employer.

Barton v   **[2003] IRLR 332 EAT**
Investec Henderson Crosthwaite Securities Ltd
In accordance with the decision of the European Court of Justice in *Brunnhofer v Bank der Österreichischen Postsparkasse AG*, there is a burden on an employer seeking to establish a material factor defence to prove that there were objective reasons for the difference; unrelated to sex; corresponding to a real need on the part of the undertaking; appropriate to achieving the objective pursued; and that it was necessary to that end; that the difference conformed to the principle of proportionality; and that that was the case throughout the period during which the differential existed.

Parliamentary Commissioner   **[2004] IRLR 22 EAT**
   for Administration v
Fernandez
The decision of the European Court of Justice in *Brunnhofer* did not alter the approach to be taken by employment tribunals, following the guidance of the House of Lords in *Strathclyde Regional Council v Wallace* and *Glasgow City*

Council v Marshall, when considering an employer's genuine material factor defence under s.1(3) of the Equal Pay Act that no requirement of objective justification arises in the absence of prima facie indirect discrimination. The Court in *Brunnhofer* was not laying down a requirement that in a case where the factor relied on by the employer is not tainted by direct sex discrimination, and no suggestion of prima facie indirect sex discrimination is raised, that it is nevertheless necessary for the employer to objectively justify the pay difference.

Schonheit v   **[2004] IRLR 983 ECJ**
Stadt Frankfurt am Main
A difference in treatment between men and women may be justified, depending on the circumstances, by reasons other than those put forward when the measure introducing the differential treatment was adopted. It is for the Member State which has introduced such a measure, or the party who invokes it, to establish before the national court that there are objective reasons unrelated to any discrimination on grounds of sex such as to justify the measure concerned, and they are not bound in that respect by the intention expressed when the measure was adopted.

Cadman v   **[2004] IRLR 971 CA**
Health and Safety Executive
There is no rule of law that the justification must have consciously and contemporaneously featured in the decision-making processes of the employer, and cannot be "after the event" arguments.

Tyldesley v   **[1996] IRLR 395 EAT**
TML Plastics Ltd
A differential which is explained by careless mistake, which could not possibly be objectively justified, amounts to a defence, provided the tribunal is satisfied that the mistake was of sufficient influence to be significant or relevant. If a genuine mistake suffices, so must a genuine perception, whether reasonable or not, about the need to engage an individual with particular experience, commitment and skills.

Methven v   **[1980] IRLR 289 CA**
Cow Industrial Polymers Ltd
The words "due to" in s.1(3) indicate that the question is one of causation, and like all questions of causation is a question of fact and degree.

Grounds for the pay difference

Bilka-Kaufhaus GmbH v   **[1986] IRLR 317 ECJ**
Weber von Hartz
A policy which applies independently of a worker's sex but in fact affects more women than men will not constitute an infringement of Article 141 if the employer shows that the policy is objectively justified on economic grounds. This requires a finding by the national court that the measures chosen by the employer correspond to a real need on the part of the undertaking, are appropriate with a view to achieving the objectives pursued and are necessary to that end.

Rainey v   **[1987] IRLR 26 HL**
Greater Glasgow Health Board
Although the European Court in the *Bilka-Kaufhaus* case referred to "economic" grounds objectively justified, read as a whole the ruling of the European Court would not exclude objectively justified grounds which are other than economic, such as administrative efficiency in a concern not engaged in commerce or business.

Cadman v   **[2004] IRLR 971 CA**
Health and Safety Executive
As reformulated by the Court of Appeal in *Barry v Midland Bank plc*, the test for objective justification set out in the *Bilka Kaufhaus* decision is whether the means used are "reasonably necessary". The difference between "necessary" and "reasonably necessary" is a significant one. The test does not require the employer to establish that the measure complained of was "necessary" in the sense of being the only course open to him.

Rainey v   **[1987] IRLR 26 HL**
Greater Glasgow Health Board
The true meaning and effect of Article 141 in the context of the employer's defence is the same as that correctly attributed to s.1(3) of the Equal Pay Act by the EAT in *Jenkins v Kingsgate (Clothing) Productions (No.2)*.

Specialarbejderforbundet   **[1995] IRLR 648 ECJ**
  i Danmark v
Dansk Industri,
  acting for Royal Copenhagen
It is for the national court to ascertain whether, in the light of the facts relating to the nature of the work carried out and the conditions in which it is carried out, equal value may be attributed to it, or whether those facts may be considered to be objective factors unrelated to discrimination on grounds of sex such as to justify any pay differentials.

Rainey v   **[1987] IRLR 26 HL**
Greater Glasgow Health Board
A difference between the woman's case and the man's must be "material", which means "significant and relevant".

Rainey v   **[1987] IRLR 26 HL**
Greater Glasgow Health Board
A relevant difference for the purposes of s.1(3) may relate to circumstances other than the personal qualifications or merits of the male and female workers who are the subject of comparison. Consideration of a difference between "her case and his" must necessarily involve consideration of all the circum-

stances of that case. These may go beyond the personal qualities by way of skill, experience or training which the individual brings to the job.

Waddington v   **[1977] IRLR 32 EAT**
Leicester Council for Voluntary
  Services
Usually the material difference within s.1(3) will be something other than the differences considered under s.1(4), and will not be differences between the things the woman does and the things the man does in the course of the work.

Davies v   **[1989] IRLR 439 EAT**
McCartneys
There is no limitation upon the factors relevant to a consideration of a defence under s.1(3). The factors which form the basis for a defence under s.1(3) can also be factors relevant in determining the demands of the jobs for the purpose of assessing equal value. However, an employer should not be allowed simply to say, "I value one demand factor so highly that I pay more," unless his true reason for so doing is one which is found by the tribunal to be genuine and not attributable to sex.

Christie v   **[2003] IRLR 670 EAT**
John E Haith
In accordance with the decision of the EAT in *Davies v McCartneys*, the mere fact that a particular factor may be relevant in the evaluation exercise to determine the question of equal value is no ground for excluding it as a defence which may be relied on by the employer under s.1(3), and may be taken into account by the tribunal in considering whether the employer's pay differential is justified or not on grounds other than sex. Therefore, an employment tribunal did not err in dismissing the appellants' equal value complaints on grounds that the physical effort and unpleasantness involved in the work of their male comparators was a genuine material difference accounting for the differential in pay within the meaning of s.1(3)

Benveniste v   **[1989] IRLR 123 CA**
University of Southampton
A material factor defence "evaporates" when the justification for it has disappeared.

Sex discrimination

British Coal Corporation v   **[1994] IRLR 342 CA**
Smith
North Yorkshire County Council v
Ratcliffe
There cannot be a "material factor" defence under s.1(3) of the Equal Pay Act in any case where the facts establish direct discrimination within s.1(1)(a) of the Sex Dis-

crimination Act, since an employer who treats a woman less favourably than a man "on the grounds of her sex" cannot assert that the difference between their terms of employment is due to a material factor which is not the difference of sex. Therefore, a "material factor" defence must fail if the employer cannot prove that the material factor relied upon was not tainted by sex.

Glasgow City Council v   **[2000] IRLR 272 HL**
Marshall
In order to discharge the burden of showing that the explanation for the variation is not tainted with sex the employer must satisfy the tribunal on several matters. First, that the proffered explanation, or reason, is genuine, and not a sham or pretence. Second, that the less favourable treatment is due to this reason. The factor relied upon must be the cause of the disparity. The factor must be "material" in a causative sense, rather than in a justificatory sense. Third, that the reason is not "the difference of sex", which is apt to embrace any form of sex discrimination, whether direct or indirect. Fourth, that the factor relied upon is a "material" difference, that is or, in a case within s.1(2)(c), may be, a significant and relevant difference, between the woman's case and the man's case.

Ministry of Defence v   **[2004] IRLR 672 EAT**
Armstrong
The concept of indirect discrimination under the Equal Pay Act is broader than that which applies under the Sex Discrimination Act. In considering s.1(3), the fundamental question is whether there is a causative link between the applicant's sex and the fact that she is paid less than the true value of her job as reflected in the pay of her named comparator. If the material cause of the pay difference between the applicant and her comparator is tainted by sex-related factors, then the defence fails. This link may be established in a variety of different ways, depending on the facts of the case. There is no necessity for an employment tribunal, as a matter of law, always to adopt a formulaic approach, consistent with the provisions of s.1(1)(b) of the Sex Discrimination Act (and since 12 October 2001, s.1(2)), in considering whether there is sex-related pay discrimination and disparate impact for the purposes of s.1(3).

Snoxell v   **[1977] IRLR 123 EAT**
Vauxhall Motors Ltd
An employer can never establish that a variation between the woman's contract and the man's contract is genuinely due to a material difference (other than the difference of sex) between her case and his when it can be seen that past sex discrimination has contributed to the variation.

E Coomes (Holdings) Ltd v   **[1978] IRLR 263 CA**
Shields
The Equal Pay Act and the Sex Discrimination Act form two complementary parts of a single comprehensive code directed against sex discrimination. Both Acts should be

construed and applied as a harmonious whole and in such a way that the broad principles which underlie the whole scheme of legislation are not frustrated by a narrow interpretation or restrictive application of particular provisions.

Specific defences

Collective agreements

Enderby v   **[1993] IRLR 591 ECJ**
Frenchay Health Authority and
   Secretary of State for Health
The fact that the respective rates of pay of two jobs of equal value, one carried out almost exclusively by women and the other predominantly by men, were arrived at by collective bargaining processes which, although carried out by the same parties, were distinct, and conducted separately and without any discriminatory effect within each group, is not sufficient objective justification for the difference in pay between those two jobs.

British Road Services Ltd v   **[1997] IRLR 92 NICA**
Loughran
Separate pay structures based on different collective agreements are not a sufficient defence under s.1(3) if the applicants are members of a class of which a "significant" number are female. The European Court's use of the term "almost exclusively" women in *Enderby* was merely a reference to the facts of that case and did not intend to propound a principle that unless the disadvantaged group could be described as being composed "almost exclusively" of females, a presumption of discrimination could not arise.

Home Office v   **[2004] IRLR 921 EAT**
Bailey
In considering whether a disparity of pay which has arisen as between two work groups by reason of a history of different arrangements for collective bargaining evidences sex discrimination, a prima facie case will be established if the advantaged group is predominantly male and the disadvantaged group is predominantly female. Where, however, the disadvantaged group is neutral in gender terms, then the situation may not be fair, but it is not prima facie discriminatory on grounds of sex.

Specialarbejderforbundet   **[1995] IRLR 648 ECJ**
   i Danmark v
Dansk Industri,
   acting for Royal Copenhagen
The fact that rates of pay have been determined by collective bargaining or by negotiation at local level may be taken into account by the national court as a factor in its assessment of whether differences between the average pay of two groups of workers are due to objective factors unrelated to any discrimination on grounds of sex.

Barber v   **[1993] IRLR 95 EAT**
NCR (Manufacturing) Ltd
Evidence explaining the historical process by which a difference in hourly rates had been arrived at did not show any objective factor which justified the result which had been produced.

Grading

National Vulcan Engineering   **[1978] IRLR 225 CA**
   Insurance Group Ltd v
Wade
A grading system according to skill, ability and experience is an integral part of good business management and as long as it is fairly and genuinely applied irrespective of sex, it cannot be held to infringe the Equal Pay Act.

Separate pay structures

British Coal Corporation v   **[1996] IRLR 404 HL**
Smith
The simple existence of separate pay structures is not in itself a defence under s.1(3). What must be determined is whether the justification for the differences in benefits received by the applicants and their comparators satisfy objective criteria and was not one which occurred because of a difference of sex.

Administrative convenience

Barry v   **[1998] IRLR 138 CA**
Midland Bank plc
Administrative convenience is an objective reason unconnected with the difference in sex.

Legal requirements

R v   **[1988] IRLR 22 DC**
Secretary of State for Social Services
   ex parte Clarke
That an employer is bound by statutory instrument to pay the salaries paid is not in itself a "material factor" defence to an equal pay claim.

Quality of work

Handels- og Kontorfunktionaerernes   **[1989] IRLR 532 ECJ**
   Forbund i Danmark v
Dansk Arbejdsgiverforening
   (acting for Danfoss)

The EC Equal Pay Directive must be interpreted as meaning that the quality of the work carried out by the worker may not be used as a criterion for pay increments where its application shows itself to be systematically unfavourable to women. Where an assessment of the quality of work results in systematic unfairness to female workers, that could only be because the employer applied the criterion in an abusive manner. It is inconceivable that the work carried out by female workers would be generally of a lower quality.

Additional obligations

Handels- og Kontorfunktionaerernes [1989] IRLR 532 ECJ
Forbund i Danmark v
Dansk Arbejdsgiverforening
(acting for Danfoss)
The EC Equal Pay Directive must be interpreted as meaning that where the adaptability of the employee to variable work schedules and places of work is used as a criterion for pay increments and this works systematically to the disadvantage of female workers who, as a result of household and family duties, may have greater difficulty than male workers in organising their working time in a flexible manner, the employer may justify the use of the criterion by demonstrating that such adaptability is important for the performance of the specific duties entrusted to the worker.

National Coal Board v   [1978] IRLR 122 EAT
Sherwin
While the mere fact that work is done at different times is irrelevant for the purposes of s.1(4), it does not follow that once like work has been established an employer, in seeking to set up an answer under s.1(3), cannot put forward as constituting a "material difference" circumstances which may include the fact that the man and the woman work at different times.

National Coal Board v   [1978] IRLR 122 EAT
Sherwin
An employment tribunal that found that a difference between the woman's pay and the pay of a man employed on like work was greater than could be justified by the fact that the man worked permanently on the night shift alone was entitled to conclude that the employers had failed to show that the difference to which the variation in pay was genuinely due was other than a difference of sex. The tribunal were therefore entitled to order that the women should be paid at the same rate as the man after making a proper, but not excessive, discount for the fact that he worked permanently at night alone.

Edmonds v   [1977] IRLR 359 EAT
Computer Services (South-West) Ltd
Higher pay because of the potential to exercise responsibility may be a "material difference" under s.1(3).

Training

Handels- og Kontorfunktionaerernes [1989] IRLR 532 ECJ
Forbund i Danmark v
Dansk Arbejdsgiverforening
(acting for Danfoss)
The EC Equal Pay Directive must be interpreted as meaning that where the worker's vocational training is used as a criterion for pay increments and this works systematically to the disadvantage of female workers, the employer may justify the use of the criterion of vocational training by demonstrating that such training is important for the performance of specific duties entrusted to the worker.

Service payments

Handels- og Kontorfunktionaerernes [1989] IRLR 532 ECJ
Forbund i Danmark v
Dansk Arbejdsgiverforening
(acting for Danfoss)
The EC Equal Pay Directive must be interpreted as meaning that the employer does not need to give any specific justification for using the worker's seniority as a criterion for pay increments, even though the criterion of seniority may result in less favourable treatment of female workers than of male workers.

Nimz v   [1991] IRLR 222 ECJ
Freie und Hansestadt Hamburg
Article 141 precludes a collective agreement from providing for the service of full-time workers to be fully taken into account for reclassification to a higher salary grade, where only one half of such service is taken into account in the case of part-time workers and the latter group comprises a considerably smaller percentage of men than women, unless the employer can prove that such a provision is objectively justified by the relationship between the nature of the duties performed and the experience afforded by the performance of those duties after a certain number of working hours have been worked. Although seniority goes hand in hand with experience which, in principle, should allow the employee to carry out his tasks all the better, the objectivity of such a criterion depends on all the circumstances in each case.

Hill v   [1998] IRLR 466 ECJ
Revenue Commissioners
Rules which treat full-time workers who previously job-shared at a disadvantage compared with other full-time workers by applying a criterion of service calculated by length of time actually worked in a post, and therefore placing them on the full-time pay scale at a level lower

than that which they occupied on the pay scale applicable to job-sharing, must in principle be treated as contrary to Article 141 and the Equal Pay Directive, where 98% of those employed under job-sharing contracts are women.

Hill v   **[1998] IRLR 466 ECJ**
Revenue Commissioners
An employer cannot justify discrimination arising from a job-sharing scheme solely on the ground that avoidance of such discrimination would involve increased costs.

Protected pay

Snoxell v   **[1977] IRLR 123 EAT**
Vauxhall Motors Ltd
Where it can be shown that there is a group of employees who have had their wages protected for causes neither directly nor indirectly due to a difference of sex, and where male and female employees, doing the same work, who are not in this "red circle" are treated alike, an employer may succeed in establishing a defence under s.1(3).

United Biscuits Ltd v   **[1978] IRLR 15 EAT**
Young
Where an employer seeks to discharge the onus of proof under s.1(3) by a "red circle" defence, he must do so with respect to each employee who, it is claimed, is within the circle. The employer must prove that at the time when the employee was admitted to the circle his higher pay was related to a consideration other than sex.

Outlook Supplies Ltd v   **[1978] IRLR 12 EAT**
Parry
It is relevant for an employment tribunal to take into account the length of time which has elapsed since a "red circle" was introduced, and whether the employer has acted in accordance with good industrial practice in the continuation of the practice, for the purpose of determining whether the employer has discharged the onus under s.1(3).

Financial constraints

Benveniste v   **[1989] IRLR 123 CA**
University of Southampton
That a woman was appointed at a lower point on a salary scale than men doing like work due to financial constraints did not constitute a material difference to justify her lower salary once the reason for the lower payment disappeared. The material difference between her case and the case of her comparators evaporated when the financial constraints were removed.

Location

Navy, Army & Air Force   **[1976] IRLR 408 EAT**
Institutes v
Varley
A difference in weekly hours of work between employees on like work in London and in Nottingham was based on a long-standing geographical distinction and was a genuine material difference within s.1(3).

Other contractual terms

Hayward v   **[1988] IRLR 257 HL**
Cammell Laird Shipbuilders Ltd
Per the Lord Chancellor [Lord Mackay]: Section 1(3) would not provide a defence to an employer against whom it was shown that a term in the woman's contract was less favourable to her than a corresponding term in the man's contract, on the basis that there was another term in the woman's contract which was more favourable to her than the corresponding term in the man's contract. At the very least, for s.1(3) to operate, it would have to be shown that the unfavourable character of the term in the woman's contract was in fact due to the difference in the opposite sense in the other term and that the difference was not due to the reason of sex.

Hours of work

Leverton v   **[1989] IRLR 28 HL**
Clwyd County Council
Where a woman's and a man's regular annual working hours, unaffected by any significant additional hours of work, can be translated into a notional hourly rate which yields no significant difference, it is a legitimate, if not a necessary, inference that the difference in their annual salaries is both due to and justified by the difference in the hours they work in the course of a year and has nothing to do with the difference in sex.

Bilka-Kaufhaus GmbH v   **[1986] IRLR 317 ECJ**
Weber von Hartz
An employer who excludes part-time workers from an occupational pension scheme is in breach of Article 141 if this exclusion affects significantly more women than men, unless the employer can show that the exclusion is based on objectively justified factors unrelated to any discrimination on grounds of sex.

Bilka-Kaufhaus GmbH v   **[1986] IRLR 317 ECJ**
Weber von Hartz
An employer may justify the exclusion of part-time workers, irrespective of their sex, from an occupational pension

scheme on the ground that it seeks to employ as few part-time workers as possible, where it is found that the means chosen for achieving that objective correspond to a real need on the part of the undertaking, are appropriate with a view to achieving the objective in question and are necessary to that end.

Kowalska v
[1990] IRLR 447 ECJ
Freie und Hansestadt Hamburg
Article 141 precludes the application of a provision of a collective agreement under which part-time workers are excluded from the benefit of a severance payment in the case of termination of the employment relationship, when it is clear that in fact a considerably smaller percentage of men than of women work part time, unless the employer shows that the provision is justified by objective factors unrelated to any discrimination on grounds of sex.

Market forces

Enderby v
[1993] IRLR 591 ECJ
Frenchay Health Authority and
Secretary of State for Health
The state of the employment market, which may lead an employer to increase the pay of a particular job in order to attract candidates, may constitute an objectively justified economic ground for a difference in pay. If the national court is able to determine precisely what proportion of the increase in pay is attributable to market forces, it must necessarily accept that the pay differential is objectively justified to the extent of that proportion. If that is not the case, it is for the national court to assess whether the role of market forces in determining the rate of pay was sufficiently significant to provide objective justification for part or all of the difference. Therefore, it must determine, if necessary by applying the principle of proportionality, whether and to what extent the shortage of candidates for a job and the need to attract them by higher pay constitutes an objectively justified economic ground for the difference in pay between the jobs in question.

Rainey v
[1987] IRLR 26 HL
Greater Glasgow Health Board
A difference in pay between a female prosthetist and her male comparator, employed on like work but recruited from the private sector on his existing terms and conditions when the prosthetic service was established prior to her employment, was "genuinely due to a material difference (other than the difference of sex) between her case and his", where the fact that the new service could never have been established within a reasonable time if the employees of private contractors had not been offered a scale of remuneration no less favourable than that which they were then enjoying was a good and objectively justified ground for offering that scale of remuneration. There was no suggestion that it was unreasonable to place the prosthetists on the particular point on the salary scale which was in fact selected, and it was not a question of the women being paid less than the norm but of the comparator being paid more because of the necessity to attract him.

Ratcliffe v
[1995] IRLR 439 HL
North Yorkshire County Council
A difference in pay, between the female school catering assistants and their male comparators employed in local government on work rated as equivalent, which resulted from a reduction in the women's wages from the local government rate because of the employer's need to tender for work at a commercially competitive rate, was not genuinely due to a material factor which was not the difference of sex. To reduce the women's wages below that of their male comparators was the very kind of discrimination in relation to pay which the Act sought to remove.

Albion Shipping Agency v
[1981] IRLR 525 EAT
Arnold
A change in an employer's trading position leading to reduced profitability was capable of constituting a defence to a woman's claim for equal pay with her male predecessor, provided the employers could show that they were not taking advantage of the complainant's sex to get the work done at a rate less than that for which a man would have worked.

EFFECT OF THE EQUALITY CLAUSE

[(1) If the terms of a contract under which a woman is employed at an establishment in Great Britain do not include (directly or by reference to a collective agreement or otherwise) an equality clause they shall be deemed to include one.

(2) An equality clause is a provision which relates to terms (whether concerned with pay or not) of a contract under which a woman is employed (the "woman's contract"), and has the effect that –

(a) where the woman is employed on like work with a man in the same employment –

(i) if (apart from the equality clause) any term of the woman's contract is or becomes less favourable to the woman than a term of a similar kind in the contract under which that man is employed, that term of the woman's contract shall be treated as so modified as not to be less favourable, and

(ii) if (apart from the equality clause) at any time the woman's contract does not include a term corresponding to a term benefiting that man included in the contract under which he is employed, the woman's contract shall be treated as including such a term;

(b) where the woman is employed on work rated as equivalent with that of a man in the same employment –

(i) if (apart from the equality clause) any term of the woman's contract determined by the rating of the work is or becomes less favourable to the woman than a term of a similar kind in the contract under which that man is employed, that term of the woman's contract shall be treated as so modified as not to be less favourable, and

(ii) if (apart from the equality clause) at any time the woman's contract does not include a term corresponding to a term benefiting that man included in the contract under which he is employed and determined by the rating of the work, the woman's contract shall be treated as including such a term;

(c) where a woman is employed on work which, not being work in relation to which paragraph (a) or (b) above applies, is, in terms of the demands made on her (for instance under such headings as effort, skill and decision), of equal value to that of a man in the same employment –

(i) if (apart from the equality clause) any term of the woman's contract is or becomes less favourable to the woman than a term of a similar kind in the contract under which that man is employed, that term of the woman's contract shall be treated as so modified as not to be less favourable, and

(ii) if (apart from the equality clause) at any time the woman's contract does not include a term corresponding to a term benefiting that man included in the contract under which he is employed, the woman's contract shall be treated as including such a term.]

EQUAL PAY ACT – s.1

(1) [Any claim in respect of the contravention of a term modified or included by virtue of an equality clause, including a claim for arrears of remuneration or damages in respect of the contravention, may be presented by way of a complaint to an employment tribunal.]

EQUAL PAY ACT – s.2

Barber v   **[1990] IRLR 240 ECJ**
Guardian Royal Exchange Assurance Group
The application of the principle of equal pay must be ensured in respect of each element of remuneration and not only on the basis of a comprehensive assessment of the consideration paid to workers.

Jämställdhetsombudsmannen v   **[2000] IRLR 421 ECJ**
Örebro Läns Landsting
In comparing the pay of midwives and a clinical technician for the purpose of Article 141, the appropriate comparison was between the monthly basic salary of the two groups. No account was to be taken of a supplement paid to the midwives for working inconvenient hours. Genuine transparency, permitting effective judicial review, is assured only if the principle of equal pay applies to each of the elements of remuneration.

Hayward v   **[1988] IRLR 257 HL**
Cammell Laird Shipbuilders Ltd
The natural meaning of the word "term" in the context of s.1(2)(c) is a distinct provision or part of the contract which has sufficient content to make it possible to compare it, from the point of view of the benefits it confers, with a similar provision or part in another contract. Therefore, on the correct construction of s.1(2)(c)(i), if in the contract of a woman and the contract of a man employed on work of equal value there is "a term of a similar kind" – ie a term making a comparable provision for the same subject-matter – the two must be compared and if, on that comparison, the term of the woman's contract proves to be less favourable than the term of the man's contract, then the term in the woman's contract is to be treated as modified so as to make it not less favourable.

Hayward v   **[1988] IRLR 257 HL**
Cammell Laird Shipbuilders Ltd
If a contract contains provisions relating to basic pay, benefits in kind such as the use of a car, cash bonuses and sickness benefits, on the natural and ordinary meaning of the word "term", all these different terms cannot be lumped together as one "term" of the contract, simply because they can all together be considered as providing for the total "remuneration" for the services to be performed under the contract.

Hayward v   **[1988] IRLR 257 HL**
Cammell Laird Shipbuilders Ltd
On the correct construction of s.1(2)(c) of the Equal Pay Act as amended, a woman who can point to a term of her con-

tract which is less favourable than a term of a similar kind in the man's contract is entitled to have that term made not less favourable irrespective of whether she is as favourably treated as the man when the whole of her contract and the whole of his contract are considered. Therefore, a woman employee on work of equal value was entitled to the same basic hourly wage and overtime rates as her comparator, notwithstanding that she received additional holidays and better sickness benefits.

Dugdale v   **[1976] IRLR 368 EAT**
Kraft Foods Ltd

An equality clause has effect so as to modify any less favourable term of the women's contract so as to make it not less favourable. It need not produce equality if, though they are engaged on like work, the payment to the men includes something affecting them and not the woman, such as working at night.

Evesham v   **[2000] IRLR 257 CA**
North Hertfordshire Health Authority

An applicant's entitlement under s.1(2)(c) to have the relevant term of her contract of employment modified so as to be not less favourable than that of her male comparator means that she should mirror her comparator on the incremental pay scale, and therefore enter the scale at the lowest level, rather than that she should be placed on the pay scale for his post at a level appropriate to her actual years of service.

Sorbie v   **[1976] IRLR 371 EAT**
Trust House Forte Hotels Ltd

The effect of an equality clause is to strike out the less favourable rate and substitute the higher rate. Once a contract of employment has been modified in accordance with an equality clause, it is a contract providing remuneration at the higher rate. That contract remains so modified until something else happens, such as a further agreement between the parties, a further collective agreement, or a further statutory modification by reason of a further operation of the equality clause. Therefore, a modification to a woman's contract providing equal pay with a male comparator did not cease to operate when the man was no longer employed on like work.

REMEDIES

(5) A woman shall not be entitled, in proceedings brought in respect of a contravention of a term modified or included by virtue of an equality clause (including proceedings before an employment tribunal), to be awarded any payment by way of arrears of remuneration or damages –
> *(a) in proceedings in England and Wales, in respect of a time earlier than the arrears date (determined in accordance with section 2ZB below), and*
> *(b) in proceedings in Scotland, in respect of a time before the period determined in accordance with section 2ZC below."*

EQUAL PAY ACT (as amended) – s.2(5)

(1) This section applies for the purpose of determining the arrears date, in relation to an award of any payment by way of arrears of remuneration or damages in proceedings in England and Wales in respect of a woman's employment, for the purposes of section 2(5)(a) above.

(2) In this section –
"concealment case" means a case where –
> *(a) the employer deliberately concealed from the woman any fact –*
> > *(i) which is relevant to the contravention to which the proceedings relate, and*
> > *(ii) without knowledge of which the woman could not reasonably have been expected to institute the proceedings, and*
> *(b) the woman instituted the proceedings within six years of the day on which she discovered the fact (or could with reasonable diligence have discovered it);*
"disability case" means a case where –
> *(a) the woman was under a disability at the time of the contravention to which the proceedings relate, and*
> *(b) the woman instituted the proceedings within six years of the day on which she ceased to be under a disability;*
"standard case" means a case which is not –
> *(a) a concealment case,*
> *(b) a disability case, or*
> *(c) both.*

(3) In a standard case, the arrears date is the date falling six years before the day on which the proceedings were instituted.

(4) In a case which is a concealment or a disability case or both, the arrears date is the date of the contravention.

EQUAL PAY ACT (as amended) – s.2ZB

(1) This section applies, in relation to an award of any payment by way of arrears of remuneration or damages in proceedings in Scotland in respect of a woman's employment, for the purpose of determining the period mentioned in section 2(5)(b) above.

(2) Subject to subsection (3) below, that period is the period of five years which ends on the day on which the proceedings were instituted, except that the five years shall not be regarded as running during –
> *(a) any time when the woman was induced, by reason of fraud on the part of, or error induced by the words or*

conduct of, the employer or any person acting on his behalf, to refrain from commencing proceedings (not being a time after she could with reasonable diligence have discovered the fraud or error), or

(b) any time when she was under a disability.

(3) If, after regard is had to the exceptions in subsection (2) above, that period would include any time more than twenty years before the day mentioned in that subsection, that period is instead the period of twenty years which ends on that day."

EQUAL PAY ACT (as amended) – s.2ZC

(2A) For the purposes of this Act a woman is under a disability –
   (a) in the case of proceedings in England and Wales, if she is a minor or of unsound mind (which has the same meaning as in section 38(2) of the Limitation Act 1980; or
   (b) in the case of proceedings in Scotland, if she has not attained the age of sixteen years or is incapable within the meaning of the Adults with Incapacity (Scotland) Act 2000.

EQUAL PAY ACT (as amended) – s.11

Preston v   **[2000] IRLR 506 ECJ**
Wolverhampton Healthcare NHS Trust
Community law precludes a national procedural rule, such as that in s.2(5) of the Equal Pay Act as amended, which provides that a claimant's entitlement to join an occupational pension scheme is limited to a period which starts to run two years prior to the commencement of proceedings in connection with the claim. A procedural rule such as in s.2(5) and reg. 12 of the Occupational Pension Regulations renders any action by individuals relying on Community law impossible in practice.

Preston v   **[2000] IRLR 506 ECJ**
Wolverhampton Healthcare NHS Trust
The fact that a worker can claim retroactively to join an occupational pension scheme does not allow him to avoid paying the contributions relating to the period of membership concerned.

Preston v   **[2001] IRLR 237 HL**
Wolverhampton Healthcare NHS Trust (No.2)
Section 2(5) of the Equal Pay Act and reg.12 cannot be relied on to defeat a claim for periods of pensionable service prior to two years before the date of the claim to be taken into account, so long as the employee pays contributions owing in respect of the period for which membership was claimed retrospectively. In accordance with the ruling of the European Court, the rule that pensionable service is to be calculated only by reference to service after a date falling no earlier than two years prior to the date of the claim is precluded by Community law. Future pension benefits, therefore, have to be calculated by reference to full and part-time periods of service subsequent to 8 April 1976, the date of the decision of the European Court in *Defrenne (No.2)*.

Levez v   **[1999] IRLR 36 ECJ**
T H Jennings (Harlow Pools) Ltd
The two-year limitation on arrears of remuneration in s.2(5) of the Equal Pay Act is precluded by Community law, even when another remedy is available, if that remedy is likely to entail procedural rules or other conditions which are less favourable than those applicable to similar domestic actions. It is for the national court to determine whether that is the case. The principle of equivalence requires that the rule at issue be applied without distinction, whether the infringement alleged is of Community law or national law, where the purpose and cause of action are similar.

Levez v   **[1999] IRLR 36 ECJ**
T H Jennings (Harlow Pools) Ltd
The fact that the limitation period laid down by s.2(5) of the Equal Pay Act applies both to a right acquired under domestic law and to claims based directly on Article 141 of the Treaty is not enough to ensure compliance with the principle of equivalence, since one and the same form of action is involved. The Equal Pay Act cannot therefore provide an appropriate ground of comparison against which to measure compliance with the principle of equivalence.

Levez v   **[1999] IRLR 764 EAT**
T H Jennings (Harlow Pools) Ltd (No.2)
Hicking v
Basford Group Ltd
The two-year limitation on arrears of remuneration in s.2(5) of the Equal Pay Act is a breach of the European Community law principle of equivalence, in that it is less favourable than those governing similar claims such as for unlawful deduction from wages and unlawful discrimination on grounds of race or disability. The two-year back pay limit is thus unenforceable as being incompatible with the UK's obligations under Community law. The six-year time limit in the Limitation Act from the date of commencement of proceedings applies to claims under the Equal Pay Act.

Levez v   **[1999] IRLR 36 ECJ**
T H Jennings (Harlow Pools) Ltd
A national rule under which entitlement to arrears of remuneration is restricted to the two years preceding the date on which the proceedings were instituted cannot be said to make the exercise of rights conferred by Community law either virtually impossible or excessively difficult, even though the expiry of such limitation periods entails by definition the rejection, wholly or in part, of the action brought.

Levez v   **[1999] IRLR 36 ECJ**
T H Jennings (Harlow Pools) Ltd
Application of s.2(5) of the Equal Pay Act, which limits an employee's entitlement to arrears of remuneration to a period of two years prior to the date on which the proceedings were instituted, is precluded by Community law in a case where the delay in bringing the claim is attributable to the fact that the employer deliberately provided the employee with inaccurate information as to the level of remuneration received by employees of the opposite sex performing like work, so that the employee had no way of determining whether she was being discriminated against or, if so, to what extent.

3. DISABILITY DISCRIMINATION

STATUTORY EXCLUSIONS AND EXCEPTIONS

Meaning of "employee"

'Employment' means, subject to any prescribed provision, employment under a contract of service or of apprenticeship or a contract personally to do any work, and related expressions are to be construed accordingly.

DISABILITY DISCRIMINATION ACT – s.68(1)

Burton v   **[2003] IRLR 257 EAT**
Higham t/a Ace Appointments

All that s.68 requires is for there to be an obligation to do work. In this case, those engaged by an employment agency under a temporary worker's contract fell within the wider definition of "employment", notwithstanding that they provided their services to the client. The obligations set out in their contract corresponded to those envisaged in s.68. The temporary worker's contract required them, when accepting an assignment, to do work. They could not substitute another person to take their place. That the work was performed for the client did not take it outside the scope of s.68.

South East Sheffield Citizens   **[2004] IRLR 353 EAT**
   Advice Bureau v
Grayson

Volunteer advisers working for a Citizens Advice Bureau were not "employees" employed under a contract of service within the meaning of s.68(1), where the volunteer agreement did not impose a contractual obligation upon the Bureau to provide work for the volunteer to do or upon the volunteer personally to do for the Bureau any work so provided such that, were the volunteer to give notice immediately terminating his relationship with the Bureau, the latter would have a remedy for breach of contract against him.

Claim in time

(1) An employment tribunal shall not consider a complaint under s.8 unless it is presented before the end of the period of three months beginning when the act complained of was done.

(2) A tribunal may consider any such complaint which is out of time if, in all the circumstances of the case, it considers that it is just and equitable to do so.

DISABILITY DISCRIMINATION ACT – Sch. 3, para. 3

Robinson v   **[2000] IRLR 904 EAT**
Post Office

An employment tribunal was entitled to find that it was not just and equitable to extend the time limit for presenting the applicant's disability discrimination complaint in respect of his dismissal, notwithstanding that his complaint was out of time because he was pursuing an internal appeal against dismissal. Parliament deliberately has not provided that the running of time should be delayed until the end of the domestic processes. When delay on account of an incomplete internal appeal is relied upon as a reason for failing to lodge a tribunal application in time, it will ordinarily suffice for the employment tribunal to put this into the balance when the justice and equity of the matter is being considered.

British Gas Services Ltd v   **[2001] IRLR 60 EAT**
McCaull

Time does not run in respect of a discriminatory dismissal until the notice of dismissal expires and the employment ceases. In dismissal cases, it is when the individual finds himself out of a job that he suffers detriment as a result of the discrimination.

MEANING OF DISABILITY

(1) Subject to the provisions of Schedule 1, a person has a disability for the purposes of this Act if he has a physical or mental impairment which has a substantial and long-term adverse effect on his ability to carry out normal day-to-day activities.

(2) In this Act "disabled person" means a person who has a disability.
DISABILITY DISCRIMINATION ACT – s.1

General approach

Goodwin v   **[1999] IRLR 4 EAT**
The Patent Office
When faced with an issue as to whether a person has a disability within the meaning of the Act, the tribunal should adopt an inquisitorial or interventionist role. There is a risk of a "Catch 22" situation, in that some disabled persons may be unable or unwilling to accept that they have a disability. Without the direct assistance of the tribunal at the hearing, there may be cases where the applicant, for a reason related to his disability, is unwilling to support the claim.

Rugamer v   **[2001] IRLR 644 EAT**
Sony Music Entertainment UK Ltd
McNicol v
Balfour Beatty Rail Maintenance
An employment tribunal is not an inquisitorial body in the same sense as a medical or other tribunal dealing with a disablement issue as part of the statutory machinery for determining benefit claims. The observations of Morison J in *Goodwin v Patent Office* that the role of tribunals in a disability discrimination case contains "an inquisitorial element" mean no more than that the tribunal is obliged to conduct the hearing in a fair and balanced manner, intervening and making its own inquiries in the course of the hearing of such persons appearing before it and such witnesses as are called before it as it considers appropriate, so as to ensure due consideration of the issues raised by, or necessarily implicit in, the complaint being made. The role of the tribunal is not thereby extended so as to place on it the duty to conduct a freestanding inquiry of its own, or to require it to attempt to obtain further evidence beyond that placed in front of it on the issues raised by the parties, or to cause the parties to raise additional issues they have not sought to rely on at all.

Goodwin v   **[1999] IRLR 4 EAT**
The Patent Office
The tribunal should adopt a purposive approach to construction, construing the statutory language in a way which gives effect to the stated or presumed intention of Parliament, but with due regard to the ordinary and natural meaning of the words in question. Explicit reference should always be made to any relevant provision of the Guidance issued by the Secretary of State or of the Code of Practice, which the tribunal has taken into account. However, the Guidance should not be used as an extra hurdle over which the applicant must jump.

Excluded conditions

(1) Subject to para. (2) below, addiction to alcohol, nicotine or any other substance is to be treated as not amounting to an impairment for the purposes of the Act.

(2) Para. (1) above does not apply to addiction which was originally the result of administration of medically prescribed drugs or other medical treatment.
DISABILITY DISCRIMINATION (MEANING OF DISABIITY) REGULATIONS 1996 – reg.3

Power v   **[2003] IRLR 151 EAT**
Panasonic UK Ltd
It is not material to a decision as to whether a person has a disability within the meaning of the Act to consider how the impairment which they have was caused. What is material is to ascertain whether the disability which they have at the material time is a disability within the meaning of the Act or whether, where it is relevant, it is an impairment which is excluded by reason of the Regulations from being treated as such a disability. In this case, the tribunal erred in not considering whether the applicant's depression had a substantial and long-term adverse effect on her ability to carry out normal day-to-day activities, but by considering instead whether alcoholism caused her depression, and concluding that her case fell within reg.3(1), which provides that "addiction to alcohol ... is to be treated as not amounting to an impairment for the purposes of the Act."

(1) For the purposes of the Act the following conditions are to be treated as not amounting to impairments:—
> *(a) a tendency to set fires,*
> *(b) a tendency to steal,*
> *(c) a tendency to physical or sexual abuse of other persons,*
> *(d) exhibitionism, and*
> *(e) voyeurism.*
DISABILITY DISCRIMINATION (MEANING OF DISABIITY) REGULATIONS 1996 – reg.4

Murray v   **[2003] IRLR 340 EAT**
Newham Citizens Advice Bureau Ltd
A condition, such as a tendency to violence, falls within reg.4 of the Meaning of Disability Regulations only where it is a freestanding condition, and not where it is a condition that is the direct consequence of a physical or mental impairment within the meaning of s.1(1). Where the consequence of a recognised illness is a tendency to violence, a potential employer may only treat the disabled person less favourably than other persons if the discrimination can be justified.

Meaning of impairment

1(1) "Mental impairment" includes an impairment resulting from or consisting of a mental illness only if the illness is a clinically well-recognised illness.

DISABILITY DISCRIMINATION ACT – Sch.1

McNicol v   **[2002] IRLR 711 CA**
Balfour Beatty Rail Maintenance Ltd
The term "impairment" in s.1 of the Act bears its ordinary and natural meaning. It is clear from Schedule 1 that impairment may result from an illness or it may consist of an illness, provided that, in the case of mental impairment, it must be a "clinically well-recognised illness". The essential question in each case is whether, on a sensible interpretation of the relevant evidence, including the expert medical evidence and reasonable inferences which can be made from all the evidence, the applicant can fairly be described as having a physical or mental impairment. Such a decision can and should be made without substituting for the statutory language a different word or form of words in an attempt to describe or define the concept of "impairment".

McNicol v   **[2002] IRLR 711 CA**
Balfour Beatty Rail Maintenance Ltd
The onus is on the applicant to prove the impairment on the conventional balance of probabilities.

Morgan v   **[2002] IRLR 190 EAT**
Staffordshire University
The possible routes to establishing the existence of mental impairment within the DDA are as follows:
(i) proof of a mental illness specifically mentioned as such in the World Health Organisation's International Classification of Diseases (WHOICD).
(ii) proof of a mental illness specifically mentioned as such in a publication "such as" that classification, presumably therefore referring to some other classification of very wide professional acceptable;
(iii) proof by other means of a medical illness recognised by a respected body of medical opinion;
(iv) proof by substantial and specific medical evidence of a mental impairment which neither results from nor consists of a mental illness.

Morgan v   **[2002] IRLR 190 EAT**
Staffordshire University
Medical notes which refer to "anxiety", "stress" and "depression" do not amount to proof of a mental impairment within the meaning of the DDA.

Morgan v   **[2002] IRLR 190 EAT**
Staffordshire University
Observed: (1) Advisers to parties claiming mental impairment must bear in mind that the onus on a claimant under the DDA is on him to prove that impairment on the conventional balance of probabilities.
(2) There is no good ground for expecting the tribunal mem-

bers (or EAT members) to have anything more than a layman's rudimentary familiarity with psychiatric classification. Things therefore need to be spelled out. What it is that needs to be spelled out depends upon which of the three or four routes is attempted. It is unwise for claimants not clearly to identify in good time before the hearing exactly what is the impairment they say is relevant and for respondents to indicate whether impairment is an issue and why it is. It is equally unwise for tribunals not to insist that both sides should do so. Only if that is done can the parties be clear as to what has to be proved or rebutted, in medical terms, at the hearing.

(3) As the WHOICD does not use such terms without qualification and there is no general acceptance of such loose terms, it is not the case that some loose description such as "anxiety", "stress" or "depression" of itself will suffice unless there is credible and informed evidence that in the particular circumstances so loose a description nonetheless identifies a clinically well-recognised illness. In any case where a dispute as to such impairment is likely, the well-advised claimant will thus equip himself, if he can, with a writing from a suitably qualified medical practitioner that indicates the grounds upon which the practitioner has become able to speak as to the claimant's condition and which in terms clearly diagnoses either an illness specified in the WHOICD (saying which) or, alternatively, diagnoses some other clinically well-recognised mental illness or the result thereof, identifying it specifically and (in this alternative case) giving his grounds for asserting that, despite its absence from the WHOICD (if such is the case), it is nonetheless to be accepted as a clinically well-recognised illness or as the result of one.

(4) Where the WHOICD classification is relied on then, in any case where dispute is likely, the medical deponent should depose to the presence or absence of the symptoms identified in its diagnostic guidelines. When a dispute is likely a bare statement that does no more than identifying the illness is unlikely to dispel doubt nor focus expert evidence on what will prove to be the area in dispute.

(5) This summary is not to be taken to require a full Consultant Psychiatrist's report in every case. There will be many cases where the illness is sufficiently marked for the claimant's GP by letter to prove it in terms which satisfy the DDA. Whilst the question of what are or are not "day-to-day activities" within the DDA is not a matter for medical evidence – *Vicary v British Telecommunication plc*, the existence or not of a mental impairment is very much a matter for qualified and informed medical opinion. Whoever deposes, it will be prudent for the specific requirements of the Act to be drawn to the deponent's attention.

(6) If it becomes clear, despite a GP's letter or other initially available indication, that impairment is to be disputed on technical medical grounds then thought will need to be given to further expert evidence, as to which see *De Keyser v Wilson*.

(7) There will be many cases, particularly if the failure to make adjustments is in issue, where the medical evidence will need to cover not merely a description of the mental illness but when, over what periods and how it can be expected to have manifested itself, either generally or to the employer in the course of the claimant's employment. Thus claimants' advis-

ers, before seeking medical evidence, must consider also whether it will be enough to prove a present impairment and whether, instead or in addition, they will need to prove it at some earlier time or times and to prove how it could, earlier or at present, have been expected to have manifested itself.

(8) The dangers of the tribunal forming a view on "mental impairment" from the way the claimant gives evidence on the day cannot be over-stated. Aside from the risk of undetected, or suspected but non-existent, play-acting by the claimant and that the date of the hearing itself will seldom be a date as at which the presence of the impairment will need to be proved or disproved, tribunal members will need to remind themselves that few mental illnesses are such that their symptoms are obvious *all* the time and that they have no training or, as is likely, expertise, in the detection of real or simulated psychiatric disorders.

(9) The tribunals are not inquisitorial bodies charged with a duty to see to the procurement of adequate medical evidence – see *Rugamer v Sony Music Entertainment UK Ltd*. But that is not to say that the tribunal does not have its normal discretion to consider adjournment in an appropriate case, which may be more than usually likely to be found where a claimant is not only in person but (whether to the extent of disability or not) suffers *some* mental weakness.

Leonard v   **[2001] IRLR 19 EAT**
Southern Derbyshire
  Chamber of Commerce

An employment tribunal misdirected themselves as to the manner in which the Guidance on the definition of disability should be applied by taking examples from the Guidance of what the applicant could do, such as being able to eat and drink, and catch a ball and then weighing that against what she could not do, such as negotiate pavement edges safely. This was inappropriate, since her ability to catch a ball did not diminish her inability to negotiate pavement edges safely.

Long-term effects

2. (1) The effect of an impairment is a long-term effect if –
    (a) it has lasted at least 12 months;
    (b) the period for which it lasts is likely to be at least 12 months; or
    (c) it is likely to last for the rest of the life of the person affected.

(2) Where an impairment ceases to have a substantial adverse effect on a person's ability to carry out normal day-to-day activities, it is to be treated as continuing to have that effect if that effect is likely to recur.
       DISABILITY DISCRIMINATION ACT – Sch. 1

Cruickshank v   **[2002] IRLR 24 EAT**
VAW Motorcast Ltd

The material time at which to assess the applicant's disability is at the time of the alleged discriminatory act, in this case the dismissal, rather than at the time of the tribunal hearing.. A claim that "an employer discriminates against a disabled per-

son" contrary to s.5 must involve an examination of what the employer knew or ought to have known of the employee's disability at the time of the actions complained of.

Greenwood v   **[1999] IRLR 600 EAT**
British Airways plc

In determining whether the effect of an impairment is likely to last for at least 12 months, as the Secretary of State's Guidance makes clear, the tribunal should consider the adverse effects of the applicant's condition up to and including the employment tribunal hearing.

Normal day-to-day activities

4. – (1) An impairment is to be taken to affect the ability of the person concerned to carry out normal day-to-day activities only if it affects one of the following –
    (a) mobility;
    (b) manual dexterity;
    (c) physical co-ordination;
    (d) continence;
    (e) ability to lift, carry or otherwise move everyday objects;
    (f) speech, hearing or eyesight;
    (g) memory or ability to concentrate, learn or understand; or
    (h) perception of the risk of physical danger.
       DISABILITY DISCRIMINATION ACT – Sch. 1

Goodwin v   **[1999] IRLR 4 EAT**
The Patent Office

The Act is concerned with a person's ability to carry out activities. The fact that a person can carry out such activities does not mean that his ability to carry them out has not been impaired. The focus of the Act is on the things that the applicant either cannot do or can only do with difficulty, rather than on the things that the person can do.

Ekpe v   **[2001] IRLR 605 EAT**
Commissioner of Police
  of the Metropolis

A tribunal inquiring as to whether an impairment affects the ability of the person concerned to carry out normal day-to-day activities should focus upon whether or not any of the abilities, or capacities, listed in para.4(1)(a) to (h) of Schedule 1 to the Act has been affected. If it has, then it must be almost inevitable that there will be some adverse effect upon normal day-to-day activities.

Ekpe v   **[2001] IRLR 605 EAT**
Commissioner of Police
  of the Metropolis

What is "normal" for the purposes of the Act may be best understood by defining it as anything which is not abnormal or unusual (or, in the words of the Guidance issued by the Secretary of State, 'particular' to the individual applicant). What is normal cannot sensibly depend on whether the majority of people do it. The antithesis for the purposes of the Act is between that which is "normal" and that which is "abnormal" or "unusual" as a regular activity, judged by an objective population standard.

Ekpe v   **[2001] IRLR 605 EAT**
Commissioner of Police
  of the Metropolis
Anything done by most women, or most men, is a normal day-to-day activity. Therefore, an employment tribunal erred in discounting the fact that the applicant could not put rollers in her hair and that she could not always use her right hand to apply make-up on grounds that neither was a "normal day-to-day activity" because they are activities carried out almost exclusively by women.

Abadeh v   **[2001] IRLR 23 EAT**
British Telecommunications plc
What is a normal day-to-day activity must be addressed without regard to whether it is normal to the particular applicant.

Law Hospital NHS Trust v   **[2001] IRLR 611 CS**
Rush
Evidence of the nature of an applicant's duties at work, and the way in which they are performed, particularly if they include "normal day-to-day activities, can be relevant to the assessment which the tribunal has to make of the applicant's case.

Cruickshank v   **[2002] IRLR 24 EAT**
VAW Motorcast Ltd
In a case where, as a result of a medical condition, the effects of an impairment on ability to carry out normal day-to-day activities fluctuate and may be exacerbated by conditions at work, the tribunal should consider whether the impairment has a substantial and long-term adverse effect on the employee's ability to perform normal day-to-day activities both while actually at work and while not at work. If, while at work, an applicant's symptoms are such as to have a significant and long-term effect on his ability to perform day-to-day tasks, such symptoms are not to be ignored simply because the work itself may be specialised and unusual, so long as the disability and its consequences can be measured in terms of the ability of an applicant to undertake day-to-day tasks.

Vicary v   **[1999] IRLR 680 EAT**
British Telecommunications plc
It is not for a doctor to express an opinion as to what is a normal day-to-day activity. Nor is it for the medical expert to tell the tribunal whether the impairments which had been found proved were or were not substantial. Those are matters for the employment tribunal to arrive at its own assessment.

Ekpe v   **[2001] IRLR 605 EAT**
Commissioner of Police
  of the Metropolis
An employment tribunal is entitled to have regard to its own observation of the applicant in determining the extent of an applicant's disability. A decision as to whether a disability has an adverse impact on normal day-to-day activities and whether that impact is substantial may properly be influenced by the behaviour of an applicant as demonstrated before the tribunal, although any tribunal considering whether to draw any conclusion from such behaviour would be expected to raise that possibility at the hearing.

Kapadia v   **[2000] IRLR 699 CA**
London Borough of Lambeth
An employment tribunal was obliged to conclude that an applicant's mental impairment had a substantial adverse effect on his normal day-to-day activities, in circumstances in which there was direct medical evidence that his anxiety, neuroses and depression would have had such an effect but for the fact that he had received medical treatment, and there was no contrary expert medical evidence or challenge to the factual bases of those opinions.

Hewett v   **[2004] IRLR 545 EAT**
Motorola Ltd
Ability to "understand", for the purposes of para.4(1)(g) is not limited simply to an ability to understand information, knowledge or instructions. A broad approach to the concept of "understanding" should be taken. Someone who has difficulty in understanding normal social interaction among people, and/or the subtleties of human nonfactual communication, such as someone with Asperger's Syndrome, can be regarded as having their understanding affected.

Recurring conditions

2(2) Where an impairment ceases to have a substantial adverse effect on a person's ability to carry out normal day-to-day activities, it is to be treated as continuing to have that effect if that effect is likely to recur.

DISABILITY DISCRIMINATION ACT 1995 – Sch.1

Swift v   **[2004] IRLR 540 EAT**
Chief Constable of Wiltshire Constabulary
In considering the application of para.2(2), a tribunal should ask itself the following questions: first, was there at some stage an impairment which had a substantial adverse effect on the applicant's ability to carry out normal day-to-day activities? Secondly, did the impairment cease to have a substantial adverse effect on the applicant's ability to carry out normal day-to-day activities, and if so when? Thirdly, what was the substantial adverse effect? Fourthly, is that substantial adverse effect likely to recur. The tribunal must be satisfied that the same effect is likely to recur and will again amount to a substantial adverse effect on the applicant's ability to carry out normal day-to-day activities.

Swift v   **[2004] IRLR 540 EAT**
Chief Constable of Wiltshire Constabulary
A substantial adverse effect is "likely to recur" if it is more probable than not that the effect will recur. Although the tribunal must be satisfied that the substantial adverse effect is likely to recur, it need not be satisfied that the recurrence is likely to last for at least 12 months. The effect of para.2(2) is that the impairment is treated as continuing for as long as its substantial adverse effect is likely to recur. Even if the impairment has ceased to have a substantial adverse effect, it "lasts" for as long as its substantial adverse effect is likely to recur.

Swift v   **[2004] IRLR 540 EAT**
Chief Constable of Wiltshire Constabulary
The question for the tribunal is whether the substantial adverse effect is likely to recur, not whether the illness is likely to recur. The Act contemplates that an illness may run its course to a conclusion but leave behind an impairment.

Substantial adverse effects

Goodwin v   **[1999] IRLR 4 EAT**
The Patent Office
"Substantial" means "more than minor or trivial" rather than "very large". The tribunal may take into account how the applicant appears to the tribunal to "manage", although it should be slow to regard a person's capabilities in the relatively strange adversarial environment as an entirely reliable guide to the level of ability to perform normal day-to-day activities.

Abadeh v   **[2001] IRLR 23 EAT**
British Telecommunications plc
It is not the task of the medical expert to tell the tribunal whether an impairment was or was not substantial. That is a question which the tribunal itself has to answer. The medical report should deal with the doctor's diagnosis of the impairment, the doctor's observation of the applicant carrying out day-to-day activities and the ease with which he was able to perform those functions, together with any relevant opinion as to prognosis and the effect of medication.

Vicary v   **[1999] IRLR 680 EAT**
British Telecommunications plc
The Guidance issued by the Secretary of State on the definition of disability will only be of assistance in marginal cases.

Vicary v   **[1999] IRLR 680 EAT**
British Telecommunications plc
Having concluded that the ability of the applicant to do a number of activities was impaired, the tribunal should have concluded that she had a disability within the meaning of the Act.

Abadeh v   **[2001] IRLR 23 EAT**
British Telecommunications plc
An assessment of disability by a Medical Appeal Tribunal is clearly relevant evidence for an employment tribunal to take into account as part of the evidence before them on the issue of disability.

Goodwin v   **[1999] IRLR 4 EAT**
The Patent Office
An employment tribunal erred in finding that a paranoid schizophrenic who was dismissed after complaints relating to his behaviour, was not a "disabled person" because the adverse effect of the impairment on his ability to carry out normal day-to-day activities was not "substantial". The applicant was unable to carry on a normal day-to-day conversation with work colleagues, which was good evidence that his capacity to concentrate and communicate had been adversely affected in a significant manner.

Effect of medical treatment

6(1) An impairment which would be likely to have a substantial adverse effect on the ability of the person concerned to carry out normal day-to-day activities, but for the fact that measures are being taken to treat or correct it, is to be treated as having that effect.

(2) In sub-paragraph (1) "measures" includes, in particular, medical treatment and the use of a prosthesis or other aid.

(3) Sub-paragraph (1) does not apply –
  (a) in relation to the impairment of a person's sight, to the extent that the impairment is, in his case, correctable by spectacles or contact lenses or in such other ways as may be prescribed; or
  (b) in relation to such other impairments as may be prescribed, in such circumstances as may be prescribed.
  DISABILITY DISCRIMINATION ACT – Sch. 1

Woodrup v   **[2003] IRLR 111 CA**
London Borough of Southwark
Para. 6(1) provides that someone is to be treated as disabled even though they are not in fact disabled (in that they suffer no substantial adverse effect on their ability to carry out normal day-to-day activities) if, without the medical treatment they are in fact receiving, they would suffer that disability. The question to be asked is whether, if treatment were stopped at the relevant date, would the person then, notwithstanding such benefit as had been obtained from prior treatment, have an impairment which would have the relevant adverse effect?

Goodwin v   **[1999] IRLR 4 EAT**
The Patent Office
In determining whether an adverse effect is substantial, the tribunal should examine how an applicant's abilities have actually been affected whilst on medication and then consider the "deduced effects" – the effects which they think there would have been but for the medication – and whether the

actual and deduced effects on ability to carry out normal day-to-day activities is clearly more than trivial.

Abadeh v   **[2001] IRLR 23 EAT**
British Telecommunications plc
Para. 6 of Schedule 1 applies only to continuing medical treatment, ie to measures that "are being taken" and not to concluded treatment where the effects of such treatment may be more readily ascertained. Where treatment has ceased, the effects of that treatment should be taken into account in order to assess the disability.

Abadeh v   **[2001] IRLR 23 EAT**
British Telecommunications plc
Where the medical evidence satisfies the tribunal that the effect of continuing medical treatment is to create a permanent improvement, the effects of that treatment should be taken into account in order to assess the disability as measures are no longer needed to treat or correct it once the permanent improvement has been established.

Woodrup v   **[2003] IRLR 111 CA**
London Borough of Southwark
In a deduced effects case similar to the present one, in which the applicant was claiming that if her psychotherapy treatment for anxiety neurosis had been discontinued, her impairment would have had a substantial adverse effect on her ability to carry out normal day-to-day activities, the applicant should be required to prove his or her alleged disability with some particularity. Ordinarily, one would expect clear medical evidence to be necessary.

Kapadia v   **[2000] IRLR 14 EAT**
London Borough of Lambeth
Counselling sessions with a consultant clinical psychologist constitute "medical treatment" within the meaning of para. 6 of Schedule 1.

Progressive conditions

8(1) Where –
> *(a) a person has a progressive condition (such as cancer, multiple sclerosis or muscular dystrophy or infection by the human immunodeficiency virus),*
> *(b) as a result of that condition, he has an impairment which has (or had) an effect on his ability to carry out normal day-to-day activities, but*
> *(c) that effect is not (or was not) a substantial adverse effect,*

he shall be taken to have an impairment which has such a substantial adverse effect if the condition is likely to result in his having such an impairment."

                   DISABILITY DISCRIMINATION ACT – Sch. 1

Mowat-Brown v   **[2002] IRLR 235 EAT**
University of Surrey
In order to determine whether an applicant's case falls within the definition relating to progressive conditions, the question to be asked is whether, on the balance of probabilities, the applicant has established that the condition in his case is likely to have a substantial adverse effect. It is not enough simply for an applicant to establish that he has a progressive condition and that it has or has had an effect on his ability to carry out normal day-to-day activities. He must go on and show that it is more likely than not that at some stage in the future he will have an impairment which will have a substantial adverse effect on his ability to carry out normal day-to-day activities. In some cases it may be possible to produce medical evidence of his likely prognosis. In other cases it may be possible to discharge the onus of proof by statistical evidence.

Kirton v   **[2003] IRLR 353 CA**
Tetrosyl Ltd
The words "as a result of that condition" should not be so narrowly construed as to exclude an impairment which results from a standard and common form of operative procedure for cancer. Impairment in this context also includes the ordinary consequences of an operation to relieve the disease. Therefore, an applicant who had an operation for prostate cancer which led to urinary incontinence fell within the definition of disability relating to a "progressive condition", notwithstanding that his incontinence was not a direct result of the progressive condition, but was a result of the surgery by which the progressive condition was treated.

EMPLOYMENT DISCRIMINATION

Meaning of "discrimination"

"(1) For the purposes of this Part, a person discriminates against a disabled person if –

> *(a) for a reason which relates to the disabled person's disability, he treats him less favourably than he treats or would treat others to whom that reason does not or would not apply, and*
>
> *(b) he cannot show that the treatment in question is justified.*

(5) A person directly discriminates against a disabled person if, on the ground of the disabled person's disability, he treats the disabled person less favourably than he treats or would treat a person not having that particular disability whose relevant circumstances, including his abilities, are the same as, or not materially different from, those of the disabled person.

DISABILITY DISCRIMINATION ACT 1995 (as amended) – s.5

Reason related to disability

H J Heinz Co Ltd v   **[2000] IRLR 144 EAT**
Kenrick
[S.3A(1)(a)] does not require the employer to have knowledge of the disability as such, or as to whether its material features fall within Schedule 1 to the Act, in order to be said to have acted for a reason which relates to the disability. There is nothing in the statutory language that requires that the relationship between the disability and the treatment should be judged subjectively through the eyes of the employer. The correct test is the objective one of whether the relationship exists, not whether the employer knew of it. Absence of knowledge of the disability, however, may be highly material to justifiability or as to the steps to be considered or taken under the duty of reasonable adjustment.

London Clubs Management Ltd v   **[2001] IRLR 719 EAT**
Hood
A disabled employee was not treated less favourably for a reason related to his disability when the employers refused to pay him sick pay, in circumstances in which sick pay was withdrawn generally for employees of his grade. The reason for the treatment was the application of the policy on sick pay. That reason did not relate to the applicant's disability.

Others to whom reason does not apply

Clark v   **[1999] IRLR 318 CA**
TDG Ltd t/a Novacold
In deciding whether the reason for less favourable treatment does not or would not apply to others, it is simply a case of identifying others to whom the reason for the treatment does not or would not apply. The test of less favourable treatment does not turn on a like-for-like comparison of the treatment of the disabled person and of others in similar circumstances. Thus, it is not appropriate to make a comparison of the cases in the same way as in the Sex Discrimination and Race Relations Acts. The Disability Discrimination Act does not contain an express provision requiring a comparison of the cases of different persons in the same, or not materially different, circumstances. The statutory focus is narrower. The result is that the reason would not apply to others even if their circumstances are different from those of the disabled person.

Clark v   **[1999] IRLR 318 CA**
TDG Ltd t/a Novacold
In the case of an employee absent from work for a disability-related reason, the correct comparison is with the treatment of employees who are not absent, rather than with an employee absent for the same time for a reason unrelated to disability.

Justification

(3) Treatment is justified for the purposes of subsection (1)(b) if, but only if, the reason for it is both material to the circumstances of the particular case and substantial.

(4) But treatment of a disabled person cannot be justified under subsection (3) if it amounts to direct discrimination falling within subsection (5).

DISABILITY DISCRIMINATION ACT 1995 (as amendeD) – S.3A

Jones v   **[2001] IRLR 384 CA**
Post Office
The statutory test for justification confines employment tribunals to considering whether the reason given for less favourable treatment can properly be described as both material to the circumstances of the particular case and substantial. The function of employment tribunals in this respect is not very different from the task which they have to perform in cases of unfair dismissal. Under s.98 of the Employment Rights Act, the tribunal's task is to adopt the range of reasonable responses approach to considering the reasonableness of a dismissal, and under [s.3A(3)] of the

DDA, it is to consider the materiality and substantiality of the employer's reason. In both cases, the members of the tribunal might themselves have come to a different conclusion on the evidence, but they must respect the opinion of the employer, in the one case if it is within the range of reasonable responses, and in the other if the reason given is material and substantial.

Jones v   **[2001] IRLR 384 CA**
Post Office
Consideration of the statutory criteria may involve an assessment of the employer's decision to the extent of considering whether there was evidence on the basis of which a decision could properly be taken. Thus if no risk assessment was made or a decision was taken otherwise than on the basis of appropriate medical evidence, or was an irrational decision as being beyond the range of reasonable responses open to a reasonable decision maker, the employment tribunal can hold the reason insufficient and the treatment unjustified.

Jones v   **[2001] IRLR 384 CA**
Post Office
Where a case involves an assessment of risk, and a properly conducted risk assessment provides a reason which is on its face both material and substantial, and is not irrational, a tribunal does not have the power to make its own appraisal of the medical evidence and decide whether the employer's assessment of risk is correct. A tribunal is not permitted to conclude that the reason is not material or substantial because the medical opinion on the basis of which the employer's decision was made is thought to be inferior to a different medical opinion expressed to the tribunal.

H J Heinz Co Ltd v   **[2000] IRLR 144 EAT**
Kenrick
The threshold for justification of disability discrimination is very low. Taking account of what the Code of Practice says about the meaning of "material to the circumstances of the particular case and substantial", if the reason for the treatment relates to the individual circumstances in question and is not just trivial or minor, then justification has to be held to exist in a case in which the employer has no duty of reasonable adjustment.

Jones v   **[2001] IRLR 384 CA**
Post Office
per Arden LJ: The standard by which the employer's reason is to be reviewed is an objective, rather than a subjective, one. "Material" denotes the quality of the connection which must exist between the employer's reason for discriminating against the employee and the circumstances of the particular case. There must be a reasonably strong connection between the reason and the circumstances. Those circumstances may include those of both the employer and employee.

Jones v   **[2001] IRLR 384 CA**
Post Office
per Arden LJ: "Substantial" means that the reason which the employer adopted as the ground for discrimination must carry real weight and thus be of substance.

Callagan v   **[2001] IRLR 724 EAT**
Glasgow City Council
In accordance with the analysis by Arden LJ in *Jones v Post Office*, there must be a causal connection between the discriminatory act and the justifying circumstances. Those justifying circumstances must be material, in the sense of relevant, and substantial, meaning more than de minimis.

Surrey Police v   **[2002] IRLR 843 EAT**
Marshall
There is nothing in the decision of the Court of Appeal in *Jones v Post Office* which bars a tribunal from making findings of fact on some of the medical evidence obtained after the employee's rejection, where parts of the evidence were relevant as to whether, at the point of decision, there was material in the medical officer's hands on which a decision such as she made could properly have been made and as to whether it was a decision open to a reasonable decision-maker on the material before her. Expert evidence, for and against, including evidence other than from the decision-maker and obtained after the decision, will often be desirable or even necessary if the decision-maker's credibility and rationality are to be examined.

Murray v   **[2003] IRLR 340 EAT**
Newham Citizens Advice Bureau Ltd
An employment tribunal should only interfere with the decision of a prospective employer where the employer's investigations are outside the reasonable range of responses by a reasonable prospective employer in the circumstances.

Murray v   **[2003] IRLR 340 EAT**
Newham Citizens Advice Bureau Ltd
If it seeks to rely upon the defence of justification, a prospective employer must show that the justification was based on material that it had before it at the time it took the relevant decision. Where the employer failed to obtain the appropriate information which may, in the event, have justified its decision, that evidence cannot provide ex post facto justification, but might be relevant to the question of compensation

Murray v   **[2003] IRLR 340 EAT**
Newham Citizens Advice Bureau Ltd
Although a prospective employer cannot be expected to carry out the rigorous investigation that might be expected of an employer who already employs a disabled person or to seek medical evidence in respect of every applicant, an employer must make such inquiries as are appropriate in the circumstances of the case. In the case of an employer who has failed to carry out reasonable investigations, a tribunal may hold that the reason was insufficient and the less favourable treatment unjustified.

Clark v   **[1999] IRLR 318 CA**
TDG Ltd t/a Novacold
Whether treatment has been shown to be justified is a question of fact to be determined on a proper self-direction on the relevant law. This includes taking into account those parts of the Code of Practice which a reasonable tribunal would regard as relevant to the determination of that question.

Callagan v   **[2001] IRLR724 EAT**
Glasgow City Council
The fact that the employer did not know the disability existed might affect the justification issue but does not preclude it. What matters is to analyse the treatment meted out by the employer. In so far as the EAT suggested in *Quinn v Schwarzkopf* that justification can never occur if the employer is ignorant of the fact of disability at the relevant time, that went too far.

London Borough of Hammersmith   **[2000] IRLR 691 EAT**
   & Fulham v
Farnsworth
Knowledge, or lack of knowledge, of an applicant's disability is not a necessary ingredient for the purposes of the test of justification.

Meaning of harassment

(1) For the purposes of this Part, a person subjects a disabled person to harassment where, for a reason which relates to the disabled person's disability, he engages in unwanted conduct which has the purpose or effect of –
     (a) violating the disabled person's dignity, or
     (b) creating an intimidating, hostile, degrading, humiliating or offensive environment for him.

(2) Conduct shall be regarded as having the effect referred to in paragraph (a) or (b) of subsection (1) only if, having regard to all the circumstances, including in particular the perception of the disabled person, it should reasonably be considered as having that effect.

DISABILITY DISCRIMINATION ACT 1995 (as amended) – s.3B

Duty to make reasonable adjustment

(1) Where –
     (a) a provision, criterion or practice applied by or on behalf of an employer, or
     (b) any physical feature of premises occupied by the employer,
places the disabled person concerned at a substantial disadvantage in comparison with persons who are not disabled, it is the duty of the employer to take such steps as it is reasonable, in all the circumstances of the case, for him to have to take in order to prevent the provision, criterion or practice, or feature, having that effect.

(2) In subsection (1), "the disabled person concerned" means –
     (a) in the case of a provision, criterion or practice for determining to whom employment should be offered, any disabled person who is, or has notified the employer that he may be, an applicant for that employment;
     (b) in any other case, a disabled person who is –
        (i) an applicant for the employment concerned, or
        (ii) an employee of the employer concerned.

(3) Nothing in this section imposes any duty on an employer in relation to a disabled person if the employer does not know, and could not reasonably be expected to know –
     (a) in the case of an applicant or potential applicant, that the disabled person concerned is, or may be, an applicant for the employment; or
     (b) in any case, that that person has a disability and is likely to be affected in the way mentioned in subsection (1).

DISABILITY DISCRIMINATION ACT 1995 (as amended) – s.4A

(1) In determining whether it is reasonable for a person to have to take a particular step in order to comply with a duty to make reasonable adjustments, regard shall be had, in particular, to –
     (a) the extent to which taking the step would prevent the effect in relation to which the duty is imposed;
     (b) the extent to which it is practicable for him to take the step;
     (c) the financial and other costs which would be incurred by him in taking the step and the extent to which taking it would disrupt any of his activities;
     (d) the extent of his financial and other resources;
     (e) the availability to him of financial or other assistance with respect to taking the step;
     (f) the nature of his activities and the size of his undertaking;
     (g) where the step would be taken in relation to a private household, the extent to which taking it would –
        (i) disrupt that household, or
        (ii) disturb any person residing there.

(2) The following are examples of steps which a person may need to take in relation to a disabled person in order to comply with a duty to make reasonable adjustments –
     (a) making adjustments to premises;
     (b) allocating some of the disabled person's duties to another person;
     (c) transferring him to fill an existing vacancy;
     (d) altering his hours of working or training;
     (e) assigning him to a different place of work or training;
     (f) allowing him to be absent during working or training hours for rehabilitation, assessment or treatment;
     (g) giving, or arranging for, training or mentoring (whether for the disabled person or any other person);
     (h) acquiring or modifying equipment;
     (i) modifying instructions or reference manuals;
     (j) modifying procedures for testing or assessment;
     (k) providing a reader or interpreter;
     (l) providing supervision or other support.

DISABILITY DISCRIMINATION ACT 1995 (as amended) – s.18B

Provision, criterion or practice

Archibald v   [2004] IRLR 651 HL
Fife Council
The duty to make an adjustment is triggered where an employee becomes so disabled that she can no longer meet the requirements of her job description. The duty applies to the job description for a post and the liability of anyone who becomes incapable of fulfilling the job description to be dismissed, as much as it applies to an employer's arrangements for deciding who gets what job or how much each is paid.

Archibald v   [2004] IRLR 651 HL
Fife Council
An applicant was placed "at a substantial disadvantage in comparison with persons who are not disabled" where her job description required her to be physically fit, which she was no longer able to meet, and that exposed her to a condition that if she was physically unable to do the job she was employed to do, she was liable to be dismissed.

Kenny v   [1999] IRLR 76 EAT
Hampshire Constabulary
An employer's duty to make a reasonable adjustment to arrangements on which employment is offered or afforded is restricted to "job related" matters. Not every failure to make an arrangement which deprives an employee of a chance to be employed is unlawful.

Kenny v   [1999] IRLR 76 EAT
Hampshire Constabulary
The statutory definition directs employers to make adjustments to the way the job is structured and organised so as to accommodate those who cannot fit into existing arrangements.

Paul v   [2004] IRLR 190 EAT
National Probation Service
The existence of a disability does not of itself substantially disadvantage a disabled person who is subject to a general requirement of clearance from an occupational health adviser. In many cases, having a disability does not adversely affect an individual's general health and an occupational health assessment will not lead to a refusal of employment unless the disability affects the applicant's ability to do the work and no reasonable adjustments can be made.

Nottinghamshire County Council v   [2004] IRLR 703 CA
Meikle
Payment of full sick pay by an employer can be an adjustment falling within the scope of [s.4A].

Kenny v   [1999] IRLR 76 EAT
Hampshire Constabulary
Employers are not under a statutory duty to provide carers to attend to their employees' personal needs, such as assistance in going to the toilet. A line has to be drawn on the extent of the employer's responsibilities in providing adjustments to accommodate a disabled employee.

When duty applies

Archibald v   [2004] IRLR 651 HL
Fife Council
The duty to make adjustments is not linked to the employee's particular employment and can arise even if there is nothing that the employer can do to prevent the disabled person from being placed at a disadvantage in their particular employment.

Archibald v   [2004] IRLR 651 HL
Fife Council
The duty to make adjustments may require the employer to treat a disabled person more favourably to remove the disadvantage which is attributable to the disability. This necessarily entails a measure of positive discrimination.

Archibald v   [2004] IRLR 651 HL
Fife Council
The comparison under [s.4A(1)] with persons who are not disabled is not confined to non-disabled people doing the same job. Therefore, the steps which the employer might have to take in order to prevent the arrangements placing a disabled employee at a substantial disadvantage in comparison with non-disabled persons include transferring her to another job, a possibility expressly contemplated by [s.18B(2)(c)].

Archibald v   [2004] IRLR 651 HL
Fife Council
The duty to take such steps as it is reasonable in all the circumstances for the employer to have to take could include transferring without competitive interview a disabled employee from a post she can no longer do to a post which she can do. The employer's duty may require moving the disabled person to a post at a slightly higher grade. A transfer can be upwards as well as sideways or downwards.

Beart v   [2003] IRLR 238 CA
H M Prison Service
The test of reasonableness under [s.4A] is directed to the steps to be taken to prevent the employment from having a detrimental effect on the disabled employee.

British Gas Services Ltd v   [2001] IRLR 60 EAT
McCaull
The test under [s.4A] is an objective one: did the employer take such steps as it is reasonable in all the circumstances

of the case for him to have to take in order to prevent the arrangements made by the employer from placing the disabled person at a substantial disadvantage in comparison with those who are not disabled? The test of whether it was reasonable for an employer to have to take a particular step does not relate to what the employer considered but to what he did and did not do. That is for the tribunal to consider. If Parliament had intended an employer to be in breach of statutory duty because he failed to consider what steps he might reasonably take, it would have so provided in the Act.

Morse v   **[1999] IRLR 352 EAT**
Wiltshire County Council
The purpose of [s.18B(2)] is to focus the mind of the employer on possible steps which it might take in compliance with its duty under [s.4A(1)], and to focus the mind of the tribunal when considering whether an employer has failed to comply with a [s.4A] duty.

Ridout v   **[1999] IRLR 628 EAT**
T C Group
The duty to make a reasonable adjustment is to be construed in the light of [s.4A(3)]. This requires a tribunal to measure the extent of the duty, if any, against the actual or assumed knowledge of the employer both as to the disability and its likelihood of causing the individual a substantial disadvantage in comparison with persons who are not disabled.

British Gas Services Ltd v   **[2001] IRLR 60 EAT**
McCaull
There is no automatic breach of the duty of reasonable adjustment because an employer is unaware of that duty. The question is what steps the employer took and did not take. An employer might take all reasonable steps as contemplated by the statute while remaining ignorant of the statutory provision itself.

Cosgrove v   **[2001] IRLR 653 EAT**
Caesar & Howie
The duty to make adjustments is upon the employer. There will be cases where the evidence given on the applicant's side alone will establish a total unavailability of reasonable and effective adjustments. It does not follow, however, that the duty on the employer should, without more, be taken to have been satisfied on the basis that neither the applicant nor her general practitioner could think of anything that would have represented a satisfactory adjustment, in circumstances in which the employers themselves had given no thought to the matter.

Ridout v   **[1999] IRLR 628 EAT**
T C Group
Tribunals should be careful not to impose upon disabled people a duty to give a long detailed explanation as to the effects of their disability merely to cause the employer to

make adjustments which it probably should have made in the first place. On the other hand, it is equally undesirable that an employer should be required to ask a number of questions as to whether a person with a disability feels disadvantaged merely to protect themselves from liability.

Failure to make reasonable adjustment

(2) For the purposes of this Part, a person also discriminates against a disabled person if he fails to comply with a duty to make reasonable adjustments imposed on him in relation to the disabled person.

(6) If, in a case falling within subsection (1), a person is under a duty to make reasonable adjustments in relation to a disabled person but fails to comply with that duty, his treatment of that person cannot be justified under subsection (3) unless it would have been justified even if he had complied with that duty.

DISABILITY DISCRIMINATION ACT 1995 (as amended) – s.3A

Clark v   **[1999] IRLR 318 CA**
TDG Ltd t/a Novacold
A claim for a breach of a duty of reasonable adjustment is not dependent on successfully establishing a claim for less favourable treatment for a reason related to disability.

Morse v   **[1999] IRLR 352 EAT**
Wiltshire County Council
A tribunal hearing an allegation of failure to make a reasonable adjustment must go through a number of sequential steps:
– it must decide whether the provisions of [s.4A] impose a duty on the employer in the circumstances of the particular case.
– if such a duty is imposed, it must next decide whether the employer has taken such steps as it is reasonable, in all the circumstances of the case, for him to have to take in order to prevent the arrangements or feature having the effect of placing the disabled person concerned at a substantial disadvantage in comparison with persons who are not disabled.
– this, in turn, involves the tribunal inquiring whether the employer could reasonably have taken any of the steps set out in [s.18B(1)]
– at the same time the tribunal must have regard to the factors set out in [s.18B(2)].

Beart v   **[2003] IRLR 238 CA**
H M Prison Service
It is not an error of law for a tribunal to have failed to follow sequentially the series of steps indicated in *Morse*, provided that it is apparent from the tribunal's decision that they properly applied themselves to considering whether the requirements of the statute were satisfied.

Mid Staffordshire General Hospitals NHS Trust v Cambridge

[2003] IRLR 566 EAT

A proper assessment of what is required to eliminate a disabled person's disadvantage is a necessary part of the duty imposed by [s.4A(1)], since that duty cannot be complied with unless the employer makes a proper assessment of what needs to be done. There must be many cases in which a disabled person has been placed at a substantial disadvantage in the workplace, but in which the employer does not know what it ought to do to ameliorate that disadvantage without making inquiries. To say that a failure to make those inquiries would not amount to a breach of the duty imposed on employers by [s.4A(1)]would render that section practically unworkable in many cases.

Morse v Wiltshire County Council

[1999] IRLR 352 EAT

The tribunal must scrutinise the explanation put forward by the employer, and reach its own decision on what, if any, steps were reasonable and what was objectively justified, and material and substantial.

DISABILITY DISCRIMINATION BY EMPLOYERS

(1) It is unlawful for an employer to discriminate against a disabled person –

(a) in the arrangements which he makes for the purpose of determining to whom he should offer employment;

(b) in the terms on which he offers that person employment; or

(c) by refusing to offer, or deliberately not offering, him employment.

(2) It is unlawful for an employer to discriminate against a disabled person whom he employs –

(a) in the terms of employment which he affords him;

(b) in the opportunities which he affords him for promotion, a transfer, training or receiving any other benefit;

(c) by refusing to afford him, or deliberately not affording him, any such opportunity; or

(d) by dismissing him, or subjecting him to any other detriment.

(3) It is also unlawful for an employer, in relation to employment by him, to subject to harassment –

(a) a disabled person whom he employs; or

(b) a disabled person who has applied to him for employment.

(4) Subsection (2) does not apply to benefits of any description if the employer is concerned with the provision (whether or not for payment) of benefits of that description to the public, or to a section of the public which includes the employee in question, unless –

(a) that provision differs in a material respect from the provision of the benefits by the employer to his employees;

(b) the provision of the benefits to the employee in question is regulated by his contract of employment; or

(c) the benefits relate to training.

(5) The reference in subsection (2)(d) to the dismissal of a person includes a reference –

(a) to the termination of that person's employment by the expiration of any period (including a period expiring by reference to an event or circumstance), not being a termination immediately after which the employment is renewed on the same terms; and

(b) to the termination of that person's employment by any act of his (including the giving of notice) in circumstances such that he is entitled to terminate it without notice by reason of the conduct of the employer.

(6) This section applies only in relation to employment at an establishment in Great Britain.

DISABILITY DISCRIMINATION ACT 1995 (as amended) – s.4

Dismissal

British Sugar plc v Kirker   **[1998] IRLR 624 EAT**

An employment tribunal was entitled to take into account the history of the applicant's treatment prior to the Disability Discrimination Act coming into force by way of background in order to determine whether or not old perceptions of the applicant's value as an employee, based on his disability, were carried through to when he was assessed for redundancy selection purposes.

H J Heinz Co Ltd v Kenrick   **[2000] IRLR 144 EAT**

An employer who does not adequately consider alternative employment or shorter hours may find that the dismissal is held not to be justified, on the basis that a reason for the dismissal such as continuing incapability would not be material to the circumstances so long as part-time or lighter duties might have fitted the bill.

Fu v London Borough of Camden   **[2001] IRLR 186 EAT**

In deciding whether an employer was justified in dismissing rather than making reasonable adjustments on the basis that they would not enable the employee off work ill to return to work, an employment tribunal should arrive at its conclusion by examining the adjustments proposed and the extent to which they could have overcome the medical symptoms which otherwise prevented the employee's return to work.

Kent County Council v Mingo   **[2000] IRLR 90 EAT**

The employers unlawfully discriminated against the applicant when, notwithstanding his disability, they treated him less favourably for the purposes of redeployment than employees at risk of redundancy. A redeployment policy of giving preferential treatment to redundant or potentially redundant employees does not adequately reflect the statutory duty on employers under the Disability Discrimination Act, since it means that those with disabilities are relatively handicapped in the redeployment system.

Nottinghamshire County Council v Meikle   **[2004] IRLR 703 CA**

A persistent failure by a local authority to carry out reasonable adjustments amounted to a fundamental breach of the obligation of trust and confidence entitling the employee to claim that she was constructively dismissed.

DISCRIMINATION BY OTHERS THAN EMPLOYERS

Discrimination against contract workers

(1) It is unlawful for a principal, in relation to contract work, to discriminate against a disabled person who is a contract worker (a "disabled contract worker") –

    (a) in the terms on which he allows him to do that work;

    (b) by not allowing him to do it or continue to do it;

    (c) in the way he affords him access to any benefits or by refusing or deliberately omitting to afford him access to them; or

    (d) by subjecting him to any other detriment.

(6) Section 4A applies to any principal, in relation to contract work, as if he were, or would be, the employer of the disabled contract worker and as if any contract worker supplied to do work for him were an employee of his.

(7) However, for the purposes of s.4A as applied by subsection (6), a principal is not required to take a step in relation to a disabled contract worker if under that section the disabled contract worker's employer is required to take the step in relation to him.

(9) In this section –

"principal" means a person ("A") who makes work available for doing by individuals who are employed by another person who supplies them under a contract made with A;

"contract work" means work so made available; and

"contract worker" means any individual who is supplied to the principal under such a contract.

DISABILITY DISCRIMINATION ACT 1995 (as amendeD) – s.4B

Abbey Life Assurance Co Ltd v Tansell   **[2000] IRLR 387 CA**

[Section 4B] does not require a direct contractual relationship between the employer and the principal. It applies to a case where there is no direct contract between the person making the work available and the employer of the individual who is supplied to do that work. The statutory definition only requires the supply of the individual to be "under a contract made with 'A'." It does not expressly stipulate who is to be the party who contracts with 'A'. Although in many cases the contract with the end-user will be made by the employer who supplies the individual, the definition in s.4B does not require that to be the case.

Abbey Life Assurance Co Ltd v Tansell   **[2000] IRLR 387 CA**

An applicant, who was employed by a company which supplied him to an agency, which in turn supplied him to an end-user, was a "contract worker" within the meaning of s.4B who could present a claim against the end-user as being a "principal".

REMEDIES

(1) A complaint by any person that another person –

> *(a) has discriminated against him in a way which is unlawful under this Part, or*
>
> *(b) is, by virtue of section 57 or 58, to be treated as having discriminated against him in such a way,*

may be presented to an employment tribunal.

(2) Where an employment tribunal finds that a complaint presented to it under this section is well-founded, it shall take such of the following steps as it considers just and equitable –

> *(a) making a declaration as to the rights of the complainant and the respondent in relation to the matters to which the complaint relates;*
>
> *(b ordering the respondent to pay compensation to the complainant;*
>
> *(c) recommending that the respondent take, within a specified period, action appearing to the tribunal to be reasonable, in all the circumstances of the case, for the purpose of obviating or reducing the adverse effect on the complainant of any matter to which the complaint relates.*

(3) Where a tribunal orders compensation under subsection (2)(b), the amount of the compensation shall be calculated by applying the principles applicable to the calculation of damages in claims in tort or (in Scotland) in reparation for breach of statutory duty.

(4) For the avoidance of doubt it is hereby declared that compensation in respect of discrimination in a way which is unlawful under this Part may include compensation for injury to feelings whether or not it includes compensation under any other head.

(5) If the respondent to a complaint fails, without reasonable justification, to comply with a recommendation made by an employment tribunal under subsection (2)(c) the tribunal may, if it thinks it just and equitable to do so –

> *(a) increase the amount of compensation required to be paid to the complainant in respect of the complaint, where an order was made under subsection (2)(b); or*
>
> *(b) make an order under subsection (2)(b).*

DISABILITY DISCRIMINATION ACT – s.8

Compensation

Buxton v [1999] IRLR 158 EAT
Equinox Design Ltd

An employment tribunal's finding that the period of loss should be one year for an employee with multiple sclerosis who was dismissed lacked a sufficient evidential basis, since it involved making a finding as to the outcome of a risk assessment in the context of a disease which has variable effects. Without medical evidence, the tribunal was not in a position to say what the outcome would be.

Purves v [2003] IRLR 420 Sheriff Principal
Joydisc Ltd

Damages for injury to feelings should be awarded in a case of discrimination in relation to goods, facilities and services on the same basis as in employment tribunal cases. Whether the ground of discrimination is race or sex or disability, and whether the context is the field of employment or some other field, a person may suffer injury to his or her feelings as a result. It would be erroneous to assume that the measure of damages in an action based on one ground or in one context must necessarily always be greater or smaller than in an action based on some other ground or in another context. The precise ground and context of the act of discrimination in respect of which damages are claimed are not of primary importance.

4. SEXUAL ORIENTATION DISCRIMINATION

EXCLUSIONS AND EXCEPTIONS

Genuine occupational requirements

(1) In relation to discrimination falling within reg.3 (discrimination on grounds of sexual orientation) –
   (a) reg.6(1)(a) or (c) does not apply to any employment;
   (b) reg.6(2)(b) or (c) does not apply to promotion or transfer to, or training for, any employment; and
   (c) reg.6(2)(d) does not apply to dismissal from any employment,
where para. (2) or (3) applies.

(2) This paragraph applies where, having regard to the nature of the employment or the context in which it is carried out –
   (a) being of a particular sexual orientation is a genuine and determining occupational requirement;
   (b) it is proportionate to apply that requirement in the particular case; and
   (c) either –
      (i) the person to whom that requirement is applied does not meet it, or
      (ii) the employer is not satisfied, and in all the circumstances it is reasonable for him not to be satisfied, that that person meets it,
and this paragraph applies whether or not the employment is for purposes of an organised religion.

EMPLOYMENT EQUALITY (SEXUAL ORIENTATION) REGULATIONS 2003 – Reg.7

R (on the application of Amicus –   **[2004] IRLR 430 HC**
  MSF section) v
Secretary of State for Trade and Industry
Regulation 7(2) is compatible with the Framework Employment Directive, even though the exception applies not only where a person does not in fact meet the requirement as to sexual orientation but also, by virtue of reg.7(2)(c)(ii), where it is "reasonable" for the employer "not to be satisfied" that the person meets it. The derogation in Article 4(1) of the Directive, which refers to a difference of treatment "based on a characteristic related to" sexual orientation, is wide enough to cover reg.7(2), even allowing for the need to construe derogations strictly. Regulation 7(2)(c)(ii) has a sensible rationale. In those cases where being of a particular sexual orientation is a genuine and determining occupational requirement, it cannot be right that an employer, having asked the plainly permissible initial question whether a person meets that requirement, is bound in all circumstances to accept at face value the answer given or is precluded from forming his own assessment if no answer is given. The requirement of reasonableness ensures that decisions cannot lawfully be based on mere assumptions or social stereotyping.

Organised religion

(3) This paragraph applies where –
   (a) the employment is for purposes of an organised religion;
   (b) the employer applies a requirement related to sexual orientation –
      (i) so as to comply with the doctrines of the religion, or
      (ii) because of the nature of the employment and the context in which it is carried out, so as to avoid conflicting with the strongly held religious convictions of a significant number of the religion's followers; and
   (c) either –
      (i) the person to whom that requirement is applied does not meet it, or
      (ii) the employer is not satisfied, and in all the circumstances it is reasonable for him not to be satisfied, that that person meets it.

EMPLOYMENT EQUALITY (SEXUAL ORIENTATION) REGULATIONS 2003 – Reg.7

R (on the application of Amicus –   **[2004] IRLR 430 HC**
  MSF section) v
Secretary of State for Trade and Industry
Regulation 7(3) is compatible with the Framework Employment Directive. The exception in reg.7(3) is very narrow. It has to be construed strictly since it is a derogation from the principle of equal treatment; and it has to be construed purposively so as to ensure, so far as possible, compatibility with the Directive. When its terms are considered in light of those interpretative principles, they can be seen to afford an exception only in very limited circumstances. The fact that the exception applies "for the purposes of an organised religion" is an important initial limitation since that is a narrower expression than "for the purposes of a religious organisation" or "an ethos based on religion or belief" as used in the Regulations relating to discrimination on grounds of religion or belief. Thus, employment as a teacher in a faith school is likely to be for the "purposes of a religious organisation" but not for the "purposes of an organised religion".

R (on the application of Amicus –   **[2004] IRLR 430 HC**
  MSF section) v
Secretary of State for Trade and Industry
The condition in reg.7(3)(b)(i) that the employer must apply the requirement "so as to comply with the doctrines of the religion" is an objective test whereby it must be shown that employment of a person not meeting the requirement would be incompatible with the doctrines of the religion. That is very narrow in scope.

R (on the application of Amicus –   **[2004] IRLR 430 HC**
  MSF section) v
Secretary of State for Trade and Industry
The condition in reg.7(3)(b)(ii), which refers to an employer

applying a requirement related to sexual orientation "because of the nature of the employment and the context in which it is carried out, so as to avoid conflicting with the strongly held religious convictions of a significant number of the religion's followers", requires careful examination of the precise nature of the employment and is to be read as an objective, not subjective, test. It will be a very far from easy test to satisfy in practice

R (on the application of Amicus –   **[2004] IRLR 430 HC**
  MSF section) v
Secretary of State for Trade and Industry
The protection against discrimination on grounds of sexual orientation relates as much to the manifestation of that orientation in the form of sexual behaviour as it does to sexuality as such.

DISCRIMINATION BY EMPLOYERS

(1) It is unlawful for an employer, in relation to employment by him at an establishment in Great Britain, to discriminate against a person –
> *(a) in the arrangements he makes for the purpose of determining to whom he should offer employment;*
> *(b) in the terms on which he offers that person employment; or*
> *(c) by refusing to offer, or deliberately not offering, him employment.*

(2) It is unlawful for an employer, in relation to a person whom he employs at an establishment in Great Britain, to discriminate against that person –
> *(a) in the terms of employment which he affords him;*
> *(b) in the opportunities which he affords him for promotion, a transfer, training, or receiving any other benefit;*
> *(c) by refusing to afford him, or deliberately not affording him, any such opportunity; or*
> *(d) by dismissing him, or subjecting him to any other detriment.*
> EMPLOYMENT EQUALITY (SEXUAL ORIENTATION)
> REGULATIONS 2003 – Reg.6

Access to benefits

Benefits defined by reference to marital status

Nothing in Part II or III shall render unlawful anything which prevents or restricts access to a benefit by reference to marital status.

EMPLOYMENT EQUALITY (SEXUAL ORIENTATION)
REGULATIONS 2003 – Reg.25

R (on the application of Amicus –   **[2004] IRLR 430 HC**
  MSF section) v
Secretary of State for Trade and Industry
Regulation 25, which has the effect that employment benefits defined by reference to marital status, such as a surviving spouse's pension, are not prohibited by the Regulations, reflects a limitation in the scope of the Directive itself. Recital 22 to the Directive, which says that "this Directive is without prejudice to national laws on marital status and the benefits dependent thereon", is of general application, covering all benefits that are dependent on marital status. It is not limited to State benefits.

DISCRIMINATION BY OTHERS THAN EMPLOYERS

Institutions of further and higher education

(1) It is unlawful, in relation to an educational establishment to which this regulation applies, for the governing body of that establishment to discriminate against a person –

(a) in the terms on which it offers to admit him to the establishment as a student;

(b) by refusing or deliberately not accepting an application for his admission to the establishment as a student; or

(c) where he is a student of the establishment –

(i) in the way it affords him access to any benefits,

(ii) by refusing or deliberately not affording him access to them, or

(iii) by excluding him from the establishment or subjecting him to any other detriment.

(3) Paragraph (1) does not apply if the discrimination only concerns training which would help fit a person for employment which, by virtue of reg.7 (exception for genuine occupational requirement etc), the employer could lawfully refuse to offer the person in question.

EMPLOYMENT EQUALITY (SEXUAL ORIENTATION) REGULATIONS 2003 – Reg.20

R (on the application of Amicus – MSF section) v   [2004] IRLR 430 HC

Secretary of State for Trade and Industry

For training to come within the exception in reg.20(3), it must be training that would only help fit a person for a relevant employment. If training has a broader purpose, as in the case of a degree course in theology, it cannot come within the exception. The expression "would help fit . . . for employment" is likewise to be strictly construed, as referring to vocational training rather than to training of a more general nature. Construed in that way, the exception has a narrow scope, being tied closely to training directed specifically and solely towards an employment to which an occupational requirement can lawfully be applied.

Notes